Exploring

Arizona's
Wild Areas

16380

D0353992

A GUIDE FOR

HIKERS • BACKPACKERS • CLIMBERS
CROSS-COUNTRY SKIERS • PADDLERS

Exploring

Arizona's
Wild Areas

SECOND EDITION
Scott S. Warren

THE MOUNTAINEERS BOOKS

Published by
The Mountaineers Books
1001 SW Klickitat Way, Suite 201
Seattle, WA 98134

First edition, 1996. Second edition, 2002.

Published simultaneously in Great Britain by Cordee, 3a DeMontfort Street, Leicester, England, LE1 7HD

Manufactured in the United States of America

Project Editor: Christine Ummel Hosler
Copyeditor: Paula Thurman
Cover and book design: Ani Rucki
Layout: Marge Mueller, Gray Mouse Graphics
Cartographer: Scott S. Warren
Photographer: Scott S. Warren

Cover photograph: *Prehistoric petroglyph in the Saguaro Wilderness*
Frontispiece: *Within Wall Street along the Chiricahua National Monument's Echo Canyon Loop*

Library of Congress Cataloging-in-Publication Data
Warren, Scott S.
  Exploring Arizona's wild areas : a guide for hikers, backpackers, climbers,
cross-country skiers, and paddlers / Scott S. Warren—2nd ed.
      p. cm.
Includes index.
  ISBN 0-89886-774-6 (pbk.)
  1. Outdoor recreation—Arizona—Guidebooks. 2. Wilderness areas—Arizona—
Directories. 3. Natural history—Arizona—Guidebooks. 4. Arizona—Guidebooks. I. Title.
  GV191.42.A7 W37 2002
  917.9104'53—dc21
                                        2002004987

 Printed on recycled paper

CONTENTS

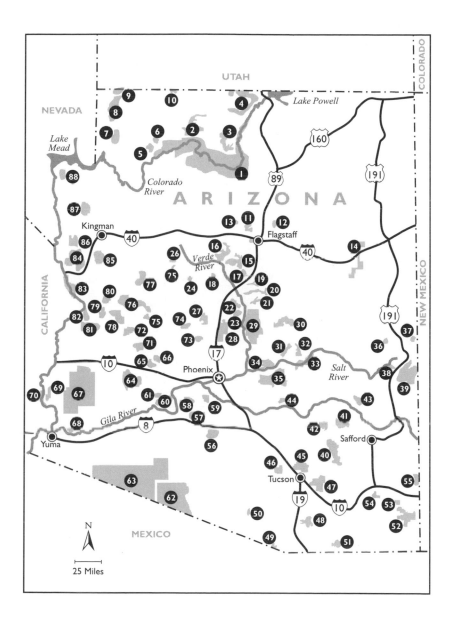

PREFACE

Unlike other western states, which are still struggling with the political headaches of setting aside wild areas, Arizona put its wilderness house in order years ago. In the early part of this century, the state began to recognize the intrinsic worth of pristine lands by setting aside several designated Primitive Areas. With the Wilderness Act of 1964, many areas were protected as part of a National Wilderness Preservation System. A great many additional parcels of national forest lands, along with a handful of Bureau of Land Management (BLM) areas, were set aside as a result of the Arizona Wilderness Act of 1984. Finally, in 1990, Arizona's congressional legislatures won passage of the Arizona Desert Wilderness Bill—a bill that added many more BLM areas to Arizona's wilderness system, as well as some parcels managed by the National Park Service and the U.S. Fish and Wildlife Service. As a result, several expanses of desert terrain were set aside in perpetuity.

Today, thanks to the efforts of federal land managers, conservation groups, thoughtful politicians, and concerned citizens, Arizona has ninety wilderness areas and one primitive area. In terms of area, these parcels of legally protected land total 4,529,862 acres. Add to this the 1,218,376 acres that fall within Grand Canyon National Park (most of which is part of a Wilderness Study Area) and the 71,100 acres included in the newly established Agua Fria National Monument and outdoors enthusiasts have one of the largest inventories of wild areas in the nation: 5,819,338 acres. These lands encompass everything from sparsely vegetated desert basins to shady pine forests, chaparral choked mesas to alpine meadows, and impressive saguaro cactus forests to verdant subalpine forests.

The eighty-eight Arizona protected wild areas described in this book are organized in a manner that should facilitate planning and undertaking a backcountry trek. Two BLM wilderness areas—Needles Eye near Globe and Coyote Mountains west of Tucson—are left out because they are not currently legally accessible. In addition, a handful of other BLM wilderness areas are covered here in combination with adjacent national forest, national park, or wildlife refuge wildernesses. This organization reflects the fact that these neighboring wilderness areas are intended as a single parcel of wild land, preserving a greater ecosystem. While backcountry in Grand Canyon National Park and Agua Fria National Monument has yet to be set aside as designated wilderness, it is mostly managed as wilderness by the National Park Service and BLM, respectively.

Established in 2000 and 2001, three expansive national monuments (the Sonoran Desert, Grand Canyon–Parashant, and Vermilion Cliffs National Monuments) include several previously existing BLM wilderness areas. Because the boundaries of these wilderness areas are well established and because land use on monument acreage in between them is not always conducive to a wilderness setting, this book will not cover

Colorful sandstone cliffs ring the Sedona area.

all lands within these monuments. Rather, it will continue to discuss only the previously established wilderness lands within.

While conducting research for this book it quickly became apparent that there is very little published information available on many of these wilderness lands. Field research and interviews with land management personnel then became especially important. Furthermore, many of Arizona's desert wildernesses are remote, difficult to reach, and completely lacking in established backcountry routes. Such challenging conditions warrant an honest assessment of your hiking abilities before you set out into these exceptionally wild lands. There are plenty of reminders throughout the book, but remember: If you are an inexperienced hiker, don't even think of entering these remote wildernesses alone.

Producing this guide to Arizona's wilderness areas was an exhausting—and, at times, frustrating—endeavor, which proved quite hard on my 4WD vehicle. But it was also a lot of fun. I jumped at every opportunity the project provided to escape the grip of winter back home (Colorado). I came to know more about the state of Arizona than I ever thought possible, and I look forward to returning to many of these places to linger for a few days or more, whenever a little R & R is in order.

I hope that this book will generate a love and respect for the land; however, I have had reservations about the unwanted publicity this guide will bring to Arizona's wilderness areas. This book provides valuable information about the fragile nature of these lands, stressing the need to tread lightly on the land. Leave nothing but footprints and take nothing but photographs. Have a safe and memorable trip, and enjoy! Arizona is an incredible state with plenty of incredible wild lands.

INTRODUCTION

The Grand Canyon and the Sonoran Desert. These two landscapes—the gaping gulch that slices across the northern third of the state and the forests of towering saguaro cactus that typify Arizona's central and southern desert basins—are uniquely Arizonian. But, there is far more to the state than these two most obvious of images. Arizona is also home to mountains that top 12,000 feet and broad plateaus that are shaded by tall ponderosa pines, spruce, and fir. Verdant riparian plant communities line stream-beds and canyon bottoms. Perfectly formed cinder cones attest to a fiery volcanic past that helped shape much of the state. Sheer cliff faces soar skyward, mesa tops drop precipitously and, yes, numerous canyons, gulches, and abysses, other than the Grand Canyon, dissect the land. It is this grand variety of topographies that Arizona's wild lands celebrate today and safeguard for tomorrow.

HOW TO USE THIS BOOK

For convenience, this book is split into four chapters, each covering a separate geographical unit. Stretching across much of the northern third of the state is the colorful canyon country of the Colorado Plateau. Bordered on the south by the Mogollon Rim and on the west by the Grand Wash Cliffs, the Colorado Plateau gives way to two more provinces. Directly below the Mogollon Rim and stretching across much of central Arizona is the Central Highlands with its midelevation mountains and occasional canyons and mesas. To the south and the west lies the Basin and Range province, where mountain ranges erupt from broad desert basins. Because of the numerous wilderness tracts found within the Basin and Range province, it has been divided into two units: the Southeastern Basin and Range and the Western Basin and Range.

The wild areas profiled in this book are all federally managed. Six national forests contain thirty-six wilderness areas and one primitive area. The Bureau of Land Management (BLM) has been charged with administering most desert lands in the West and oversees forty-seven wilderness areas in Arizona. National parks and monuments in the state include many thousands of acres of designated wilderness within them. Although the backcountry of Grand Canyon National Park has not yet won designation as wilderness, it is managed as wilderness, and therefore is included in this book. A fourth federal agency—the U.S. Fish and Wildlife Service—also administers wilderness land in Arizona. This agency oversees some of the most arid terrain in the state within two monstrously large wildlife refuges and two smaller ones.

The Maps

A locator map in the table of contents shows the general location of the eighty-eight areas covered in this book. Each chapter begins with its own regional map, and a more

Opposite: *Near the summit of Wasson Peak in Saguaro National Park*

detailed map of each wilderness accompanies the individual wilderness area descriptions. On the wilderness area maps, wild lands are indicated by gray shading, well-established trails are marked with a thick dashed line, and secondary routes mentioned in the text are shown as a dotted line. Roads leading to wilderness areas are indicated according to their general condition. Drainages, mountain summits, and other natural features are also shown. The maps in this book are intended to be general guides for these areas and are not suitable for navigation in the wilderness. Be sure to acquire the appropriate topographic maps, a land management agency map, and any other suitable maps of the area before heading out.

Information Blocks

Each section begins with an information block, which provides information at a glance. **Location** indicates driving distance to the wilderness (not air miles) from the nearest town or city. **Size** indicates the actual size of the area in acres. **Status** indicates the unit's official designation and the year it was established. Most areas in this book are wilderness areas, but one primitive area, one national park (the Grand Canyon), and one national monument (Agua Fria) are also listed. **Terrain** summarizes the type of topography you can expect to find in the wild area. **Elevation** cites the lowest and highest elevations of the wild area. **Management** indicates the government agency that administers the land. Some areas are administered by more than one agency. **Topographic maps** lists each of the 7.5-minute USGS maps that cover the area.

The Text

The text begins with a brief introduction to the area. The **Seasons** heading covers recommended times of the year to visit the wilderness. While every attempt has been made to be accurate here, the weather is at least as fickle in Arizona as in other western states. Generally speaking, these recommendations are directly tied to the area's elevation. You can pretty much count on summers being too hot for safe hiking in areas below 3,000 feet. Between 3,000 feet and 5,000 feet, the climate may be such that year-round hiking is possible, although summers can still be hot. Areas between 5,000 feet and 7,000 feet see some snow and cold temperatures in the winter, and fairly warm temperatures in July and August. Wilderness lands above 7,000 feet have a well-defined off-season when snow precludes hiking altogether.

Each entry includes a **Plants and Wildlife** section, which briefly describes the ecological features of the area: its plant communities, perhaps some unusual or endangered species of plants and animals, and the more common species of wildlife that you might expect to see. The **Geology** section summarizes some of the geological occurrences that have helped shape the wilderness. You may do well to carry along some field books about its geology.

Under the **Activities** heading you will learn about the best ways to visit the wilderness area. With one exception (Salt River Canyon), all wilderness areas are most readily accessible to hikers. Directions for accessing the wilderness and descriptions

MAP LEGEND

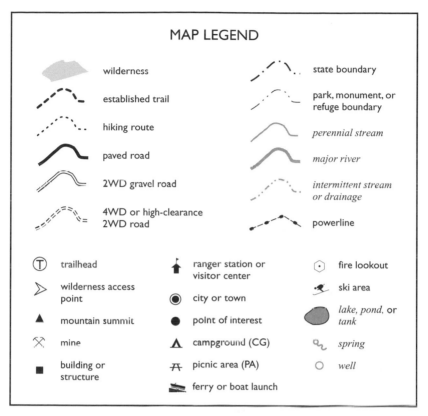

wilderness		state boundary
established trail		park, monument, or refuge boundary
hiking route		*perennial stream*
paved road		*major river*
2WD gravel road		*intermittent stream or drainage*
4WD or high-clearance 2WD road		powerline

Ⓣ	trailhead	⚑	ranger station or visitor center	⬡	fire lookout
⟩	wilderness access point	◉	city or town	⚒	ski area
▲	mountain summit	●	point of interest	◖	*lake, pond,* or *tank*
✕	mine	▲	campground (CG)	℺	*spring*
■	building or structure	𝝥	picnic area (PA)	○	*well*
		⛴	ferry or boat launch		

of the possible hiking routes within each are covered in the **Hiking** section. As with other western states, many of Arizona's national forest wildernesses feature established trails. Somewhat unique to Arizona, though, are the dozens of desert wilderness areas that feature no established hiking routes. This is largely due to the fact that these desert areas are remote and the BLM continues to manage them in as pristine a condition as possible. Despite the lack of established trails, signs, and such, these areas are mostly open to hiking because they feature natural corridors such as canyon bottoms and washes and because the terrain is sparse enough not to impede travel. While this text describes some of the most obvious hiking possibilities, it is not all-inclusive, nor should it be. Frankly, if you are an expert hiker (and only expert hikers should attempt to visit such areas), you do not need to be guided every step of the way.

In the handful of wilderness areas high enough to receive regular deposits of snow, backcountry ski touring is a possibility. **Cross-Country Skiing** sections are included, where appropriate. Although nearly all of Arizona's wildernesses include precipitous cliffs, some areas are particularly popular with rock climbers and are mentioned in **Rock Climbing** sections in the text. Lastly, despite Arizona's overall aridity, some of its desert wilderness lands are blessed with interesting stretches of river. These sections include a **River Running** entry.

WILDERNESS ETIQUETTE

As set forth in the Wilderness Act of 1964, wilderness is a place where "the earth and its community of life are untrammeled by man, where man himself is a visitor who does not remain." In practice, this simple belief has translated into individual parcels of land, within which certain rules and regulations determine which activities are acceptable and which are not. The most important of these regulations is that mechanical transport is banned. In addition to motorized vehicles, this prohibition also applies to

The Grand Canyon at sunset

all-terrain bicycles, or mountain bikes, and hang gliders. Simply put, travel within wilderness areas is restricted to foot, pack animal, or nonmotorized water craft. Contrary to what a few mountain bicyclists who have chosen to ignore this rule believe, bicycles do constitute a mechanical means of transport and, no matter how environmentally friendly they may be, bikes do not belong in designated wilderness lands. Fortunately, Arizona has plenty of interesting backcountry terrain that is legally accessible to mountain bikes.

Along with mechanical means of transport, the Wilderness Act of 1964 also bans chain saws, generators, electric toothbrushes, and other motorized devices from wilderness lands. Livestock grazing is acceptable in wilderness lands (though not in national parks). Timber cutting and mining are not allowed. Commercial outfitters can operate within the specific rules of each wilderness area. While hunting is prohibited in all national parks, and fishing is prohibited in many national parks, both are perfectly acceptable on wilderness lands. Camping is not a problem; however, some areas may restrict the use of campfires or restrict camping in environmentally sensitive areas. And pets are generally allowed, although some wildlife breeding areas may be closed to dogs. Pets are not allowed in the backcountry areas of most national parks and monuments. Where they are permitted, pets should be kept under restraint at all times so that they do not disrupt wildlife and other hikers.

Beyond these basic regulations, all visitors to Arizona's backcountry should follow some additional commonsense rules that relate to no-trace hiking and camping. These include:

- Do not build fires; use a stove instead.
- Avoid camping in sensitive areas.
- Camp at least 100 feet from trails and other hiking routes.
- Camp at least 0.25 mile from any spring or water hole—this is state law.
- Never cut standing trees, dead or alive.
- Do not leave behind any structures or nails.
- Do not dig holes and trenches or level tent sites.
- Bury all human waste at least 200 feet from water sources.
- Use biodegradable soap well away from streams.
- Travel in small groups to avoid degrading fragile wilderness lands.
- Do not cut across switchbacks.
- Avoid walking on fragile areas such as microbiotic or cryptogamic soil.
- Pack out all litter.

While most backpackers are savvy enough to follow these rules in the backcountry, they may not always think to do so when camped at trailheads or at dispersed sites along backroads. Of course, all trash should be hauled away. Use preexisting campsites when possible. Do not drive off established roads. Camp well away from streams, springs, and such (state law prohibits camping within 0.25 mile of any spring). If you really need a fire, use preexisting fire rings. Remember to bury all human waste in a hole at least 6 inches deep. In effect, leave all camp areas as clean or cleaner than you found them.

SAFETY FIRST

Because of its rugged and remote backcountry, Arizona can be a hazardous place for hikers. By following some commonsense precautions, however, you can avoid most hazards altogether. While the text below outlines some of these dangers, it is no substitute for experience when it comes to a safe and enjoyable excursion. To find out more about backcountry safety, read the following books:

Wilderness Basics: The Complete Handbook for Hikers & Backpackers, 2nd edition. The San Diego Chapter of the Sierra Club. Seattle: The Mountaineers, 1993.

Mountaineering: The Freedom of the Hills, 6th edition. Don Graydon and Kurt Hanson, eds. Seattle: The Mountaineers, 1992.

Desert Hiking. David Ganci. Berkeley: Wilderness Press, 1993.

Keep Your Cool

One of the greatest dangers facing outdoor enthusiasts visiting Arizona's backcountry is the heat. From late spring through early fall, temperatures in the low desert elevations easily top 100 degrees, and even exceed 115 degrees during hot spells. At these temperatures, the body can quickly become dehydrated, leading to fatigue, exhaustion, heat stroke, and death. The best thing to do is to avoid exerting yourself in the heat altogether. If you do find yourself out in such conditions, drink plenty of water—a gallon per person per day is the minimum amount—and be sure to drink often. Sometimes you may not think about it until it is too late. If you begin to feel dizzy, have a headache, your skin is cool, pale, and sweaty, and you lack energy, then you are probably suffering from heat exhaustion—a condition that will shortly lead to heat stroke. If this happens, rest in a cool and shady place, drink plenty of water, then seek medical attention as quickly as possible.

A second hazard in the desert and the mountains is severe sunburn. Although it is often little more than a painful nuisance, sunburn can become serious. To prevent sunburn, wear light-colored clothing and a broad-brimmed hat to protect your face, ears, and neck. Apply plenty of sunblock (SPF 15 or higher) to exposed skin.

Hypothermia

Yes, hypothermia is a very real hazard for hikers in Arizona. The weather here may change quite rapidly and temperatures drop significantly as soon as the sun goes down, especially at higher elevations. Hypothermia results from exposure to cold and damp conditions. This combination can cause the body's core temperature to drop to dangerous levels. Symptoms include uncontrollable shivering, impaired judgment, failing speech, weakness, and severe drowsiness. The best way to treat this killer is to prevent it from ever happening at all. As a precaution, carry extra clothing (synthetic fleece and wool are best: they stay warm even when wet), rain gear, and plenty of high-energy food. If someone in your party does show signs of hypothermia, get him or her into dry, warm clothing immediately, then into a warm sleeping bag if possible. If all else fails, have another person strip and get into the sleeping bag with the victim to

Vultee Arch is a popular sight for hikers in the Red Rock–Secret Mountain Wilderness.

provide warmth. Administer warm liquids and high-energy food and get the victim to a doctor as soon as possible.

Lightning

The threat of lightning is considerable in much of Arizona. Violent thunderstorms rake across much of the state on many a summer afternoon. These sudden storms are not uncommon during other times of the year as well. To avoid being struck by lightning, move away from higher, exposed terrain as the storms roll in. Watching the weather helps, but these storms can build in a matter of an hour or less. Should you find yourself in an exposed location, look for a low-lying or flat area away from trees and crouch down. If you are caught out in the open, away from shelter, crouch down on all fours, hands and feet planted on the ground. Tents are not safe but cars are. Deep caves are safe while shallow alcoves are not.

Flash Floods

Another threat that Arizona's varied weather poses is flash floods. Sudden, heavy rains can send a wall of water crashing down washes and canyon bottoms. Rain falling many miles away may produce flash floods that hikers may not know about until it is too late. When hiking along streambeds and other prone areas, keep in mind the possibility of flash floods and make sure you can get to higher ground. Additionally, do not try to drive across flooded roads or streambeds; this is how many deaths occur. Sit tight on higher ground until the waters recede. Never camp in a wash.

Wildlife

While there are lions, not tigers, but, yes, bears, in Arizona's backcountry, the chances of them bothering you are quite rare, especially if you take a few precautions. As black bears are becoming more and more used to the presence of people, they are more apt to enter a camp in their search for a free handout. To avoid this less-than-ideal contact, hang your food from trees 10 feet off the ground and 4 feet away from the trunk, and well away from camp. As for mountain lions: there have been a few isolated attacks on people in the past, but they have nearly always resulted when a cat has grown used to living near a populated area. Generally, these elusive creatures are quite shy and will go to great lengths to avoid contact with people.

A more common creature to worry about is the rattlesnake. Found throughout Arizona, these venomous serpents can pose a hazard to hikers who may not be paying attention, especially when hiking cross-country in desert locales. Rattlesnakes will almost always let you know they're nearby with a shake of their tail. Because they cannot control body temperature, rattlers are likely to keep cool under rocks or in alcoves during the day, so be careful where you put your hands and feet during rest stops. Snakebites are treatable. If you should be bitten, seek medical assistance at once. This holds true with scorpion stings and black widow spider bites. Keep in mind that rattlesnakes are an important part of the ecological community and should be left alone. Chances are they will head the opposite way as soon as possible when confronted by

Within the depths of Buckskin Gulch

a hiker. Consider carrying a snakebite kit in your pack, available at outdoor stores.

Two additional hazards posed by Arizona's wildlife have become prevalent in just the last decade. One is the hantavirus, a deadly disease that is spread through contact with the droppings and urine of deer mice and other rodents. A swift killer, hantavirus came into the limelight during an epidemic that occurred in the Four Corners area in 1993. At that time an unknown ailment had taken several lives in short succession. Quick action by local health officials identified the virus and its source, but an effective cure has yet to be found. To avoid contracting hantavirus, keep away from rodents, their tunnels and dens, and places they may inhabit, such as old cabins. Backpackers should sleep in a tent and keep all food in rodent-proof containers.

A second, new hazard is the influx into Arizona of Africanized, or "killer," bees. In the few years since these aggressive insects were introduced to Brazil, they have spread northward all the way to the American Southwest. An angry swarm killed one person in Texas, and several people have been attacked in the Phoenix and Tucson

Cottonwood branches along Kanab Creek

areas. It is not that the sting of this exotic strain of bee is any worse than that of normal bees, nor do they go looking for victims. It is simply that these bees will defend their hives with incredible ferocity. Since killer bees are here to stay, residents of and visitors to the deserts of the Southwest (it is thought that the insect will not be able to establish itself in colder climates north of the desert areas) must learn to live with them. The number one rule is to avoid beehives altogether. If you find yourself near a hive, move slowly away and do not swat at the insects. Keep dogs close by you, since they may rile bees if they get close. And, if you are attacked, run like mad. An adult can often run faster and farther than a bee can fly. Keep in mind, however, that they may pursue a victim for up to half a mile. Once you are far enough away, try to remove the stingers as quickly as possible and seek medical help immediately.

Giardia

While not deadly, *Giardia lamblia,* a microorganism found in most surface water, is a common ailment for hikers who do not take the proper precautions to treat water before drinking it. Giardia can cause severe diarrhea, bloating, and nausea, symptoms that may not appear until weeks later. To avoid contracting Giardia, the best solution is to boil your water (at least 3 minutes for every 1,000 feet in elevation) before drinking it or use a filter (but beware: not all filters are small enough to remove Giardia cysts). Most chemical treatments do not work against Giardia.

Once the ailment has been contracted, only treatment administered by a doctor will cure it.

Losing Your Way

No matter how experienced a hiker you are, it is very easy to get lost or hurt in Arizona's wilderness areas. While experience is the best way of preventing this unfortunate situation, seasoned hikers are still prone to losing their way or becoming hurt in Arizona's backcountry. To prevent such a predicament, hikers of all abilities should not travel alone. Before setting out, be sure to let someone know about your travel plans: where you are going, when you will be back, etc. Good maps are a must when leaving civilization behind, as are good equipment, a suitable food supply, plenty of water, and a good first-aid kit. If you do become lost or injured, remain calm and stay in one place to wait for help.

Be Prepared

It is a deceptively simple thing to say that a little planning can go a long way toward insuring a fun and successful trip into the backcountry. But it is true.

When preparing for a wilderness outing, you should first take a good look at the gear you plan to take. When considering Arizona's heat, bring light-colored clothing that will protect you from the sun, yet keep you as cool as possible. A wide-brimmed hat is a good idea. No matter where or when you are hiking, bring suitable rain gear, such as a poncho and waterproof pants. Sturdy and comfortable hiking shoes are a must. A comfortable pack in which you can store your gear is an important item and, if you are heading out overnight, a good tent, sleeping bag, and pad are required.

To supplement these items, there is also a list of ten essential items that hikers should always carry. They include:

1. Extra clothing for keeping warm and dry
2. Extra food for extra energy
3. Sunglasses
4. Knife
5. Fire starter material, such as a candle
6. First-aid kit
7. Matches in a weatherproof container
8. Flashlight with extra batteries and bulb
9. Map or maps
10. Compass and the skills to use it

Sunglasses are a particularly important item to take into the desert, where the wind can carry a lot of sand. Sunglasses can protect your eyes from blowing sand as well as from the glare of the sun.

A NOTE ABOUT SAFETY

Safety is an important concern in all outdoor activities. No guidebook can alert you to every hazard or anticipate the limitations of every reader. Therefore, the descriptions of roads, trails, routes, and natural features in this book are not representations that a particular place or excursion will be safe for your party. When you follow any of the routes described in this book, you assume responsibility for your own safety. Under normal conditions, such excursions require the usual attention to traffic, road and trail conditions, weather, terrain, the capabilities of your party, and other factors. Because many of the lands in this book are subject to development and/or change of ownership, conditions may have changed since this book was written that make your use of some of these routes unwise. Always check for current conditions, obey posted private property signs, and avoid confrontations with property owners or managers. Keeping informed on current conditions and exercising common sense are the keys to a safe, enjoyable outing.

The Mountaineers Books

Opposite: *The Colorado River flows through the Inner Gorge.*

chapter 1 **Colorado Plateau**

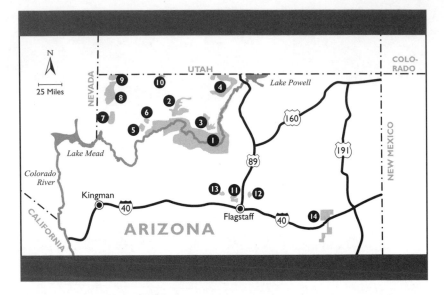

Spanning the Four Corners region, the Colorado Plateau is a highly scenic collection of canyons, mesas, mountains, and plateaus. And certainly, Arizona's share of it is as intriguing as the rest. Highlighted by the Grand Canyon, several tracts of wilderness edge up to this great abyss; among them Kanab Creek, Saddle Mountain, Mount Logan, and Mount Trumbull. Whereas these wild areas extend wilderness protection beyond the boundaries of Grand Canyon National Park, they also embrace natural features of an area known as the Arizona Strip—the part of the state that falls north of the canyon. Other wilderness areas within the Strip include Paria Canyon–Vermilion Cliffs, Grand Wash Cliffs, Paiute, Beaver Dam Mountains, and Cottonwood Point.

Embracing sections of the Painted Desert in the northeastern part of the state is Petrified Forest Wilderness, which falls within a national park by the same name. And encompassing the forested and alpine peaks that spike the skyline around Flagstaff are Kachina Peaks, Strawberry Crater, and Kendrick Mountain Wildernesses. From deep canyon bottoms and stretches of arid desert to the highest reaches of the state, the Colorado Plateau offers up Arizona's most diverse selection of wild lands.

Grand Canyon National Park

Location: 80 miles N of Flagstaff
Size: 1,218,376 acres
Status: National park (1919)
Terrain: Canyons and plateaus
Elevation: 1,600 feet to 8,827 feet
Management: NPS
Topographic maps: Bright Angel, Grand Canyon, Phantom Ranch, Cape Royal, Grandview Point, Bright Angel Point, Vulcans Throne, Vulcans Throne SE, Whitmore Rapids, Mount Trumbull SE, Mount Trumbull NE, Mount Logan, Hancock Knolls, Little Park Lake, Columbine Falls, Bat Cave, Tincanebitts Point, Mount Dellenbaugh, Whitmore Point SW, Whitmore Point SE, Snap Canyon East, Snap Canyon West, Snap Draw, Whitmore Point, Yellow John Mountain, Devils Slide Rapids, Travertine Rapids, Separation Canyon, Spencer Canyon, Granite Park, Price Point, Amos Point, Quartermaster Canyon, Quaking Aspen, Tapeats Amphitheater, Fishtail, Kanab Point, Hitson Tank, Hancock Knolls, Fern Glen Canyon, S B Point, Havasu Falls, Fossil Bay, Powell Plateau, King Arthur Castle, Kanabownits Spring, Little Park Lake, Gateway Rapids, Yunosi Point, Topocoba Hilltop, Explorers Monument, Havasupai Point, Shiva Temple, Piute Point, Navajo Bridge, Bitter Springs, Emmett Wash, North Canyon Point, Buffalo Tanks, Buffalo Ranch, Tatahatso Point, Nankoweap Mesa, Point Imperial, Cape Solitude, Walhalla Plateau, Cape Royal, Desert View, Tusayan East

For wilderness enthusiasts, the Grand Canyon offers an inexhaustible number of opportunities to explore one of the most spectacular settings on earth. A mile deep in places and more than 8 miles wide, the canyon offers an incredible smorgasbord of geological wonders and biological communities. While most of the nearly 5 million annual visitors to Grand Canyon National Park simply gawk at the big hole from overlooks along the South and North Rims, some do venture into its depths. Of those that do, the majority use three major routes to descend into the canyon: the Bright Angel, South Kaibab, and North Kaibab Trails. Beyond these trails, however, are numerous other routes, which access various corners of the park. While considerably more rugged than the above-mentioned routes, these secondary trails are a real pleasure for those experienced hikers who come well prepared. In addition to hiking trails, the Grand Canyon can also be explored by boat. The 277-mile section of the Colorado River that runs between Lees Ferry and Pearce Ferry on Lake Mead is perhaps the most coveted stretch of wild waterway in the nation. Currently, some 1,109,257 acres of Grand Canyon National Park are included in a Wilderness Study Area. This text, however, takes into consideration the entire park, since all backcountry portions of national park lands are maintained to offer a wilderness experience.

Seasons

While much of the Grand Canyon may be enjoyed year-round, there are seasonal restrictions on use in many areas. From November to the middle of May, the North Rim is closed by heavy snowfalls. Winter on the South Rim is rarely severe enough to make trails impassable, although they may become icy. You can, however, expect subfreezing temperatures from November to March at higher elevations. During the winter, temperatures at the canyon bottom are usually a pleasant 60 or 70 degrees, but during the summer season they often top the 100-degree mark. Any trip between May and October should take into account these conditions. The best times for hiking in the canyon are generally the months of March through May and late September through October.

Plants and Wildlife

Given the nearly 6,000 feet of elevation change between the canyon bottom and the North Rim, it is no surprise that a diverse selection of plants grows in Grand Canyon National Park. Of the seven life zones found in North America, four are represented here. Beginning in the lowest elevations of the canyon is the Lower Sonoran Zone, which supports black brush, Mormon tea, saltbush, yucca, agave, ocotillo, and various cactus. The Upper Sonoran Zone features pinyon pine, juniper, cliffrose, rabbitbrush, and sagebrush. Characteristic of the Transition Zone are forests of ponderosa pine and Gambel oak, which may be seen along portions of both the South and North Rims. The highest life zone in the park is the Canadian Zone, found only at the higher-elevation North Rim. Plants living in this life zone receive more moisture and enjoy a cooler environment in summer. Characteristic vegetation includes beautiful forests of blue

Blooming yucca along the Tonto Trail

spruce, Engelmann spruce, Douglas fir, and quaking aspen. Within the Grand Canyon is the verdant riparian zone, found along secondary streams, springs, and, after the completion of the Glen Canyon Dam in 1963, portions of the Colorado River. Prior to this time, spring runoff often scoured the banks of the river clean of growth. Today, an exotic species of water-loving plant known as tamarisk, or saltcedar, now chokes many shoreline areas, crowding out willow and other species.

Wildlife in the Grand Canyon includes mule deer, which, during the early part of the twentieth century, suffered greatly from the wildlife management policy of the day. To boost the deer population on the Kaibab Plateau, hundreds of mountain lions were killed. The deer population grew so large that thousands of them died from starvation. Mule deer populations on the plateau have since stabilized, and mountain lions are once again an important predator species within Grand Canyon National Park. Desert bighorn sheep live in the more rugged reaches of the canyon. Among the species of rodents that reside within the park is the Abert squirrel, which lives on the South Rim, and the Kaibab squirrel, which lives only on the North Rim. Bird species include great-horned owls, red-tailed hawks, golden eagles, turkeys, and distinctive-sounding canyon wrens. A variety of lizards haunt the more arid portions of the canyon, as do rattlesnakes. One species unique to the canyon is the Grand Canyon rattlesnake. Swimming among the waters of the Colorado River are eighteen different species of fish, including catfish, trout, and an endangered species known as the humpbacked chub.

Geology

Nearly 2 billion years of the earth's history are exposed in the Grand Canyon, offering an in-depth look at the geologic processes that continue to shape North America. Beginning on the rim and descending into the canyon, the youngest sedimentary rock at the Grand Canyon is Kaibab Limestone. It was deposited in a shallow sea about 250 million years ago. This limestone sits atop the 260 million-year-old Toroweap Formation. Coconino Sandstone is next. Heavily crossbedded, this 270 million-year-old formation resulted from sand dunes. Farther down, the Hermit Shale is a deep red stone, which dates back 280 million years. The Supai Group, a collection of different siltstones and sandstones, is 300 million years old. The Redwall Limestone constitutes one of the most imposing cliff faces in the canyon. It was formed 330 million years ago and is embedded with marine fossils. The Temple Butte Limestone dates back 370 million years. Muav Limestone is next. It was deposited in a shallow sea about 530 million years ago. The Bright Angel Shale is about 540 million years old and forms the Tonto Platform—an obvious bench that runs within much of the canyon. Next in line is the Tapeats Sandstone, which is about 10 million years older. Below this formation is a 250 million-year gap in the record that John Wesley Powell called the Great Unconformity. It resulted from an extended period of erosion. Below that is the Grand Canyon Supergroup, a collection of rock layers set at an angle by uplifting. It represents a period of deposition that took place between 800 and 1,200 million years ago. And finally, forming the Inner Gorge of the Grand Canyon, is the oldest of the Grand Canyon's rock types: the Vishnu schist. Dating back nearly 2 billion years, this dark metamorphic rock is thought to be the remains of a Precambrian mountain range. In places, it is streaked with impressive veins of rose-colored Zoroaster granite.

About 65 million years ago, the Colorado Plateau began rising due to forces deep within the earth. While geologists are not certain how long ago the Grand Canyon began to form, it is thought to have appeared only within the last 6 million years. Sporadic volcanic activity about 1 million years ago has added to the complexity of the canyon's geologic story. One of these lava flows helped shape the Toroweap area in the western portion of the park.

History

The Grand Canyon was inhabited by prehistoric hunter-gatherers as early as 2000 B.C. Evidence of their passage has been found in remote caves within the canyon, where small split-twig figurines made of willow were placed. Depicting deer or sheep, these figurines may have been used as ritual offerings to ensure a good hunt. During more recent times—beginning around A.D. 500—the Grand Canyon was home to two additional groups. In the east, early Pueblo people, formerly known as the Anasazi, built scattered cliff dwellings, while the canyon's western portion was home to the Cohonina people, who had retained more of a hunter-gatherer tradition. By A.D. 1150, a contraction of these prehistoric cultures led to the abandonment of the canyon. By A.D. 1300, the Cerbat people had moved into the South Rim area from the lower deserts to the south. The Cerbats are the ancestors of the Havasupai and Hualapai who still live in the canyon today. Other Indian groups that moved into the vicinity of the canyon in the centuries that followed were the Navajo and the Southern Paiute.

In 1540, the Spanish explorer Coronado led the first expedition into the American Southwest from what we now know as Mexico. Branching off from the main party, a scouting party eventually found themselves on the South Rim. After three days of searching for a way down to the Colorado River, which seemed so close, they gave up in frustration. Other Spanish expeditions were no more successful. The 1776 Dominguez–Escalante Expedition passed just north of the canyon while returning to what is now New Mexico after its failed attempt to find a route to Spanish missions in California. The first Anglo-American to gaze upon the canyon may have been mountain man James Ohio Pattie in the early 1800s, but no record exists to back the claim. During the second half of the nineteenth century, various American expeditions made feeble attempts at learning the canyon's secrets, but it was not until 1869 that the first complete exploration of the canyon took place. That was when a Civil War veteran, Major John Wesley Powell, and his small contingent set out in wooden boats to float through the canyon. Not knowing what lay ahead, their voyage cut across one of the last remaining blank spots on the map. Repeating the feat two years later, Powell's float trips contributed greatly to our knowledge of the Southwest.

In 1908, President Theodore Roosevelt set aside portions of the canyon as a national monument. Then, eleven years later, Woodrow Wilson signed the bill that turned the canyon into a national park. In 1975, a stroke of Gerald Ford's pen nearly doubled the size of the park.

ACTIVITIES
Hiking

Although day trips into the Grand Canyon backcountry are not restricted, overnight hikes require a permit from the National Park Service. These permits must be obtained by mail, often months in advance. They are especially hard to come by for such popular routes as the Bright Angel, South Kaibab, North Kaibab, and Grandview Trails. Because of their popularity, camping along these routes is restricted to backcountry campgrounds. For more information about backcountry permits, visit or write the Backcountry Office, Grand Canyon National Park, P.O. Box 129, Grand Canyon, AZ 86023, or call (520) 638-7875 between 1:00 P.M. and 5:00 P.M.

South Rim

Beginning along the South Rim, a number of trails drop into the canyon's depths. The easiest (a relative term where Grand Canyon hiking is concerned) and most heavily used route is the Bright Angel Trail, which begins near Bright Angel Lodge at the western end of Grand Canyon Village. This well-developed trail drops 4,400 feet in nearly 8 miles. Because of its almost constant descent, many hikers get into trouble thinking that this is an easy hike. Going down is, in fact, relatively easy, but hiking back out is another story. You can count on all Grand Canyon return hikes taking twice as long as the hike down. Within the first 3 miles, the Bright Angel Trail switchbacks several times. Two rest houses are found along the way; one at mile 1.6 and the other at mile 3.1. Drinking water is available at these facilities from mid-May to mid-October. About 4.5 miles in, the trail reaches the Indian Garden Campground, a good place for novice hikers to turn around or spend the night. Water is also available here. From Indian Garden, a nice side hike continues 2.2 miles to Plateau Point, which is perched on the edge of the Inner Gorge. Beyond the campground, the Bright Angel Trail drops into the Inner Gorge by way of the Devils Corkscrew. The trail reaches the river 7.8 miles from the trailhead, at which point the River Trail begins. It, in turn, follows the Colorado River upstream for 1.2 miles before reaching Silver Bridge, which accesses Bright Angel Campground and historic Phantom Ranch. A second bridge, the vintage Kaibab Suspension Bridge, crosses the river less than a mile upstream. Hikers using the Bright Angel Trail should be aware that mule trains carrying both tourists and gear use this trail frequently and will likely be encountered. If you encounter a mule train, you are required to step well off the trail until it passes.

A second popular route to the canyon bottom is the South Kaibab Trail. Dropping roughly the same number of feet as the Bright Angel Trail, the South Kaibab Trail does it in 6.4 miles. It is steeper and there is no water along the way and very little shade, so come prepared. From Yaki Point, which is a couple of miles east of Grand Canyon Village, the trail drops down Cedar Ridge before reaching the Tonto Platform. From there, it descends into the Inner Gorge. The route reaches the river at the Kaibab

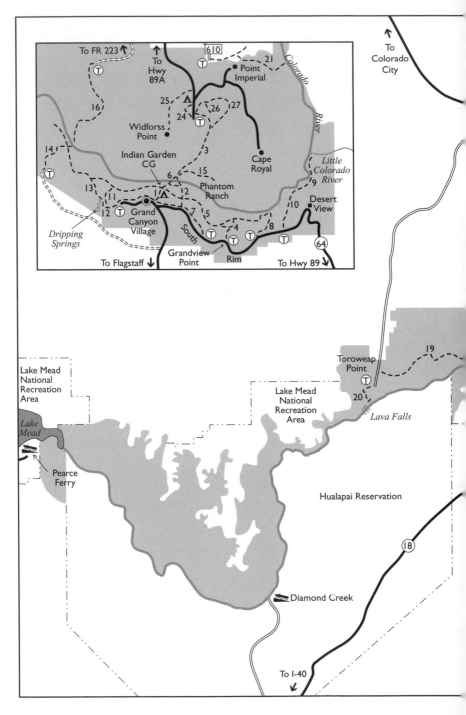

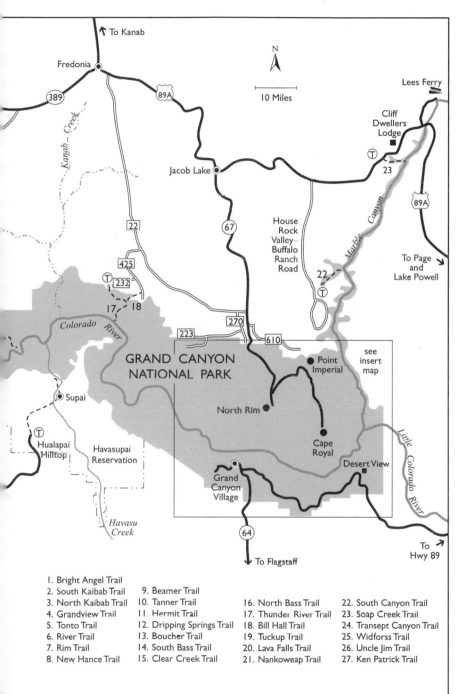

To Kanab

Fredonia

389

89A

Kanab Creek

Jacob Lake

22

67

425

232

17 18

Colorado River

GRAND CANYON
NATIONAL PARK

Supai

Hualapai
Hilltop

Havasupai
Reservation

Havasu
Creek

N

10 Miles

Lees Ferry

Cliff
Dwellers
Lodge

23

89A

House
Rock
Valley–
Buffalo
Ranch
Road

22

Marble Canyon

To Page
and
Lake Powell

223

270

610

see
insert
map

Point
Imperial

North Rim

Cape
Royal

Desert View

Grand
Canyon
Village

Little Colorado River

64

To Flagstaff

To
Hwy 89

1. Bright Angel Trail
2. South Kaibab Trail
3. North Kaibab Trail
4. Grandview Trail
5. Tonto Trail
6. River Trail
7. Rim Trail
8. New Hance Trail

9. Beamer Trail
10. Tanner Trail
11. Hermit Trail
12. Dripping Springs Trail
13. Boucher Trail
14. South Bass Trail
15. Clear Creek Trail

16. North Bass Trail
17. Thunder River Trail
18. Bill Hall Trail
19. Tuckup Trail
20. Lava Falls Trail
21. Nankoweap Trail

22. South Canyon Trail
23. Soap Creek Trail
24. Transept Canyon Trail
25. Widforss Trail
26. Uncle Jim Trail
27. Ken Patrick Trail

The Grand Canyon as seen from the South Rim

Suspension Bridge, then crosses the river to continue 0.5 mile to the Bright Angel Campground. A possible round-trip hike follows both the South Kaibab and Bright Angel Trails.

While other trails enter the canyon from the South Rim, none are as developed and easy to follow as the Bright Angel and South Kaibab Trails. In the eastern portion of the park, the 9-mile New Hance Trail begins a short distance west of Desert View and drops 4,660 feet to Tanner Rapids, where it connects with the Beamer Trail. Unmaintained, the New Hance Trail is rugged, sometimes indistinct, and steep. The Beamer Trail continues upstream for 9 miles, to reach the mouth of the Little Colorado River. It also heads downstream from Tanner Rapids for a few miles, to reach the end of the New Hance Trail and the start of the Tonto Trail. Dropping about 5,000 feet in 8 miles, the rugged New Hance Trail is accessed a mile southwest of Moran Point. Like other trails, the New Hance route is steep, hard to follow in places, and quite rugged: in other words, for experienced hikers only.

Farther west, at Grandview Point, the Grandview Trail makes its way into the canyon. Dropping 2,600 feet in 3 miles, this popular trail reaches Horseshoe Mesa, the site of a backcountry campground. The remains of some old mines remind hikers that the mesa was a source of copper for many centuries—from prehistoric times, when the early Puebloan people collected the bluish ore for paint, until the turn of the century, when prospector Pete Berry and the Cameron brothers extracted high-grade ore from the ground. From Horseshoe Mesa, it is possible to drop into Hance Creek to the east or descend west into Cottonwood Creek. Both of these routes reach the Tonto Trail within a few miles. In somewhat better shape than the Tanner and New Hance Trails, the Grandview Trail is easier to follow, although it is steep in spots, and there are some dangerous exposures along the way.

West of Grand Canyon Village, West Rim Drive leads to Hermits Rest and the start of the Hermit Trail. West Rim Drive is closed to private vehicles from late May through September, but a free shuttle bus transports visitors between the village and Hermits Rest. From road's end, the Hermit Trail (named for a hermit who lived below the rim) drops about 1,500 feet in 1.25 miles to reach Hermit Basin, where it connects with the 1.5-mile Dripping Springs Trail—a nice spring nestled in a grotto. Beyond the turnoff for Dripping Springs, the Hermit Trail drops deftly into Hermit Gorge. The route then descends sharply along a set of switchbacks known as the Cathedral Stairs. In all, the 8.5-mile Hermit Trail descends 4,300 feet and is steep in places. Within 1.5 miles of the Colorado River, the Hermit Trail intersects the Tonto Trail, which it then follows for a while. One possible round-trip hike would be to follow the Hermit Trail to the Tonto Trail, turn west, and then take up the 6.5-mile Boucher Trail. From Boucher Creek, the Boucher Trail climbs around the head of Travertine Canyon and then on to Yuma Point, before connecting with the Dripping Springs Trail.

Several miles west of the Hermit Trail, the South Bass Trail descends into the canyon from the end of a 28-mile drive on dirt roads. In 7 miles, this route descends 4,400 feet via Bass Canyon. As the South Bass Trail nears the river, it, too, intersects the Tonto Trail. The Tonto Trail follows its namesake—the Tonto Platform—for 95 miles. As a prominent bench within the Grand Canyon, the Tonto Platform offers a wonderful avenue along which to hike. But it is also arid and can be very hot. Comparatively speaking, it is somewhat level, although the trail often strays far from a straight course to skirt around side drainages. Nevertheless, this trail offers a scenic, east-west avenue across much of the park. Beginning at the end of the New Hance Trail, the Tonto Trail continues west all the way to Garnet Canyon. Besides the New Hance Trail, access routes to the Tonto Trail include the Grandview, South Kaibab, Bright Angel, Hermit, Boucher, and South Bass Trails. Distances along the Tonto between these trails vary greatly. It is 10 miles, for instance, from the New Hance Trail to the Grandview Trail, 5 miles from the South Kaibab Trail to the Bright Angel Trail, and 30 miles between Hermit and Bass. Planning a hike along the Tonto would depend on how much time you have for the hike and which portion of the canyon you want to see. One interesting hike, nearly 30 miles long, accesses the Tonto Trail by way of the Grandview Trail. Following the Tonto Trail west, it then climbs back out of the canyon on the South Kaibab. Although water is available at some springs, it is best to check with the National Park Service for a current list of reliable water sources.

North Rim

The number of trails that drop to the Colorado River from the North Rim are fewer than those on the south, but they are considerably less crowded. The primary trail on this side of the canyon is the 14.2-mile North Kaibab Trail. Following Bright Angel Creek for most of the way, this route takes in some spectacular sights. After dropping into Roaring Springs Canyon, the trail passes by impressive Roaring Springs. It then takes up perennial Bright Angel Creek, a waterway with a ribbon of verdant riparian growth. A little beyond the halfway point a 0.25-mile side trail leads to Ribbon Falls. Within the last few miles to Phantom Ranch the route follows the Box, an interesting corridor through walls of Vishnu schist. Like the South Kaibab and Bright Angel Trails, the North Kaibab Trail is well maintained and is utilized by mule trains.

A nice side route that turns off the North Kaibab Trail less than a mile north of Phantom Ranch, the 8-mile Clear Creek Trail climbs 1,500 feet in the first 2 miles, then levels off to follow the Tonto Platform eastward to the Clear Creek drainage. Clear Creek is a perennial stream that flows from the north. Eight miles upstream from trail's end is Cheyava Falls, the highest waterfall in the canyon. The Colorado River is 5 miles downstream.

Reaching Bass Rapids from a remote trailhead on the North Rim is the North Bass Trail. Approximately 14 miles long, this rugged route drops more than 5,300 feet. From Swamp Point, this trail descends to Muav Saddle, and then into Muav Canyon. Following White Creek for a while, it then takes up Shinumo Creek. In the last couple of miles the trail leaves the canyon bottom to avoid tangled growth. The start of this trail is reached by turning off Arizona Highway 67 at the Kaibab Lodge onto Forest Road (FR) 22. Follow it for a short distance to FR 270. Turn left and continue to FR 223. Follow this road west for several miles to FR 223A, then turn west on Swamp Ridge Road and follow it to Swamp Point.

Farther west in the canyon, the 17-mile Thunder River Trail drops into Tapeats Creek, which it follows to Tapeats Rapids on the Colorado River. Along the way, the route follows its namesake—a river that gushes from Thunder Spring before dumping into Tapeats Creek 0.5 mile later. Trail considerations include the lack of water for the first 10 miles and the fact that Tapeats Creek may be impossible to cross during spring runoff. Variations on this hike include a side route to Deer Creek, which branches off in Surprise Valley, and the Bill Hall Trail, a route that descends from Monument Point to the Thunder River Trail. The trailhead for the Thunder River Trail is located at Indian Hollow, which is reached by driving FR 22 for 18 miles to FR 425. Follow this road south for about 10 miles to FR 232.

West of the Thunder River Trail, Kanab Creek offers access to the Colorado River by way of Kanab Creek Wilderness. (See entry on Kanab Creek.)

The rather lengthy Tuckup Trail starts out about 5 miles east of Toroweap Point, then meanders for more than 60 miles along arid benches and around the heads of several canyons, before reaching Boysag Point to the east. A side route drops from the approximate halfway point of this trail, down Cottonwood and Tuckup Canyons, to reach the river. Needless to say, any hike along the rugged and often indistinct

Tuckup Trail requires considerable stamina and sound backcountry travel skills.

More of a route delineated by cairns than an actual trail, the Lava Falls Trail offers access to the most famous of Grand Canyon rapids. Although less than 2 miles long, the route drops 2,300 feet, making it one of the most difficult hikes in the canyon. Because it is so steep, plan on most of the day to complete this hike and expect some perilous sections of loose rock along the way. Do not attempt this hike alone. Wear sturdy hiking boots (which should go without saying in the Grand Canyon and all other rugged territory). Don't count on finding any drinking water; you'll have to pack it in. Remember, too: temperatures climb above 100 degrees in a hurry. Enough said. With any luck you may reach Lava Falls just as a boating party is preparing to run them. The Lava Falls Trail starts out a few miles west of Toroweap Point. In one of the more remote sections of the park, Toroweap is reached by driving more than 60 miles of gravel road south from Arizona Highway 389 near Fredonia. The sheer dropoff offers one of the most spectacular views of the canyon in the park.

Some easy trails on the North Rim also promise a true wilderness experience. The leisurely Transept Canyon Trail follows the canyon rim for 1.5 miles, from Grand Canyon Lodge to North Rim Campground. The 5-mile Widforss Trail heads south from a trailhead to a point by the same name. The 2.5-mile Uncle Jim Trail sets out from the North Kaibab trailhead to reach Uncle Jim Point east of Grand Canyon Lodge at the North Rim. And the 6-mile Ken Patrick Trail follows the Uncle Jim Trail for 0.5 mile before dropping to meet the North Kaibab Trail below. Except for the Ken Patrick Trail, all of these trails are easy and take you through some lovely forests of aspen, fir, and spruce.

Marble Canyon

East of the North Kaibab Trail, a number of side canyons access the Marble Canyon section of the park from the North Rim. Nankoweap Canyon is one. Beginning at Saddle Mountain, the 14-mile Nankoweap Trail descends along Tilted Mesa before dropping into Nankoweap Canyon. Rugged stretches and steep grades make this a difficult hike. To reach the Nankoweap Trail, drive south on House Rock Valley–Buffalo Ranch Road from US Highway 89A. When you reach Kaibab National Forest, follow FR 445 to the trailhead.

South Canyon offers a shorter but similarly difficult route into the canyon, upstream from Nankoweap Canyon. In 6 miles, the trail drops 2,700 feet along a rugged canyon bottom. Near the mouth of South Canyon, you will have to contour north for some distance before descending the Redwall Limestone Formation. Like the Nankoweap Trail, South Canyon is accessed from House Rock Valley–Buffalo Ranch Road. Farther north, not far from the Marble Canyon Bridge over the Colorado River, is Soap Creek. Although the route starts out on BLM land, it soon enters the national park. The trailhead is located about a mile west of Cliff Dwellers Lodge, just off US Highway 89A. About 4.5 miles in length, the Soap Creek Trail follows its namesake to Soap Creek Rapids on the Colorado River. Along the way, an extensive boulder fall must be negotiated, as well as a pour-off that must be skirted by way of the south canyon wall. This route is moderately difficult.

Indian Land Access

Although falling outside the national park boundary, some additional routes warrant mention here because they offer unique views of the Grand Canyon. A number of short but rugged routes drop into Marble Canyon from the Navajo Nation to the east. These include Jackass Canyon, Salt Water Wash, and Shinumo Wash, among others. A permit from the Navajo Nation is required since these are all located on tribal land. A longer, maintained trail drops into Havasu Canyon from Hualapai Hilltop. The fabled home of the Havasupai Indians, this canyon is a virtual paradise with its splendid waterfalls. The Indian village of Supai, complete with restaurant, motel, school, and post office, is an 8-mile hike from the trailhead, while the falls and campground area are 2 miles farther. A permit must be obtained from the Havasupai Indian Tribe. Call (520) 448-2121 or write Havasupai Tourist Enterprise, Supai, AZ 86435. Horse packing services are also available.

Safety

Water is available at some springs and along some drainages in the Grand Canyon National Park, but it should be treated before drinking. Given the great elevation changes within the canyon, hikers should expect strenuous hiking conditions throughout. Many areas are very remote, so use extreme caution when traveling along park trails. Keep in mind that all historical and archaeological artifacts are protected by law and should be left alone. Be sure to obtain a backcountry permit before setting out on overnight excursions.

Rafters tackle Lava Falls.

River Running

Float trips down the Colorado River offer an entirely different look at the Grand Canyon. Within the 277 river miles between Lees Ferry and Pearce Ferry, the Colorado descends through 160 rapids for a total drop of 1,900 feet. This stretch of the river actually includes two different sections. The first is a run of 225 miles, from Lees Ferry to Diamond Creek, and the second covers 52 river miles, from Diamond Creek to Pearce Ferry. Most of the second stretch now includes water stilled by Hoover Dam.

Downstream from Lees Ferry, the first rapid of significance is Badger Rapid at mile 8. Soap Creek Rapid is located at mile 11. At mile 52 is Nankoweap Rapid, a drop of 25 feet. The Little Colorado River joins the Colorado 9 miles after Nankoweap, and Hance Rapid drops the river 30 feet at mile 77. At mile 87 is Bright Angel Creek and Phantom Ranch. There is actually a pay phone here, and it is not uncommon for some boat passengers to cut their trip short by hiking out to the South Rim along the South Kaibab or Bright Angel Trails. Crystal Rapid, while dropping only 17 feet, greatly challenges river runners at mile 98. Tapeats Rapids is located at mile 133 and, saving the best for last, is Lava Falls, which drops 37 feet. Located at mile 180, Lava Falls is the last big water before reaching Diamond Creek, 45 miles beyond. Because Diamond Creek to Pearce Ferry drops a mere 100 feet in 53 miles, the thrills and spills are not up to snuff. For oar-powered trips, you should plan on a minimum of 18 days to complete this expedition—longer if you want to do some hiking along the way. Motor-powered excursions can make the trip in 8 days. Private trips can be planned, but permits are often years in coming due to a lengthy waiting list. For information about obtaining a permit write: Attn: River Permits Office, Grand Canyon National Park, P.O. Box 129, Grand Canyon, AZ 86023; or call (520) 638-7843.

2 Kanab Creek Wilderness

Location: 28 miles S of Fredonia
Size: 68,596 acres
Status: Wilderness area (1984)
Terrain: Canyons and mesas
Elevation: 3,800 feet to 6,168 feet
Management: Kaibab NF and BLM (Arizona Strip Field Office)
Topographic maps: Jumpup Point, Big Springs, Toothpick Ridge, Gunsight Point, Grama Spring, Sowats Spring, Fishtail, Kanab Point

As the longest drainage on the north side of the Grand Canyon, Kanab Creek has cut a dramatic canyon that snakes south from Utah and across the Arizona Strip. Colorful rock faces and deep gorges reward those who visit this wilderness. Add to this the promise of solitude, and you have a truly unique hiking experience on the Colorado Plateau. Spanning both national forest and BLM lands, Kanab Creek Wilderness is

Bleached bones in Kanab Canyon

accessible from several points. Because the southern end of the area is bounded by Grand Canyon National Park, extended backpacking trips to the Colorado River require a backcountry permit from the National Park Service.

Seasons
The lower elevations of this wilderness are free from snow year-round, although roads leading to the higher eastern side become snowed in from November to March. Summertime temperatures can be quite hot, especially from June to August.

Plants and Wildlife
Watered by springs in places and intermittent streams in others, Kanab Creek Wilderness includes scattered riparian communities of cottonwood trees, single-leaf ashes, tamarisk, and hanging gardens of columbine and maidenhair fern. Pinyon pines and junipers are found on the mesa tops, while desert shrub blackbush is most common in the lower-elevation deserts. Mule deer are common in the wilderness, as are coyotes, rabbits, and squirrels. Mountain lions also roam the wilderness, as do bobcats and foxes. Additionally, desert bighorn sheep have been reintroduced into the wilderness.

Geology
Kanab Creek has etched a deep canyon system into a variety of colorful rock formations. Constituting the upper canyon walls are exposures of Kaibab Limestone and the Toroweap Formation. Supai Sandstone creates many of the canyon walls directly above the stream bottoms. Downstream from the wilderness area, in Grand Canyon National Park, cliffs composed of Redwall Limestone define the Kanab Creek drainage.

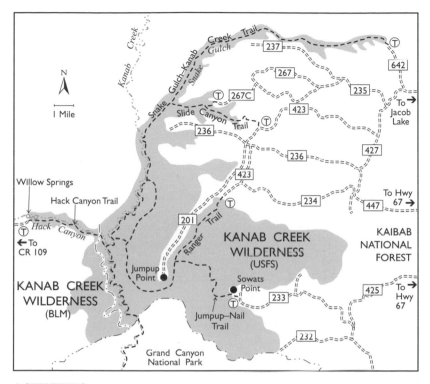

ACTIVITIES
Hiking

A half dozen trails access Kanab Creek Wilderness. One of these, the 21.5-mile Snake Gulch–Kanab Creek Trail, follows Snake Gulch before joining up with the Kanab Creek drainage. Since this trail mostly follows canyon bottoms, the going is easy. The unmaintained Slide Canyon Trail leaves Snake Gulch a couple of miles upstream from the Kanab Creek/Snake Gulch confluence. It continues eastward for 7 miles to reach Forest Road (FR) 267C, which in turn may be accessed via Jacob Lake or Fredonia. The starting point for the Snake Gulch–Kanab Creek Trail can also be reached from these two communities. Just east of Fredonia, turn south onto FR 22 and continue to FR 423. Follow this route for a little more than a mile, then turn right on FR 642. From Jacob Lake, drive west on FR 461 to where it meets FR 462, which connects to the above mentioned FR 22.

From the bottom end of the Snake Gulch–Kanab Creek Trail, the Ranger Trail leaves the canyon bottom and continues east to Lawson Canyon. The trail then circles around Jumpup Point before dropping into Jumpup Canyon. It then continues 4 miles to the eastern boundary of the wilderness. Along its 17-mile length, the Ranger Trail encounters a few tricky stretches, but the going is mostly easy. To reach the trailhead, drive south and west on above-mentioned FR 423 to FR 235. Follow this road for 7 miles to where it becomes FR 423 again. Continue for another 8 miles to road's end.

Adding to the network of backcountry routes within the northeastern portion of the wilderness is the 6-mile Jumpup–Nail Trail, which drops from Sowats Point to a junction with the Ranger Trail in the bottom of Jumpup Canyon. To reach Sowats Point, drive south on the above-mentioned FR 22 to FR 425. Turn right and continue to FR 233. Follow this high-clearance, 2WD road to its end. This trail is very steep and rocky where it drops off Sowats Point.

Adding 6,700 acres to the U.S. Forest Service portion of Kanab Creek Wilderness is the BLM-administered Kanab Creek Wilderness. Included in this section is Hack Canyon—a major side drainage and handy access route for hikers. From the Willow Springs trailhead, the Hack Canyon Trail follows its namesake for 5 miles before reaching Kanab Creek. From here, it is possible to follow Kanab Creek upstream or down for as many miles as you wish. Both Hack Canyon and this portion of Kanab Creek are usually dry, but some springs along Kanab Creek may have water. From the mouth of Hack Canyon, it is 10.5 miles to the mouth of Jumpup Canyon. Downstream from this point is Grand Canyon National Park, where it is possible to continue 16 miles to the Colorado River. You will need a backcountry permit from the park service to do so, and you should expect to scramble over rock faces. To reach the start of the Hack Canyon Trail, drive west from Fredonia to County Road 109, the road to Toroweap Point (see map of Grand Canyon National Park). Follow this gravel road 23 miles south to a sign for Hack Reservoir. Turn left and follow this secondary road for 9.5 miles to its end. The last few miles of this drive require a 4WD vehicle.

Although water is usually available at springs, seeps, potholes, and in some stretches of streambed, it is important to pack along plenty since these sources are few and far between. Watch for flash floods along all canyon bottoms in Kanab Creek Wilderness, and keep in mind that these floods can originate far upstream, even when it is clear where you are. Also keep in mind that unmaintained roads that approach the wilderness may be closed and that hikers may have to walk to the trailheads.

3 Saddle Mountain Wilderness

Location: 70 miles SW of Page
Size: 40,610 acres
Status: Wilderness area (1984)
Terrain: Canyons and forested mesa tops
Elevation: 6,000 feet to 8,800 feet
Management: Kaibab NF
Topographic maps: Dog Point, Cane, Point Imperial, Little Park Lake

Encompassing a portion of the Kaibab Plateau's eastern slope, Saddle Mountain Wilderness features an interesting collection of canyons and plateau rims. Included here are extensive forests of pinyon pine and juniper, along with timberlands of pine, spruce,

Along the North Canyon Trail

fir, and aspen. A stretch of perennial stream within the wilderness is home to a rare species of trout. The area's namesake, 8,424-foot Saddle Mountain, is named for a pronounced dip in its profile.

Seasons

The best time to visit Saddle Mountain Wilderness is from May to October, when its highest elevations are typically free of snow. It is possible to hike the canyon bottoms, which cut westward into the Kaibab Plateau, at any time of year, provided the approach roads are not muddy.

Plants and Wildlife

Across the lower east end of the wilderness are found the upper reaches of grasslands, which stretch across adjacent House Rock Valley. Extensive forests of pinyon pines and junipers soon take over, however. These also include Gambel oak and locust. Moving up in elevation, ponderosa pine becomes more frequent and in the upper reaches of the wilderness—along the rim of the plateau—is found a montane mix of Douglas fir, Engelmann spruce, and aspen. Mule deer are quite common, as are coyotes, jackrabbits, and Kaibab squirrels. Mountain lions have been spotted in the area, as have numerous species of raptors. Additionally, bison occasionally wander into the eastern end of the wilderness from the state-managed House Rock Wildlife Area. This is thought to be the only U.S. Forest Service wilderness with bison. Thanks to a successful transplanting effort, threatened Apache trout are found in the perennial creek that flows through the upper end of North Canyon.

Geology

Capping the Kaibab Plateau is a layer of Kaibab Limestone, a buff-colored rock that features numerous fossils. Beneath the Kaibab Limestone, and exposed in the walls of canyons that dissect the wilderness, are subsequent layers of sedimentary rock that date back to the Paleozoic era.

ACTIVITIES
Hiking

All three trails that traverse Saddle Mountain Wilderness may be accessed by way of House Rock Valley to the east and along national forest roads that turn off Arizona Highway 67—the paved route to the North Rim of the Grand Canyon. Beginning in the northern third of the wilderness is the seldom used and often faded North Canyon Trail, which climbs from 6,130 feet to 8,800 feet in 7 miles. Following its namesake drainage the entire way, this route stays close to the streambed, which, along the lower elevations, is usually dry. Higher up, the North Canyon drainage features a perennial stream in which fish and game officials have transplanted the threatened Apache trout. The North Canyon Trail mostly follows an easy-to-moderate grade. As it approaches the upper reaches of the canyon, it intersects with the lower end of the 1.5-mile East Rim Trail which, in turn, climbs to reach the canyon rim a mile north of where the North Canyon Trail tops out. To reach the lower trailhead for the North Canyon Trail, drive 21.5 miles west from the Marble Canyon on US Highway 89A. Turn south on House Rock Valley–Buffalo Ranch Road (FR 8910), then drive 17.3 miles to Forest Road (FR) 631. Turn right and follow this high-clearance, 2WD road 3.3 miles west to the signed trailhead. To reach the upper trailhead, drive 26.5 miles south on Arizona Highway 67 from Jacob Lake. Turn left onto FR 611 and continue east for 2.7 miles.

Heading up South Canyon from the House Rock Valley side of the wilderness is the difficult-to-follow South Canyon Trail. In 2.5 miles, this trail climbs some 2,000 feet to reach the plateau above. The upper end of the South Canyon Trail is reached by driving south from Jacob Lake to FR 611. Drive 1.4 miles east to FR 610, then turn right. Follow FR 610 for 7.5 miles to the signed trailhead. The lower end of the South Canyon Trail is accessed by driving 23 miles south on the House Rock Valley–Buffalo Ranch Road to FR 211. Follow this high-clearance, 2WD road south for 2 miles to where it ends and an old road, which is now closed to vehicles, begins. Hike 2 miles up this route to reach the start of the South Canyon Trail.

From the end of House Rock Valley–Buffalo Ranch Road, the Nankoweap Trail begins its ascent to the Nankoweap Rim, and eventually the end of the above-mentioned FR 610. In 4 miles, this trail climbs some 2,300 feet along moderate to steep grades. Upon reaching the Nankoweap Rim in 2.5 miles, the route intersects Grand Canyon National Park's Nankoweap Trail, which eventually drops into Marble Canyon to the

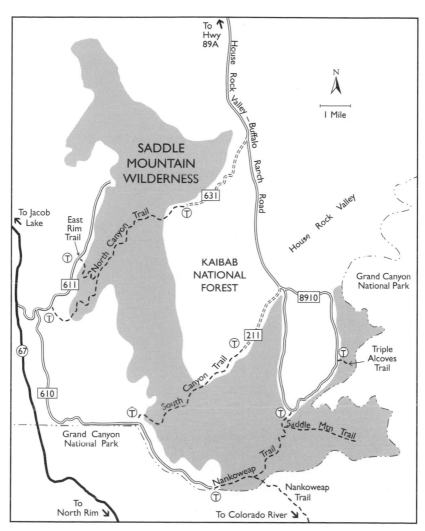

east. Because of this connection, the Kaibab National Forest's Nankoweap Trail sees heavy use in the spring and fall. Branching off from the Nankoweap Trail, about a mile in from House Rock Valley–Buffalo Ranch Road, is the 6-mile-long Saddle Mountain Trail. Maintaining a mostly level grade along a pinyon-pine-and-juniper-covered bench, this easy route heads east to offer some incredible views into Marble Canyon and north across House Rock Valley. A short route that similarly offers spectacular views into Marble Canyon is the Triple Alcoves Trail. It heads east from FR 8910 for 0.5 mile.

Water is occasionally found in springs and along some streambeds within Saddle Mountain Wilderness. It should be treated, however, before drinking. Watch for lightning along the rim areas of the wilderness, especially during the summer.

4 Paria Canyon-Vermilion Cliffs Wilderness

Location: 30 miles NW of Page
Size: 112,500 acres
Status: Wilderness area (1984)
Terrain: Desert canyons and mesas
Elevation: 3,200 feet to 7,200 feet
Management: Vermilion Cliffs NM, BLM (Arizona Strip and Kanab Field Offices)
Topographic maps: Bridger Point, Wrather Arch, Water Pockets, Ferry Swale, Lee's Ferry, House Rock, Emmett Hill, Emmett Wash, Bitter Springs, Navajo Bridge, The Big Knoll, One Toe Ridge, House Rock Spring, Coyote Buttes, Poverty Flat, West Clark Bench

Encompassing two distinctly different features of the Colorado Plateau, Paria Canyon–Vermilion Cliffs Wilderness offers some of the most memorable hiking opportunities in the Four Corners region. Perhaps best known of the wilderness area's two attractions is the narrow Paria River Canyon. For more than 30 miles, this abyss winds its way southeast from Utah to Lees Ferry and the Colorado River. In places, the canyon walls tower hundreds of feet skyward while barely 20 feet apart. Also spectacular are the dramatic Vermilion Cliffs. Of the wilderness area's 112,500 acres, some 90,000 acres fall within Arizona and about 20,000 acres lie north of the Arizona-Utah border. The wilderness currently falls within the newly created Vermilion Cliffs National Monument.

Box elder leaves in spring

A hiker in Buckskin Gulch

Seasons

Although it is possible to visit Paria Canyon–Vermilion Cliffs Wilderness throughout the year, the best seasons for hiking are spring and fall. Summer months can be hot and, while winters are usually snow-free at the lower elevations, nights can be cold and the almost constant wading through the Paria River is too icy for comfort. March, April, May, and June are the busiest times of the year.

Plants and Wildlife

Across the drier sections of the wilderness grow pinyon pine and juniper, Mormon tea, sagebrush, cliffrose, and a variety of other hardy plant species. Desert grasslands sweep up to the base of the Vermilion Cliffs, and a variety of deciduous trees grow along the perennially flowing Paria River and adjacent springs. These include willow, cottonwood, and box elder, among others. Mule deer are common. Desert bighorn sheep were reintroduced to the area in the 1980s. Pronghorn antelope may be spotted below the Vermilion Cliffs, while coyotes, bobcats, and mountain lions live throughout the area. Four species of fish are native to the Paria River.

Geology

Within Paria Canyon, sheer walls of red Navajo Sandstone are the main attraction. Only a few feet wide in places and several hundred feet deep, the Paria Canyon is often referred to as a slot canyon. The river itself carries plenty of gray sediment. This is bentonite, which the waterway picks up farther upstream. Bentonite is actually decomposing volcanic ash. Navajo Sandstone also forms the upper portion of the Vermilion Cliffs. Below it are layers of Kayenta Sandstone, the Moenave Formation, Wingate Sandstone, the Chinle Formation, and the Moenkopi Formation.

History

Panels of prehistoric rock art indicate that the early Puebloan people inhabited the Paria River Canyon more than 900 years ago. The first Europeans to visit the canyon were members of the Spanish Dominguez–Escalante Expedition, which passed through the area in 1776, trying to find a route between New Mexico and California missions. Mormon settler John D. Lee was sent to Lees Ferry to establish a boat crossing on the Colorado River in 1871 and, along with his son and two others, was the first Anglo-American to travel the length of the canyon.

ACTIVITIES
Hiking

The premier hike in this wilderness—and certainly the one that brings the area periodic recognition in national magazines—takes hikers through Paria River Canyon downstream from the White House trailhead to Lees Ferry. Some 38 miles long, this route passes through the incredible, 4-mile long Narrows, where the canyon walls are barely 20 feet apart but shoot straight up for 500 feet or more. This hike is easy, as it is generally level (the entire route descends 1,100 feet in all). Countless stream crossings must be made, though, so it is best to bring extra shoes. Although the water in the river is not potable, springs along the way are good sources of drinking water. About 7 miles in is the mouth of the even narrower Buckskin Gulch. It is possible to continue up this side canyon for either 13.5 miles to the Wire Pass trailhead or 16.3 miles to the Buckskin trailhead. Along the Buckskin Gulch bottom, hikers must contend with very narrow passages, rock jams, and pools of water. The Wire Pass and Buckskin trailheads are located along high-clearance, 2WD House Rock Valley Road, which runs south from US Highway 89 to US Highway 89A. The White House trailhead is accessed along US Highway 89, 30 miles west of Page in Utah. The Lees Ferry trailhead is reached by driving south from Page to where US Highway 89A turns west from US Highway 89. When you reach Marble Canyon Bridge, turn north and drive 6 miles to

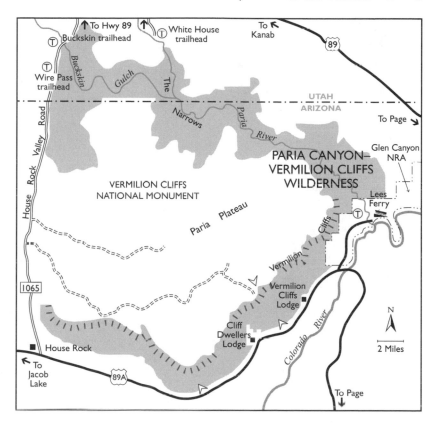

Lees Ferry. A fee of $5.00/person/day (as of summer 2001) is charged and overnight reservations are required. A reservation may be obtained from: Arizona Strip Interpretive Association, 345 East Riverside Drive, St. George, UT 84790; 435-688-3200. Campfires and the burning of trash are not permitted in the canyon. Camping near archaeological sites or springs is prohibited. The canyon gets very crowded, especially during holiday weekends. Shuttle arrangements may be made (for a fee) with local shuttle services. The BLM provides a list of these services.

If crowds are not to your liking, then consider visiting the Vermilion Cliffs portion of the wilderness, where a number of cross-country hikes explore the base of the cliffs. You can begin your hike at almost any point along US Highway 89A. Several springs, complete with riparian plant life, are found along the base of the cliffs.

Hikers visiting Paria River Canyon and Buckskin Gulch should be mindful of flash floods, especially in June, July, and August. You can pick up additional information from the BLM concerning this hazard. Water is available at several springs, but it should be treated before drinking. Be aware that all archaeological and historical artifacts are strictly protected by law and should be left alone.

5 Mount Logan Wilderness

Location: 67 miles S of Fredonia
Size: 14,650 acres
Status: Wilderness area (1984)
Terrain: Forested mountains
Elevation: 5,000 feet to 7,866 feet
Management: Grand Canyon–Parashant NM, BLM (Arizona Strip Field Office)
Topographic maps: Mount Logan, Cold Spring

Encompassing a portion of the volcanic Uinkaret Mountains, Mount Logan Wilderness offers both highly interesting geology and some beautiful forests. The second highest summit in the area, 7,866-foot Mount Logan is reached via a cherry-stemmed 4WD road. The rest of the wilderness is not quite as accessible, but nevertheless worth visiting. Mount Logan Wilderness now falls within the newly created Grand Canyon–Parashant National Monument.

Seasons
Mount Logan Wilderness is usually accessible between April and November, but that period may be extended somewhat, depending on the severity of snowfall and how early in the season it arrives. Summers are nice, as the wilderness area's high elevation and cool pine forests temper the otherwise hot temperatures that envelope much of the Arizona Strip.

Plants and Wildlife
Much of Mount Logan Wilderness features ponderosa pine forests. Pinyon pines and junipers grow in the lower reaches of the wilderness, along with sagebrush and grasses. Locust trees grow along canyon bottoms and on north-facing slopes. Gambel oak is common in many locations. Quaking aspen grows in a few scattered locations. Among the native wildlife of the area are mule deer, coyotes, and mountain lions. Turkeys were transplanted here in 1961, and the tassel-eared Kaibab squirrel was introduced into the region in the early 1970s.

Geology
Mount Logan Wilderness encompasses an area of relatively recent volcanic activity, which took place about 1 million years ago. Mount Logan itself is capped with dark basaltic rock, but other peaks in the area, such as Mount Emma to the south, are extinct cinder cones. Lava flows that seem as if they cooled just last year are also found in the area. Adding interest to the topography is an area of considerable erosion known as Hells Hole. Opening up just west of the Mount Logan summit, this deeply incised drainage reveals colorful layers of the Moenkopi and Chinle Formations.

Looking into Hells Hole

History

Along with Mount Trumbull, Mount Logan was named by Major John Wesley Powell to honor a United States senator. Powell first visited the area in 1870, during an investigation into what became of the three men who left Powell's first expedition down the Colorado River. He was accompanied by Jacob Hamblin, a Mormon missionary who figured prominently in the history of the area. Four years later, Mormon settlers began cutting timber on the slopes of Mount Logan and nearby Mount Trumbull to supply beams for the construction of the temple in St. George, Utah.

ACTIVITIES
Hiking

Perhaps of greatest interest to first-time visitors to the wilderness is the summit of Mount Logan. To reach this point from Fredonia, drive 8 miles west on Arizona Highway 389 to Mount Trumbull Road (County Road 109). Turn left and drive 46.3 miles south on this well-maintained gravel road to the signed right-hand turn for Mount Trumbull (onto County Road 5). Continue up this road for 7 miles to a BLM administrative site (a work station and crew quarters), which is in the vicinity of Nixon Spring. Turn left on BLM Road 1044 (a 4WD road) and drive 4.2 miles to reach the wilderness boundary. Turn right and continue northwest toward the Mount Logan summit. The wilderness boundary parallels this road to the south. In about 2 miles the road peters out. Park here and follow an old trail of sorts less than 0.5 mile to the top. From this 7,866-foot summit, you will enjoy a grand vista of much of the Arizona Strip. Looking northwest, the view extends all the way to the Pine Valley Mountains, which rise behind St. George, Utah. Extending west, the panorama sweeps across Shivwits Plateau, while directly west you can peer into the colorful depths of Hells Hole. The Grand Canyon lies to the south.

Other explorations into the wilderness offer a look at the depths of Hells Hole itself or access to the cinder cones that rise in the southern portion of the wilderness. Hells Hole may be reached via the above-mentioned BLM Road 1044. Upon reaching the wilderness boundary, 4.2 miles south of the Nixon Spring area, turn left and continue southwest for about 2 miles to where the extremely rough, 4WD Slide Mountain–Hells Hollow Road turns right. Follow this route west for approximately 4.5 miles to where it reaches the drainage bottom in Hells Hollow. Because this road is cherry-stemmed out of the wilderness, it divides it in two. Upon reaching Hells Hollow, begin hiking upstream along the drainage bottom. This may be followed for a few miles into the heart of Hells Hole.

To access Slide Mountain and Mount Emma, in the southern portion of the wilderness, walk along old Slide Mountain Road, which branches off Slide Mountain–Hells Hollow Road. Because it falls within the wilderness, Slide Mountain Road is closed

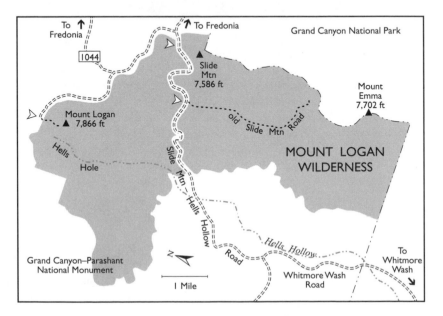

to vehicles. It is about 3 miles from Slide Mountain–Hells Hollow Road to Slide Mountain. From there, it is possible to continue south along the crest of the range for another 3 miles or so, to reach Mount Emma. Mostly forested, this ridgeline forms the boundary between Mount Logan Wilderness and Grand Canyon National Park.

Use extreme caution when hiking cross-country within this and all other backcountry areas. Don't expect to find water within Mount Logan Wilderness. Be wary of lightning during the afternoon thundershowers that frequent the area during the summer months.

6 Mount Trumbull Wilderness

Location: 62 miles S of Fredonia
Size: 7,880 acres
Status: Wilderness area (1984)
Terrain: Forested mountains
Elevation: 5,600 feet to 8,029 feet
Management: Grand Canyon–Parashant NM, BLM (Arizona Strip Field Office)
Topographic maps: Mount Trumbull NW, Mount Trumbull NE, Mount Trumbull SE

Although small and remote, Mount Trumbull Wilderness encompasses an interesting portion of the Arizona Strip. Characterized by both pinyon pine/juniper forests and taller stands of ponderosa pine, this wilderness includes one trail that accesses the scenic Mount Trumbull summit. These attributes, combined with the fact that you will probably have the entire wilderness area to yourself on most days, make it a special place to visit. Mount Trumbull Wilderness now falls within the newly created Grand Canyon–Parashant National Monument.

Seasons
Mount Trumbull Wilderness is usually free of snow from April to November, give or take a few weeks. Summertime is usually nice, with temperatures in the low 90s.

Plants and Wildlife
The lower elevations of the wilderness are characterized by stands of pinyon pine and juniper. Manzanita grows in scattered patches, as do mountain mahogany and cliffrose. Higher up, shady forests of ponderosa pine predominate. These areas also support some Gambel oak and a few hidden groves of aspen. Wildlife includes mule deer, coyotes, mountain lions, Kaibab squirrels, and wild turkeys. Not native to the area, turkeys and Kaibab squirrels were introduced within the last few decades. Golden eagles have also been spotted here, as well as other birds of prey.

A hiker approaches the summit of Mount Trumbull.

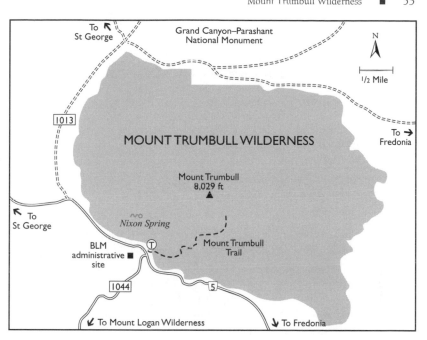

Geology

Volcanic in origin, Mount Trumbull is actually a plateau capped by an old basalt flow, as evidenced by the many exposures of dark basaltic rock found on the mountaintop. At 8,029 feet, Mount Trumbull is the highest summit within the Uinkaret Mountains.

ACTIVITIES
Hiking

The Mount Trumbull Trail begins along County Road 5 across from a BLM administrative site. To reach this trailhead, drive 8 miles west from Fredonia on Arizona Highway 389. Turn left on County Road 109 (Mount Trumbull Road) and drive 46.3 miles on this good gravel road to County Road 5. Turn right and drive another 7 miles. The 2.7-mile hike to the Mount Trumbull summit climbs from 6,500 feet to 8,029 feet. The actual trail continues for about 1.5 miles around the south slope of the mountain before eventually fading away. By this point, however, you are among open pine forests, and it is not difficult to continue to the top of the mountain. You will know you are on the summit when you reach the remains of an old weather station and a U.S. Geological Survey marker. From different vantage points on or near the summit, it is possible to spy the Torowcap section of the Grand Canyon, nearby Mount Logan, and much of the Arizona Strip.

Don't expect to find water within the wilderness. It is available, however, at a faucet that flows with water piped down from Nixon Spring, which is north of the Mount Trumbull trailhead. Watch for lightning when visiting the exposed summit area.

7 Grand Wash Cliffs Wilderness

Location: 50 miles S of St. George, Utah
Size: 37,300 acres
Status: Wilderness area (1984)
Terrain: Desert canyons and mesas
Elevation: 2,800 feet to 6,700 feet
Management: Grand Canyon–Parashant NM, BLM (Arizona Strip Field Office)
Topographic maps: St. George Canyon, Cane Springs SE, Last Chance Canyon, Olaf Knolls, Mustang Point, Grand Gulch Bench

Located in an extremely isolated portion of the Arizona Strip, Grand Wash Cliffs Wilderness is strictly for those who are looking for solitude and are willing to really work for it. From St. George, Utah, it is a 50-mile drive along backroads of every description. Once you get there, however, you will enjoy not only one of the most lonesome parcels of wilderness in Arizona but you will also be treated to some incredible desert topography. Grand Wash Cliffs Wilderness now falls within the newly created Grand Canyon–Parashant National Monument.

Seasons
Summers are hot in this portion of the Arizona Strip, and winter snows often render approach roads difficult, if not impossible, to drive. Spring and autumn are the best times of the year for a visit.

Plants and Wildlife
Because of its location along the interface between two different desert biomes, Grand Wash Cliffs Wilderness supports a wide variety of plant communities. Most noticeable along the lower and middle elevations are Joshua trees—a strictly Mojave Desert species. Unfortunately, other native plants along the lower west end of the wilderness were wiped out by wildfires and have since been replaced by cheatgrass and other exotic species. Along the middle bench and higher east side of the wilderness are forests of pinyon pine and juniper, as well as sagebrush, yucca, and pricklypear cactus. Wildlife of the area includes mule deer, desert bighorn sheep, coyotes, mountain lions, bobcats, desert tortoises, and golden eagles.

Geology
Encompassing a 12-mile-long stretch of the Grand Wash Cliffs, this wilderness actually marks the western end of the Colorado Plateau. Within this geological cross-section of the plateau are a variety of rock formations: Kaibab Limestone, Toroweap Limestone, Coconino Sandstone, Callville Limestone, and Pakoon Limestone. The

A yucca along the Grand Wash Cliffs

Grand Wash Cliffs run along the north–south-trending Grand Wash Fault. The cliffs themselves include a lower and upper section.

ACTIVITIES
Hiking
Two portions of Grand Wash Cliffs Wilderness are readily accessible to hikers. Because the lower slopes of the wilderness are mostly open, they lend themselves well to a variety of cross-country hikes. This area can be accessed from the Grand Wash Road, which

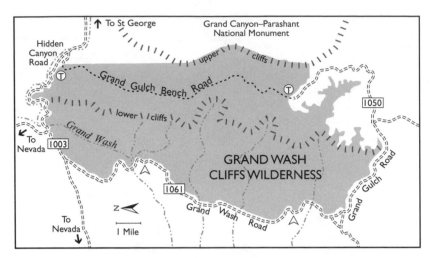

runs the length of the wilderness area's western boundary. One strategy might be to hike east from the road to one of the many canyons that dissect the lower cliffs. Following the length of the middle bench for approximately 12 miles is the Grand Gulch Bench Road. Gated on both ends, this road is closed to most vehicles (ranchers and BLM officials occasionally use it for administrative purposes); it makes for a great hiking route. To reach the north end of Grand Gulch Bench Road, drive 23.6 miles south from St. George, Utah, on BLM Road 1069 to Wolf Hole Valley. Turn right on BLM Road 1004, drive 0.4 mile to BLM Road 101 and then turn left. Drive 6.8 miles to BLM Road 1032. Bear left again, and drive 9.2 miles to where BLM Road 1034 turns off to the left. Drive another 6.6 miles on this road to BLM Road 1003 (Hidden Canyon Road) and turn right. Until this point, the roads are either good gravel or high-clearance 2WD routes. Hidden Canyon Road, however, is strictly for 4WD vehicles. After turning right, drive 4.2 miles to where a faded track branches left. Follow this route for 0.5 mile, to where a cable is strung across the road. The southern trailhead for Grand Gulch Bench Road is located along BLM Road 1050 (Grand Gulch Road). The above-mentioned Grand Wash Road (BLM Road 1061) can be accessed by continuing about 4.5 miles west on Hidden Canyon Road from the northern terminus of Grand Gulch Bench Road. Grand Wash Road also intersects Grand Gulch Road (currently impassable due to flash floods) at the southwestern corner of the wilderness. Be sure to check with the BLM office in St. George, Utah, before heading out. The agency publishes the Arizona Strip District Visitor Map, which includes most roads, topographic lines, and other features of the entire Arizona Strip. Also keep in mind that roads in this remote area may be impassable for long periods, due to washouts and other mishaps.

Water is not usually found within Grand Wash Cliffs Wilderness. Be wary of lightning in exposed locations and flash flooding along washes and canyon bottoms. Hiking cross-country in this and all other wild lands can be hazardous. Do not attempt to drive to Grand Wash Cliffs Wilderness without extra provisions and a good 4WD vehicle.

8 Paiute Wilderness

Location: 16 miles SW of St. George, Utah
Size: 87,900 acres
Status: Wilderness area (1984)
Terrain: Desert and forested mountains
Elevation: 2,000 feet to 8,012 feet
Management: Grand Canyon–Parashant NM, BLM (Arizona Strip Field Office)
Topographic maps: Mountain Sheep Spring, Purgatory Canyon, Littlefield, Mount Bangs, Elbow Canyon, Wolf Mountain West, Mustang Knoll, Canes Spring, Jacobs Well

At 87,900 acres, Paiute Wilderness encompasses a large parcel of the pristine Virgin Mountains. Rising from an elevation of 2,000 feet to 8,000 feet, this wilderness embraces several ecosystems, from arid desert lands to tall ponderosa pines. Given the breadth of topographies and climates found within this wilderness, the area holds plenty of interest for backcountry enthusiasts. A portion of Paiute Wilderness now falls within the newly created Grand Canyon–Parashant National Monument.

Seasons

While lower elevations of Paiute Wilderness are often too hot for hiking in the summer, the higher terrain remains relatively pleasant from May through October. Winter days are comfortable in the lower reaches, but snow and wet roads make access to the higher terrain difficult, if not impossible. Spring and fall are the best times to enjoy all portions of the wilderness.

Plants and Wildlife

The low areas of Paiute Wilderness include Joshua trees, creosote bushes, and sagebrush. Pinyon pine and juniper grow among the area's middle elevations, while ponderosa pine and white fir are found in the highest reaches of the range. Gambel oak and manzanita are also found in places, as are some riparian plant communities. Wildlife in the wilderness includes desert bighorn sheep, which live in the lower elevations, and mule deer, which thrive higher up. Coyotes, mountain lions, a variety of ground squirrels, desert tortoises, and a variety of birds of prey also inhabit the wilderness. Along its northern boundary, the Virgin River darts in and out of the Paiute Wilderness, adding some riparian species of plants to the area's diverse array of plant communities, including thickets of tamarisk.

Geology

Rising along the boundary between Arizona's Basin and Range province and the Colorado Plateau, the rugged Virgin Mountains were formed as a faulted anticline. While

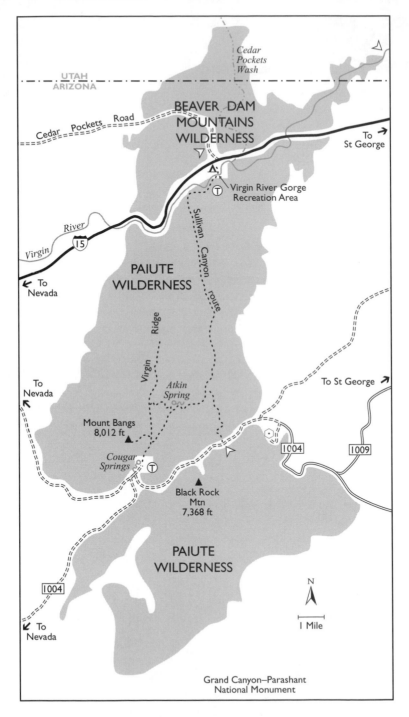

Cedar Pockets Wash

UTAH
ARIZONA

BEAVER DAM MOUNTAINS WILDERNESS

Cedar Pockets Road

To St George

Virgin River Gorge Recreation Area

Sullivan Canyon route

Virgin River

15

To Nevada

PAIUTE WILDERNESS

Virgin Ridge

Atkin Spring

To Nevada

To St George

Mount Bangs 8,012 ft

Cougar Springs

1004

1009

Black Rock Mtn 7,368 ft

PAIUTE WILDERNESS

1004

To Nevada

N

1 Mile

Grand Canyon–Parashant National Monument

The Virgin River flows along the northern boundary of the Paiute Wilderness.

outcrops of Precambrian gneiss, schist, and pegmatite are found in places, a variety of sedimentary rocks—sandstone, limestone, and siltstone—are exposed in the depths of the Virgin River Gorge, which runs along the wilderness area's northern boundary. Across the southern portion of the Paiute Wilderness is the basalt-capped Black Rock Mountain.

ACTIVITIES
Hiking

A few routes offer intrepid hikers a variety of ways to access Paiute Wilderness. Because these routes are not maintained, they can be difficult to find in places. The longest of the routes follows Sullivan Canyon to Mount Bangs. To access this route, drive 16 miles southwest from St. George, Utah, on Interstate 15 to the Virgin River Gorge Recreation Area. Exit here and drive to the campground that is south of the highway. From the facility's upper loop, follow a trail down to the Virgin River. After fording the river (this may be impossible during periods of heavy runoff), follow the south bank 1.5 miles downstream to the mouth of Sullivan Canyon. Turn up the canyon and follow the drainage bottom for about 8 miles to a fork in the canyon. Head up the right-hand fork and continue for another 2 miles to Atkin Spring. The route then climbs up the head of the canyon to eventually top a ridge just east of Mount Bangs. From this point, it is another mile to the summit. A second trail heads north from a point just east of the Mount Bangs summit along the Virgin Ridge for a few miles.

A considerably shorter route also accesses Mount Bangs from the south. The trade-off here, though, is the long and rough drive that must be made to reach its remote trailhead. A few miles south of St. George, turn off Interstate 15 at Black Rock Road (BLM Road 1009). Follow this high-clearance 2WD road south for 19.6 miles to where it intersects BLM Road 1004. Turn right, and drive 13.3 miles west to where a right turn leads about a mile up a side canyon to the Cougar Springs trailhead. From here, a hiking route follows an old road for about a mile to a saddle just east of the Mount Bangs summit. From this point, it is another mile to the summit.

Because the cherry-stemmed BLM Road 1004 climbs up and over Black Rock Mountain, it divides Paiute Wilderness in two. The last 5 miles to the Cougar Springs trailhead may require a 4WD vehicle, and the road is closed in winter. An old road, now closed to vehicles, turns north from BLM Road 1004 about 9 miles west of the BLM Road 1009/Road 1004 intersection. Continuing less than 0.5 mile, this side road reaches a corral, beyond which an old trail drops north into the head of Sullivan Canyon. You may also discover some cross-country routes that head south or north into the wilderness from BLM Road 1004.

Because of rugged topography, hiking within Paiute Wilderness should only be attempted by experienced hikers. Although water can be found at some springs, it is best to pack in all that you will need. Watch for lightning on the higher summits and ridges.

9 Beaver Dam Mountains Wilderness

Location: 16 miles SW of St. George, Utah
Size: 19,600 acres
Status: Wilderness area (1984)
Terrain: Desert mountains and canyons
Elevation: 2,000 feet to 4,629 feet
Management: BLM (Arizona Strip Field Office)
Topographic maps: Mountain Sheep Spring, Purgatory, Littlefield

Despite its name, Beaver Dam Mountains Wilderness is a land of very arid mountains. Vegetation in the area features Joshua trees, along with other desert species. A portion of the Virgin River flows through the wilderness. Wildlife is varied, and the area is surprisingly easy to access, thanks to Interstate 15, which borders the wilderness to the south and a cherry-stemmed, high-clearance road that cuts across the middle portion of the area. Of the wilderness area's 19,600 acres, 2,600 acres are in Utah and 17,000 acres are in Arizona.

One of the many Joshua trees in the Beaver Dam Mountains Wilderness

Seasons

Quite hot in the summer, the Beaver Dam Mountains are best visited in late fall, winter, and spring. Besides pleasurable hiking conditions, spring also brings a short but memorable river-running season.

Plants and Wildlife

Most prominent in the Beaver Dam Mountains are the stands of Joshua trees. Other desert plants that grow in the area include cholla, yucca, and creosote bush. Riparian plants that grow along the Virgin River include tamarisk. Wildlife includes desert bighorn sheep, mule deer, coyotes, mountain lions, jackrabbits, and desert tortoises. The endangered woundfin minnow is found in the Virgin River. The Beaver Dam Mountains were named for some beaver dams that are found in a drainage along the west side of the range.

Geology

Rising along the transition between the Basin and Range province and the Colorado Plateau, the Beaver Dam Mountains are quite complex. Severely faulted and folded throughout, this range includes both Precambrian rock and a variety of younger sedimentary layers. From Interstate 15, near the Virgin River Gorge Recreation Area, it is possible to see the severe displacement that has taken place along the Grand Wash Fault, which runs north through the Beaver Dam Mountains.

ACTIVITIES
Hiking

No trails enter the Beaver Dam Mountains but the terrain is mostly open to hiking. Access to the wilderness is easy, thanks to the Virgin River Gorge Recreation Area along Interstate 15 and Cedar Pockets Road, which dissects the wilderness into two units. To reach this access point, drive 16 miles southwest from St. George, Utah, on Interstate 15, to the Virgin River Gorge Recreation Area exit. From the highway, high-clearance 2WD Cedar Pockets Road heads north and for the next 7 miles is bordered on either side by Beaver Dam Mountains Wilderness. One route possibility would explore the gentler *bajadas* that slope away from the mountains to the south and west. Or you might be able to drop into Cedar Pockets Wash.

Hiking cross-country in this desert land can be hazardous. Use extreme caution. Water is not available in Beaver Dam Mountains Wilderness. Watch for flash floods along canyon washes.

River Running

In spring, the Virgin River occasionally flows with enough volume to support a short but action-packed rafting season. For a period of a few weeks, between February and April, river runners can float all or part of the scenic Virgin River Gorge. About 5 miles of this sinuous corridor falls within Beaver Dam Mountains Wilderness. Rafters put in at Bloomington, which is just south of St. George, Utah, and take out at either the Virgin River Gorge Recreation Area, for a trip of about 21 river miles, or in Littlefield, Arizona, which adds another 16 miles to the journey. Because the Virgin River drops quite rapidly, its rapids are thrilling, to say the least. Permits are not required, but it is a good idea to first check with the BLM for updated information about river conditions. Commercial rafting services are also available. As the Virgin River is still free-flowing, it has been recommended for federal wild and scenic river designation.

10 Cottonwood Point Wilderness

Location: 1 mile E of Colorado City
Size: 6,860 acres
Status: Wilderness area (1984)
Terrain: Cliffs and mesa tops
Elevation: 5,100 feet to 6,443 feet
Management: BLM (Arizona Strip Field Office)
Topographic maps: Colorado City, Moccasin

Dominated by 1,000-foot-high abutments that are part of the colorful Vermilion Cliffs, Cottonwood Point Wilderness offers a scenic backdrop for travelers in this part of the Arizona Strip. No trails exist within the wilderness, but some areas, especially along the foot of the cliffs, are open to hiking. Cottonwood Point Wilderness serves as an extension of Utah's much larger Canaan Mountain Wilderness Study Area.

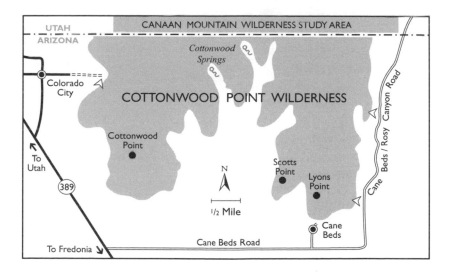

The Vermilion Cliffs rise in the Cottonwood Point Wilderness.

Seasons

Summer afternoons can be hot here, reaching temperatures of up to 100 degrees. Winters bring a little snow and freezing temperatures at night. Spring and fall are perhaps the best times to visit.

Plants and Wildlife

Cottonwood Point Wilderness mostly features stands of pinyon pine and juniper, as well as sagebrush, Mormon tea, and pricklypear cactus. Some riparian growth—such as cottonwood and willow—is found along Cottonwood Canyon, which effectively slices the wilderness in two. Wildlife includes mule deer, coyotes, a mountain lion or two, and such birds of prey as golden eagles, goshawks, prairie falcons, and peregrine falcons.

Geology

The primary feature of Cottonwood Point Wilderness is the Vermilion Cliffs, which run for many miles across the Arizona Strip. Although this geological formation includes several different layers of sedimentary rock in other places, within this wilderness the cliffs consist almost entirely of Navajo Sandstone.

ACTIVITIES
Hiking

Although three sides of Cottonwood Point Wilderness are close to public roads, access is not quite as easy as it might seem, because private lands lie in the way. The quickest access is found just east of Colorado City. To reach the wilderness boundary, walk east from the town cemetery along an old road for about 0.25 mile. A second access point can be found by driving south from Colorado City to Cane Beds Road. Turn left, and drive east to Cane Beds/Rosy Canyon Road. Turn left again and drive north into Rosy Canyon. Because the wilderness boundary is located within 0.25 mile of the road in places, it is an easy matter to hike cross-country to the foot of the cliffs. After accessing the wilderness from either of these points, it is possible to then hike along the foot of the cliffs for some distance.

Water is not readily available in Cottonwood Point Wilderness. Watch for lightning if you do happen to reach the higher points of the wilderness. Cross-country hiking here, as in all backcountry locations, should be attempted only by experienced hikers.

11 Kachina Peaks Wilderness

Location: 7 miles N of Flagstaff
Size: 18,960 acres
Status: Wilderness area (1984)
Terrain: Forested and alpine mountains
Elevation: 7,400 feet to 12,643 feet
Management: Coconino NF
Topographic maps: Humphreys Peak, White Horse Hills, Sunset Crater West

Kachina Peaks Wilderness, near Flagstaff, stands out for a number of reasons. First, the range's summit—12,643-foot Humphreys Peak—is the highest point in the state. Second, this wilderness features Arizona's only true arctic-alpine ecosystem. Because of this, the area is home to many species of plants found nowhere else in the state, and

An aspen-ringed meadow along the Kachina Trail

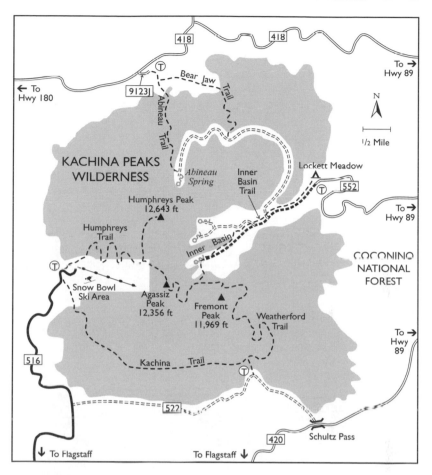

even one that grows nowhere else in the world. Add to its natural wonders a number of well-maintained trails, and you have one of Arizona's more memorable wilderness areas.

Seasons

Because the San Francisco Peaks are snow-covered from October through May, hikers must limit their visits to the summer and early fall seasons. June may see lingering patches of snow in the highest terrain, as well. Alpine flowers bloom in July, and the area's many aspen stands begin their autumn color change in September.

Plants and Wildlife

The San Francisco Peaks offer a wonderful lesson in how ecosystems change according to elevation. Characteristic of the lowest elevations, around 7,000 feet, are stands of ponderosa pine growing alongside patches of Gambel oak. Above 8,000 feet, in the Canadian Life Zone, are Engelmann spruce, subalpine fir, Douglas fir, and aspen. At the 9,500-foot level, the Hudsonian Life Zone replaces the Canadian Zone with its clusters of gnarled and stunted spruce trees known as *krummholz*. Above 11,500 feet, the Arctic-Alpine Life Zone takes hold. Among the fragile plants that grow in this area is *Senecio franciscanus,* a small species that grows nowhere else in the world.

Wildlife of the San Francisco Peaks includes mule deer, elk, mountain lions, black bears, and coyotes. One smaller creature that you will see a lot of is the tassel-eared Abert squirrel, which favors the pine forests of the lower elevations.

Geology

The fact that these mountains are actually the remains of an extinct volcano is quite evident from a distance, as it is easy to visualize a much larger conical shape in the steep slopes of the range. Geologists believe that this extinct volcano exploded about 2 million years ago, much in the same way that Mount St. Helens did in 1980. In the years since, glaciers have been at work sculpting these summits. Today, they offer the best examples of glaciation in the state.

History

Given their prominence on the northern Arizona skyline, it is no wonder that the San Francisco Peaks also figure prominently in the beliefs of the area's Native Americans.

Aspen bark

To the Navajo, whose large reservation lies to the east and northeast, the range constitutes the sacred mountain of the west—one of four directional summits that bound their homeland. To the Hopi, who live northeast of Flagstaff, atop mesas surrounded by the Navajo Nation, the San Francisco Peaks are the home of the Kachinas—beneficial spirits who bring rain to the arid Hopi mesas. The Hopi believe that for half the year, the Kachinas live among these mountains, while the other half is spent visiting the Hopi villages. Both tribes consider the mountains sacred.

ACTIVITIES
Hiking

The area's premier hike, the Humphreys Trail, accesses the 12,643-foot summit of Humphreys Peak. To reach the trailhead, drive 7 miles north of Flagstaff, on US Highway 180, to Forest Road (FR) 516. Turn right and follow this paved road 7.4 miles to park at the Snow Bowl Ski Area. Because this trail climbs nearly 4,000 feet in 4.5 miles, it is a strenuous hike. After 3 miles, the trail reaches an 11,800-foot saddle, which connects Humphreys Peak with Agassiz Peak to the south. From here, the Weatherford Trail follows an old road southeast for 8.7 miles to a trailhead at Schultz Pass, which is located along FR 420. This route once ferried Model T Fords to the upper reaches of the range. From the saddle, the Humphreys Trail continues north for another mile, along the rocky treeless slopes of the peak. Because this alpine environment is very fragile, hikers are required to stay on the trail all the way to the summit, and camping is prohibited. Check with rangers at Coconino National Forest for the exact boundaries of the closure. Humphreys Peak is the highest point for hundreds of miles around, so you will gain a real sense of being on top of the world from the summit.

Also leaving from the Snow Bowl is Kachina Trail, which traverses forest lands along the range's southern slopes. Some 5 miles long, Kachina Trail spans elevations between 8,000 and 9,200 feet. Along the way it encounters scenic meadows, aspen glades, ponderosa pine forests, some old-growth Douglas fir trees, and more. The grades are easy, and the possibility of seeing wildlife is good. The lower end of the Kachina Trail is reached after hiking 2 miles north on the above-mentioned Weatherford Trail from Schultz Pass.

Another popular hiking area in the San Francisco Peaks is the Inner Basin. The network of short trails here is actually cherry-stemmed from the wilderness. This is because the Inner Basin is a major source of drinking water for Flagstaff, and these routes also serve as access roads to springs in the Inner Basin. While you may encounter maintenance trucks along the way and see pump houses and other developments in the area, the hiking is still quite nice. From a camping area at Lockett Meadow, the Inner Basin Trail climbs steadily for about 2 miles before reaching the Inner Basin itself. It then climbs towards Fremont Saddle to meet up with the above-mentioned Weatherford Trail. Within the Inner Basin, several side trails continue to springs (most of which are enclosed for the city water system) farther up. To reach Lockett Meadow, drive 12 miles north from Flagstaff, on US Highway 89, to an unmarked left turn. Follow this graded route for 1.2 miles, turn right, and then continue 3.3 miles to the campground.

Receiving comparatively little use are the Abineau and Bear Jaw Trails, which form a 6-mile loop across the northern slope of the peaks. To reach the trailhead, drive 12 miles north from Flagstaff on US Highway 89. Turn left on FR 420 which is across from the turnoff for Sunset Crater. Turn right on FR 522. Continue 1.5 miles, turn left on FR 418, and follow it for 11 miles to FR 9123J. Drive a short distance farther to the trailhead. The two trails split a short distance from the trailhead. By keeping right, you will follow the Abineau Trail, which climbs 2,000 feet in nearly 2 miles. The trail that bears left is the 2-mile-long Bear Jaw Trail. It traverses some gentle foothills before climbing through ponderosa pine and aspen stands. The two trails are connected on top by a 2-mile stretch of service road that accesses Abineau Spring. Since this road is cherry-stemmed from the wilderness, you may see an occasional maintenance truck or mountain bike along it.

Water is found throughout Kachina Peaks Wilderness but it should be treated before drinking. Watch for lightning and rapidly changing weather in these mountains. Hikers have died in the past due to lightning strikes.

Cross-Country Skiing

Cross-country skiing can be superb in Kachina Peaks Wilderness given enough snow cover. One trail that is easily reached is the above-mentioned Kachina Trail, which sets out from the Snow Bowl. Because the Humphreys Trail is steep and narrow, it may prove difficult to ski for all but expert skiers. If you don't mind skiing 6 miles along FR 420, you could also try the Weatherford Trail. The Inner Basin offers some great backcountry skiing, but access may be blocked in winter by 4.5 miles of unplowed roads. Be very wary of avalanches on all steep slopes.

12 Strawberry Crater Wilderness

Location: 20 miles NE of Flagstaff
Size: 10,141 acres
Status: Wilderness area (1986)
Terrain: Forested ridges and volcanic formations
Elevation: 5,500 feet to 6,653 feet
Management: Coconino NF
Topographic map: Strawberry Crater

Although small and seldom visited, Strawberry Crater Wilderness embraces a truly fascinating feature of northern Arizona's unique geology. Born of fiery volcanic explosions that occurred in the not-so-distant past, Strawberry Crater includes a cinder cone and a large lava flow, both of which date back about 700 years.

A barren hillside in the Strawberry Crater Wilderness

Seasons

Spring, summer, and fall are good times for hiking in Strawberry Crater Wilderness. Winters, however, typically bring significant snowfall to the area.

Plants and Wildlife

Strawberry Crater Wilderness includes both pinyon pine/juniper and ponderosa pine forests. Other plants growing in the area include Gambel oak and Mormon tea. Because the soil of the area—a mix of dark volcanic cinder—does not hold moisture well, trees and plants tend to grow at well-spaced intervals. Wildlife species of the area include mule deer, elk, coyotes, bobcats, an occasional mountain lion, and various birds of prey.

Geology

As one of more than 600 volcanic craters and cones found in the expansive San Francisco Mountains Volcanic Field, Strawberry Crater is a prime example of the relatively recent volcanic activity that shook what is now north-central Arizona. Last active

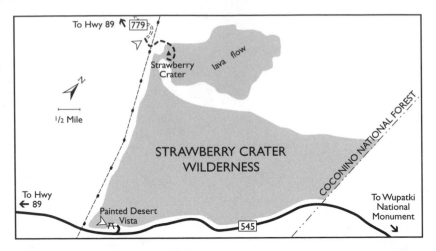

between A.D. 1065 and A.D. 1220, the San Francisco Mountains Volcanic Field actually dates back much earlier than that. In addition to the crater, other interesting features of the wilderness include a large lava flow that fans out to the northwest from the crater and the ubiquitous cinder terrain with its dark, volcanic soil. For a more detailed explanation of the geological processes of the area, stop at the nearby Sunset Crater Volcano National Monument.

ACTIVITIES
Hiking
One trail that is less than a mile long enters Strawberry Crater Wilderness from the west to climb the north side of the crater itself. It can be reached by driving north from Flagstaff on US Highway 89 to Forest Road (FR) 546, which turns east from the highway nearly 4 miles north of the turnoff for Sunset Crater Volcano and Wupatki National Monuments. After driving 1.5 miles east on FR 546, continue east on FR 779 for another 4 miles to its end, near a power transmission line. Heading south from this point, the powerline forms the western boundary of the wilderness. Be sure not to stray off the established route to the top, however, as it leaves lasting scars on the cinders.

Beyond this established route, much of Strawberry Crater Wilderness lends itself well to backcountry explorations because trees and plants tend to be spaced apart. The entire southeastern boundary of the wilderness is bordered by a 6-mile stretch of FR 545 (the paved Sunset Crater Volcano/Wupatki Road). The best access point along the road is found at the Painted Desert Vista, adjacent to the southern corner of the wilderness. From the Painted Desert Vista, cross-country hikes go north and northeast into forested, yet geologically interesting, terrain for as far as you like.

No water is found in Strawberry Crater Wilderness, so bring plenty. Watch for lightning during the summer thunderstorm season.

13 Kendrick Mountain Wilderness

Location: 21 miles NW of Flagstaff
Size: 6,510 acres
Status: Wilderness area (1984)
Terrain: Forested mountains
Elevation: 7,800 feet to 10,418 feet
Management: Kaibab NF and Coconino NF
Topographic maps: Kendrick Peak, Moritz Ridge

Although small, Kendrick Mountain Wilderness is a gem of an area. Not only does the mountain's summit offer an unobstructed 360-degree view but the trails to the top course through both old-growth forests and montane meadows. An extensive forest fire devastated parts of the wilderness in 2000, effectively making one trail unusable.

Seasons

Winter arrives on Kendrick Mountain in October and does not relinquish its grip until May. Wildflowers bloom in July and August, while aspen forests turn brilliant yellow by late September.

Plants and Wildlife

At the lowest elevations of the wilderness, ponderosa pine dominates, but higher up lush stands of Douglas fir, white fir, and Engelmann spruce are prevalent. Occasional patches of aspen often side up to small subalpine meadows, where ferns can be plentiful. Besides mule deer and elk, Kendrick Mountain is also home to black bears, coyotes, mountain lions, Mexican spotted owls, and northern goshawks.

Geology

Like the San Francisco Peaks to the east, Kendrick Mountain is one of many dormant volcanoes in the San Francisco Mountains Volcanic Field. Geologists believe Kendrick erupted less than 2 million years ago. From the summit, it is possible to pick out many smaller vents, which formed perfectly shaped cinder cones. The dark rock that makes up the surrounding Coconino Plateau is mostly basalt.

History

Since the early part of this century, the summit of Kendrick Mountain has been the site of a fire lookout. Although the current lookout tower is not too old, a relic of earlier days is found in a small cabin 0.25 mile east of the summit. Dating back to 1912, this structure housed lookout crews until the 1930s. The cabin is now listed on the National Register of Historic Places.

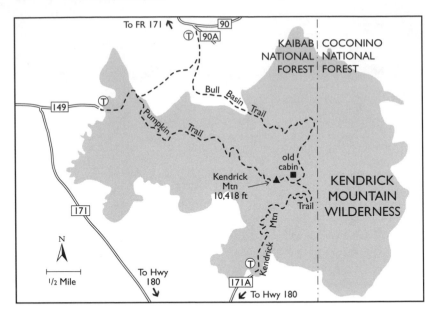

ACTIVITIES
Hiking

Of the three trails that climb to the top of Kendrick Mountain, the shortest and most popular is the 3.5-mile Kendrick Mountain Trail. Although the route climbs 2,700 feet, it is well laid out and surprisingly easy. Be sure to note the change in forest types— from ponderosa pine to mixed fir and spruce—as the trail gains in elevation. To reach the start of the Kendrick Mountain Trail, drive 15 miles north from Flagstaff on US Highway 180 to mile marker 230. Follow Forest Road (FR) 245 west for 3.1 miles to FR 171. Turn right and continue a little more than 3 miles to FR 171A. Follow it for 0.5 mile to the trailhead. The Kendrick Mountain Trail was mostly untouched by the 2000 fire.

A second route to the top, which was severely damaged by the fire, is the 4.5-mile Bull Basin Trail. Beginning at a trailhead northwest of the wilderness, this route climbs 2,400 feet along the mountain's north slope. Its trailhead is located on FR 90A, which is reached by driving past the Kendrick Mountain trailhead on FR 171. Upon reaching FR 144, turn right and continue to FR 90. Follow it for 5 miles to 90A.

The longest route to the top is the 5.5-mile Pumpkin Trail, which climbs 2,900 feet up the mountain's western slope. Thanks to a 1-mile connecting trail, it can be used in conjunction with the Bull Basin Trail to make an 11-mile loop hike. The Pumpkin trailhead is located just off FR 149.

Water is not readily found in the wilderness, so be sure to pack plenty before you set out. Watch for lightning on the summit, especially during the frequent afternoon thunderstorms in the summer.

14 Petrified Forest Wilderness

Location: 25 miles E of Holbrook
Size: 50,260 acres
Status: Wilderness area (1970)
Terrain: High desert and washes
Elevation: 5,400 feet to 6,235 feet
Management: NPS
Topographic maps: Kachina Point, Little Lithodendron Tank, Pinta, North Mill Well, Chinde Mesa, Pilot, Adamana, Agate House

Petrified Forest National Park preserves a fascinating collection of petrified wood scattered across some barren yet beautiful desert terrain. Most visitors experience the park's wonders from scenic pullouts along the 28-mile-long park road. Beyond this paved road, however, lie 50,260 acres of wilderness divided into two separate units. In the southeastern corner of the park is a 7,240-acre section of wilderness often referred to as Rainbow Forest Wilderness. A much larger parcel of wilderness, encompassing 43,020 acres of the Painted Desert, can be found in the northern half of the park. It is often referred to as Painted Desert Wilderness.

Seasons
Summers are hot, often too hot for comfortable hiking, while winters typically bring cold temperatures and occasional snow—although not enough to preclude hiking. Late fall and spring are best for a visit to Petrified Forest Wilderness.

Plants and Wildlife
Despite its rather barren appearance, Petrified Forest National Park supports some interesting plant communities. Shortgrass prairie ecosystems may be found among the higher mesa tops. This is the westernmost extension of their range. In more barren places, where clay soil predominates and salts are found in high concentrations, two plants—four-winged saltbush and greasewood—actually thrive. They are able to secrete excess salt taken up through their roots through special pores. Sagebrush grows in some places, and tamarisk and a few other riparian plants grow along wash bottoms. Pronghorn, mule deer, coyotes, bobcats, jackrabbits, and prairie dogs all live in the park.

Geology
In contrast with its present desert environment, this region was once a vast floodplain laced with streams and creeks during Triassic times. Giant reptiles and amphibians roamed about and tall trees grew to the south along the headwaters of these streams.

Prehistoric petroglyphs in Petrified Forest National Park

On occasion, floods washed the trunks of these trees down to the floodplain, where they were eventually entombed by deposits of silt, mud, and volcanic ash. The wood tissues were eventually encased or replaced with silicon which, in turn, turned to quartz. Some 225 million years later, wind and water erosion have exposed this treasure trove of fossilized trees and animal bones. Adding to the scenic wonder of the park is the multicolored Chinle Formation, a soft, crumbly, multilayered rock laid down during the Triassic period, which has created the reds, yellows, whites, and grays of the aptly named Painted Desert.

History

It is not known whether the park's prehistoric inhabitants—the Ancestral Puebloan people, who lived here between 2,000 and 700 years ago—were as impressed by the area's fossilized treasures as were the first white visitors, 150 years ago. Army survey parties circulated stories about the Painted Desert and "its trees turned to stone" during the mid-nineteenth century. A few decades later, settlers exploited the area's natural resources by selling petrified wood as souvenirs. The dwindling supply of petrified

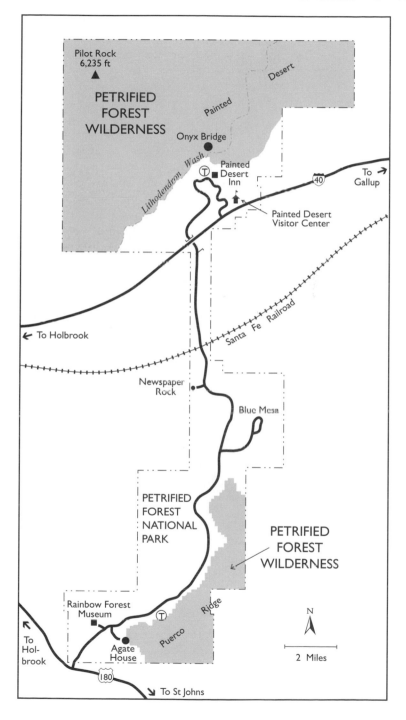

wood prompted President Theodore Roosevelt to establish Petrified Forest National Monument in 1906. Over the years, other areas were added, then, in 1962, the national monument was given national park status by Congress. In 1970, 50,260 acres of the park's backcountry was set aside as wilderness.

ACTIVITIES
Hiking
No trails are found within Petrified Forest Wilderness, but then none are really needed as the terrain is open and easy to travel across. The National Park Service requires that hikers obtain a backcountry use permit for overnight stays at either Rainbow Forest Museum or Painted Desert Visitor Center. If you intend to hike into the southern unit of the wilderness, you should begin at a parking area located a few miles north of the south entrance to the park. For exact directions, be sure to inquire at Rainbow Forest Museum. While you can reach the wilderness boundary in about a mile, continue a little farther and you will soon access Puerco Ridge, which runs along the park boundary. For explorations into the Painted Desert unit of the wilderness, hikers should begin at the Kachina Point trailhead located behind Painted Desert Inn. One unmarked route heads 2 miles north from the trailhead to Onyx Bridge. It first crosses Lithodendron Wash (which delineates the wilderness boundary) before heading up a small side canyon to a long petrified log that spans the wash bottom. Beyond Onyx Bridge, the Painted Desert spans north, east, west, and southwest for many miles. Longer hikes here are limited only by your ability and desire to hike cross-country.

Water is not available in the backcountry, and shade is at a premium. Watch for rattlesnakes and occasional flash floods in the wash bottoms. All natural items (petrified wood and fossils included), along with cultural resources such as pottery and other artifacts, are strictly protected within Petrified Forest National Park and should not be removed from the park. Petrified wood is on sale outside the park (specimens of which were collected on private property).

Opposite: *Red Rock–Secret Mountain Wilderness*

chapter 2 **Central Highlands**

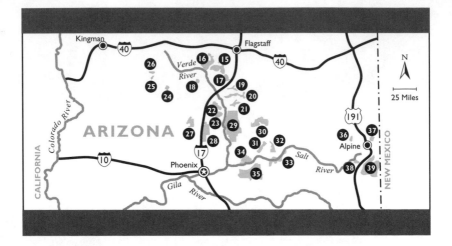

As the Mogollon Rim breaks across nearly the entire breadth of the state, it not only defines the southern edge of the Colorado Plateau but it also opens up to some interesting wild areas, be it in the form of red rock scenery, cactus-studded deserts, or timber-covered mountains.

In the central portion of the state, the Mogollon Rim reveals its colorful core in the Red Rock–Secret Mountain, Sycamore Canyon, and Munds Mountain Wildernesses, all of which side up to the Sedona area. A bit farther to the south and southeast the Woodchute, Wet Beaver, West Clear Creek, and Fossil Springs Wildernesses reveal additional features of the area. As the topography eventually gives way to the lower desert basins, the isolated Cedar Bench and Pine Mountain Wildernesses take in rugged areas west of the Verde River, while Granite Mountain, Apache Creek, Juniper Mesa, and Castle Creek are found farther to the west. The recently established Agua Fria National Monument encompasses some interesting mesa tops and canyon systems east of Interstate 17.

East of the Verde River the sizeable Mazatzal Wilderness takes in a mountain range by the same name, while Four Peaks Wilderness rises to the south. Hellsgate, Salome, Sierra Ancha, and Salt River Canyon Wildernesses embrace some incredibly rugged topography within the Salt River basin. And south of the Salt River is found the highly scenic and historically mysterious Superstition Wilderness.

Summing up the Central Highlands in the far eastern portion of Arizona are four wilderness tracts: Mount Baldy, Escudilla, Bear Wallow, and the Blue Range. So wild and expansive is the total sum of these areas and the lands in between that the area has been the site of a fairly successful reintroduction project of the Mexican gray wolf. Timbered canyons, ridges, and mountains abound as roads and other developments are few.

15 Red Rock–Secret Mountain Wilderness

Location: 1 mile N of Sedona
Size: 43,950 acres
Status: Wilderness area (1984)
Terrain: Red rock canyons and mesas
Elevation: 4,500 feet to 7,196 feet
Management: Coconino NF
Topographic maps: Loy Butte, Wilson Mountain, Munds Park, Sycamore Basin, Dutton Hill, Mountainaire

The primary draw to the Sedona area is its incredible red rock scenery. Fortunately, much of it—especially those canyons and mesas north and northwest of town—is included in Red Rock–Secret Mountain Wilderness. Beginning just beyond the city limits, this somewhat convoluted wilderness area includes such landmarks as Wilson Mountain, Secret Mountain, Boynton Canyon, and the West Fork of Oak Creek, among many others. Several established trails enable hikers to enjoy most portions of the wilderness.

Along the Wilson Mountain Trail

Colorful cliffs within the Red Rock–Secret Mountain Wilderness

While roads and other developments constitute the wilderness area's boundary to the south, west, and east, the Mogollon Rim forms a natural boundary line to the north.

Seasons

For the most part, the lower elevations of Red Rock–Secret Mountain Wilderness are open year-round, although occasional snow and cold temperatures can prove uncomfortable during the coldest winter months and temperatures around the 100-degree mark are common in July and August. The higher terrain along the top of the Mogollon Rim is usually snowed in and inaccessible from December to late March.

Plants and Wildlife

Flora in Red Rock–Secret Mountain Wilderness ranges from pinyon pine and juniper forests in the lower elevations to ponderosa pine and Douglas fir higher up. Century plants, different varieties of cactus, and yucca grow in scattered places in the lower elevations. Riparian communities of cottonwood, box elder, velvet ash, Arizona walnut, and bigtooth maple grow along the West Fork of Oak Creek. A variety of oaks are abundant across the wilderness, as well. Among the species of wildlife that reside in the wilderness are mule deer and white-tailed deer, elk at high elevations, javelina in the canyon bottoms, coyotes, mountain lions, bobcats, badgers, black bears, rabbits, and Abert squirrels.

Geology

A number of colorful formations that underlie the southern edge of the Colorado Plateau are exposed within the 2,500-foot-high topography of Red Rock–Secret Mountain Wilderness. Most prominent from town are the brilliant red cliffs of the Supai Formation. Above that are Coconino Sandstone, Kaibab Limestone, and a cap of volcanic basalt. An area of special note is the scenic Oak Creek Canyon, which borders the wilderness to the east.

History

Although pristine throughout, Red Rock–Secret Mountain Wilderness is not without its historical treasures. Most notable are the scattered cliff dwellings and rock art panels left by the Sinagua Indians prior to A.D. 1300. Representative of more recent history are the dilapidated remains of Secret Cabin. Located on the isolated top of Secret Mountain, this interesting structure was, by some accounts, built by Mormon polygamists. Still other stories say it was a hideout for horse thieves.

ACTIVITIES
Hiking

Red Rock–Secret Mountain Wilderness offers an impressive array of backcountry trails, most of which may be hiked in a day. Beginning near Sedona, an interesting route is the 3-mile Brins Mesa Trail. Climbing easily to the top of its namesake, this trail eventually

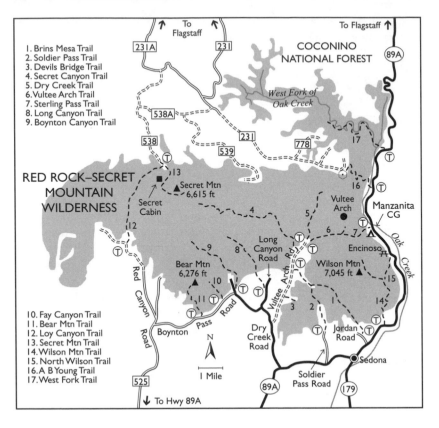

1. Brins Mesa Trail
2. Soldier Pass Trail
3. Devils Bridge Trail
4. Secret Canyon Trail
5. Dry Creek Trail
6. Vultee Arch Trail
7. Sterling Pass Trail
8. Long Canyon Trail
9. Boynton Canyon Trail

10. Fay Canyon Trail
11. Bear Mtn Trail
12. Loy Canyon Trail
13. Secret Mtn Trail
14. Wilson Mtn Trail
15. North Wilson Trail
16. A B Young Trail
17. West Fork Trail

reaches a trailhead along Vultee Arch Road. To reach the trailhead, turn north from downtown Sedona on Jordan Road and drive about a mile. Connecting with the Brins Mesa Trail is the Soldier Pass Trail. About 2 miles in length, this route begins at the end of Soldier Pass Road and gently ascends a low ridge to the north. Shortly after the pass, it connects with the Brins Mesa Trail.

A few miles west of downtown Sedona, Dry Creek Road accesses a far greater number of trails. About 2 miles north of Arizona Highway 89A, Vultee Arch Road (Forest Road [FR] 152) branches off to access a number of trailheads. A little more than 4 miles long, this road is passable to most vehicles when dry. The first trail you reach is the 0.9-mile Devils Bridge Trail, which climbs steeply to one of several natural arches in the Sedona area. The short approach road to the trailhead requires a 4WD vehicle. The second trail accessed along Vultee Arch Road is the far end of the above-mentioned Brins Mesa Trail. Beyond it is the start of the Secret Canyon Trail. Heading west from the road, this route follows its namesake drainage for 5 miles or more, before reaching the canyon's rugged upper end. From the end of Vultee Arch Road, two additional trails enter the wilderness: The Dry Creek Trail continues north for 2 miles along the Dry

Creek drainage. Heading east from the trailhead is the 1.7-mile Vultee Arch Trail. Climbing an easy grade along the bottom of Sterling Canyon, this popular trail reaches a viewpoint from which Vultee Arch can be spied. The natural arch was named after aviation pioneer Gerard Vultee, who died in a plane crash about a mile north of the arch in 1938. Within the last 0.25 mile, the Vultee Arch Trail intersects the 2.4-mile Sterling Pass Trail, which crosses a narrow pass, then drops into Oak Creek Canyon, where it reaches a trailhead near Manzanita Campground.

Shortly after the Vultee Arch Road turns north, Dry Creek Road connects with Long Canyon and Boynton Pass Roads, which, a little farther east, access trails in the western portion of the wilderness. A right turn on Long Canyon Road takes you to the start of the trail of the same name. For 3 easy miles, this route follows an old road into a scenic drainage. A mile or so up Boynton Pass Road is the very popular Boynton Canyon Trail. Some 2.5 miles long, this easy route first skirts around a large resort before dropping back into the canyon bottom. This hike is very scenic and wildlife seems to be plentiful. A shorter trail enters Fay Canyon, the next drainage south from Boynton Canyon. About a mile long, this trail passes Fay Canyon Arch near the canyon's mouth. Just past Boynton Pass, 2-mile-long Bear Mountain Trail climbs about 2,000 feet to the top of Bear Mountain.

While Boynton Pass Road eventually reaches the far west side of Red Rock–Secret

A small ring of stones created by New Age believers near Boyton Canyon

Mountain Wilderness, a more direct route from town follows Arizona Highway 89A about 10 miles west to Red Canyon Road (FR 525). By following this good dirt road north for 10 miles, you will reach the start of one of the longest and most strenuous hikes in the wilderness: the trail up Secret Mountain. This hike starts out following 5-mile-long Loy Canyon Trail and climbs 1,700 feet to reach a small saddle that connects Secret Mountain with the Mogollon Rim. From the saddle, it is a short climb to the flat top of Secret Mountain, across which you can hike another 3 miles to access several vista points along the southern end of the mountain. Of note is the antiquated Secret Cabin, which is nestled among ponderosa pines near a small spring. The saddle at the head of Loy Canyon is only 0.25 mile from the end of FR 538. While this approach offers easy access to Secret Mountain, it is a rather lengthy drive from Flagstaff to this point on gravel and dirt roads.

North of Sedona, some interesting trails enter the wilderness from trailheads along Arizona Highway 89A, as it snakes up Oak Creek Canyon. The first is the 5.6-mile Wilson Mountain Trail. Climbing 2,300 feet, this excursion offers spectacular views in many directions. When you reach the relatively flat summit of Wilson Mountain, the trail continues north to a small stock pond. The Wilson Mountain Trail begins 1.5 miles north of Sedona at Midgley Bridge. A side route—the 2-mile-long North Wilson Trail—begins farther up Oak Creek Canyon at Encinoso Picnic Ground. It connects with the Wilson Mountain Trail on First Bench, about 3 miles from the Midgley Bridge trailhead.

About 8.5 miles north of Sedona, the A. B. Young Trail begins its ascent to the East Pocket from Bootlegger Campground. This strenuous 2.4-mile trail climbs from an elevation of 5,200 feet to 7,196 feet. As it ascends nearly three dozen switchbacks, hikers are rewarded by the spectacular scenery that opens up along the way. The trail ends at the East Pocket Fire Lookout, an interesting wooden structure. This is one of several active fire towers along the Mogollon Rim.

Ten and a half miles north of Sedona, hikers will find one of the most spectacular riparian areas in the state: the West Fork of Oak Creek Canyon. From a trailhead and parking area (a use fee is charged), the trail continues downstream along the main fork of Oak Creek for a short distance before turning up the West Fork drainage. Here, canyon walls soar straight up and a perennial stream ripples along the canyon bottom. Wildlife is plentiful but so, too, are people. This beautiful canyon is easily accessed, so it often sees more than 300 hikers per day. Because of its unique plant community, the first few miles of the canyon are included in the Oak Creek Research Natural Area. For the same reason, camping is prohibited along the first 6 miles of the canyon. While an established trail extends for about 4 miles up West Fork Oak Creek Canyon, it is possible to continue through the rest of the canyon (a 14-mile hike in all) to FR 231. This would require a lot of bushwhacking, swimming, and boulder hopping.

Water is found at some springs and in creeks, but it should be treated before drinking. Watch for lightning along the exposed Mogollon Rim. Remember, all artifacts are strictly protected by law.

16 Sycamore Canyon Wilderness

Location: 23 miles W of Sedona
Size: 55,937 acres
Status: Wilderness area (1972)
Terrain: Red rock canyons and mesas
Elevation: 3,600 feet to 7,000 feet
Management: Coconino NF, Kaibab NF, and Prescott NF
Topographic maps: Loy Butte, Sycamore Basin, Sycamore Point, Bill Williams Mountain SE, Clarkdale

As with nearby Oak Creek Canyon, Sycamore Canyon offers an impressive look at the colorful rocks that underlie the Mogollon Rim. Unlike Oak Creek Canyon, though, Sycamore Canyon has been left in a truly wild state. Where there is a highway in Oak Creek Canyon, there are only a handful of wilderness trails in Sycamore Canyon. Where there are campgrounds, summer homes, small resorts, and the like in Oak Creek, Sycamore Canyon is home to deer, mountain lions, and black bears.

Seasons

Although it is possible to visit portions of Sycamore Canyon Wilderness year-round, winters may bring snow to the higher areas, and summers are often hot within the canyon itself. The best times to visit are from April through June and September through mid-November.

Plants and Wildlife

The most widespread plant community in Sycamore Canyon is the pinyon pine and juniper woodlands. These arid forests also include thick patches of shrub live oak, scattered manzanita, and a variety of cacti. Along stream bottoms, verdant riparian communities of willow, cottonwood, and sycamore are common. Ponderosa pine, Douglas fir, and Gambel oak grow at the highest elevations. Sycamore Canyon is home to mule deer, javelinas, ring-tailed cats, black bears, coyotes, bobcats, and mountain lions, among others. Golden eagles and hawks may be seen soaring high above, and a variety of songbirds, including the canyon wren, are common sights among the tangle of brush below.

Geology

From canyon bottom to rim, Sycamore Canyon displays several geologic formations that are also found in the Grand Canyon. They include Redwall Limestone, the Supai Formation, the Toroweap Formation, and Kaibab Limestone. The Mogollon Rim in this area is capped by a layer of dark basalt.

Along the Dogie Trail in the Sycamore Canyon Wilderness

ACTIVITIES
Hiking

Most trails within Sycamore Canyon Wilderness are found on its east side, which falls under the jurisdiction of the Coconino National Forest. Beginning at Sycamore Pass, the 5-mile Dogie Trail drops into beautiful Sycamore Basin before reaching Sycamore Creek. Shortly after, it intersects the Sycamore Trail, which is just inside the Prescott National Forest. A left turn here will lead several miles south toward the mouth of the canyon, while a right turn will take you 3 miles to the historic Taylor Cabin. Two miles beyond the cabin, the trail connects with the Winter Cabin and Taylor Cabin Trails. Branching left, the 5-mile Winter Cabin Trail continues upstream before climbing out of the canyon, where it then reaches the end of Forest Road (FR) 538A on the Mogollon Rim. From Winter Cabin, the Dorsey Spring Trail continues north past Dorsey Spring before reaching the Geronimo Spring Trail, which drops from a trailhead on the rim above to a spring by the same name. Turning right from the northern end of the Syca-more Trail, the Taylor Cabin Trail climbs 1,800 feet in 2 miles to reach the end of FR 538B, which is also on the rim. If you want to return to the vicinity of Sycamore Pass,

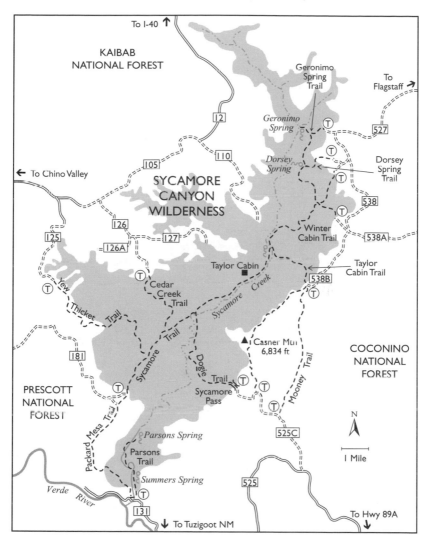

it is possible to follow a powerline road for 7 miles over Casner Mountain. You could also drop down Mooney Canyon via the Mooney Trail. The upper ends of these trails can be reached from Flagstaff by driving Turkey Butte Road (FR 231) 18 miles to FR 538. Follow it for nearly 5 miles to reach its various side roads. To reach the Sycamore Pass trailhead, drive 10 miles west of Sedona on Arizona Highway 89A to Red Canyon Road (FR 525). Follow it north for 3.4 miles to FR 525C. Turn left and drive 9 miles to Sycamore Pass. Except for the last 0.5 mile, this road is passable to most vehicles.

At the far southern end of the wilderness, the last 3 miles or so of Sycamore Canyon come alive with perennial waters that flow from Parsons and Summers Springs. Snaking through this incredible riparian environment is the 3.7-mile Parsons Trail. To protect this delicate area, camping is not allowed downstream from Parsons Spring. To reach the Parsons Trail, drive 10.5 miles north on FR 131 from the road to Tuzigoot National Monument. Turn north after the bridge, at which point this road roughly follows the east side of the Verde River.

Also starting out from the end of FR 131 is the Packard Mesa Trail. In 5 miles, this moderately difficult route climbs about 1,200 feet to reach the above-mentioned Sycamore Trail 0.5 mile south of Sycamore Tank. Although the Sycamore Trail actually begins west of the wilderness boundary, it can be picked up at the wilderness boundary from the end of FR 181. FR 181 branches off Perkinsville Road (FR 354), which is accessed from Chino Valley to the southwest. A high-clearance 2WD vehicle is needed to reach this remote trailhead. From the end of FR 181, the Sycamore Trail continues north for 2 miles before reaching the 5.3-mile Yew Thicket Trail. Difficult to follow in places, this trail can be reached from the Williams area by driving FR 173, 354, 105, and 125. The last 6 miles of this drive require a 4WD vehicle. A little more than a mile north of the Yew Thicket Trail, the Sycamore Trail also connects with the lower end of the difficult-to-follow 4.2-mile Cedar Creek Trail, which is also accessed from Williams to the northwest. In another 2 miles, the Sycamore Trail reaches the normally dry Sycamore Creek and the above-mentioned Dogie Trail. By combining the Sycamore Trail with the Packard Mesa Trail to the south and the Winter Cabin and Cedar Creek trails to the north, it would be possible to spend several days following much of the 21-mile length of the wilderness.

Although Sycamore Creek is not always running, water can occasionally be found at various springs and pools. Be sure to treat it before drinking, and check with the Forest Service about availability. Watch for lightning along the exposed canyon rims and mesa tops.

17 Munds Mountain Wilderness

Location: 1 mile E of Sedona
Size: 18,150 acres
Status: Wilderness area (1984)
Terrain: Red rock canyons and mesas
Elevation: 3,600 feet to 6,825 feet
Management: Coconino NF
Topographic map: Munds Mountain

Encompassing red-rock country southeast of Sedona, Munds Mountain Wilderness offers a colorful collection of canyons, mesas, and spires. Its namesake rises high above the town in a series of vermilion buttresses, while Jacks Canyon slices deeply through the heart of the wilderness itself. Perhaps the best-known landmark within the

Looking across the Sedona area from the Munds Mountain Wilderness

wilderness, however, is Bell Rock, which is revered by New Age followers as a vortex. Like a handful of other vortexes that are reportedly located in the Sedona area, the Bell Rock vortex is believed to be a source of spiritual energy.

Seasons

Munds Mountain Wilderness can be visited at any time of the year, although summer-time temperatures sometimes top 100 degrees. Winter brings occasional snow to the lower elevations but it rarely lasts. Snowfall does accumulate on the higher canyon rims, however.

Plants and Wildlife

The dominant trees growing in Munds Mountain Wilderness are pinyon pine, juniper, and shrub live oak. Some canyon bottoms feature thick stands of Arizona cypress and occasional alligator juniper. Gambel oak and ponderosa pine grow at higher

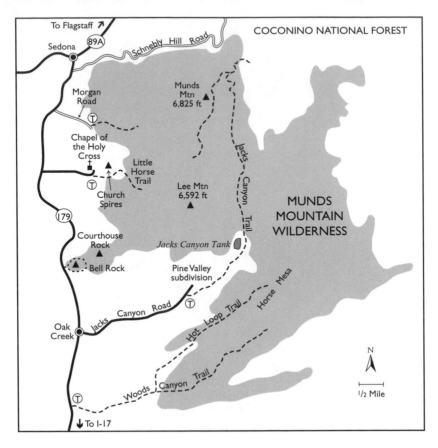

elevations; Douglas fir favors wetter, north-facing slopes. Wildlife includes deer, javelinas, coyotes, and perhaps a mountain lion or two.

Geology

The geology of Munds Mountain Wilderness, as it is elsewhere in the Sedona area, is quite vivid. Constituting many of the spires and buttes in the area is the 900-foot-thick Schnebly Hill Formation. This brilliant red rock was deposited by water and wind in a seashore environment. Another prominent formation is Coconino Sandstone. Capping the Mogollon Rim, which runs along the eastern and southern boundary of the wilderness, is dark basalt that resulted from recent volcanic activity.

ACTIVITIES
Hiking

A number of trails enter the wilderness from the west, offering a variety of hiking experiences. About 6 miles in length, the Jacks Canyon Trail starts at a trailhead east of the small town of Oak Creek. To reach it, drive 6 miles south from Sedona on Arizona

Highway 179 to Oak Creek. Turn left on Jacks Canyon Road and drive 2.6 miles to the entrance of the Pine Valley subdivision. There is a small parking area on the right-hand side of the road. The route begins by climbing gently along the canyon bottom. After 1.5 miles, the trail reaches Jacks Canyon Tank. It then enters Munds Mountain Wilderness just beyond. Continuing up the canyon bottom for another 4 miles, the trail begins a final steeper ascent to the head of the canyon. At the top of the small saddle, the Jacks Canyon Trail follows the ridge to the east, where it reaches the Mogollon Rim and the wilderness boundary. By turning left at the saddle, you can reach the top of Munds Mountain, which lies less than a mile south.

A second maintained route, the Hot Loop Trail, climbs to the top of Horse Mesa, where some nice views are possible. This route ascends 2,000 feet in 6 miles. The trailhead is about 1.5 miles south of the turnoff for Jacks Canyon Road. The less-traveled Woods Canyon Trail follows the bottom of Woods Canyon for 4 miles. This route branches off the Hot Loop Trail just before the wilderness boundary, about 2 miles in from the trailhead.

A number of short, unofficial trails that are directly adjacent to Sedona also access portions of Munds Mountain Wilderness. Because they are not regularly maintained, the routes may be hard to find in places. One of them follows an old jeep road up Margs Draw from Sombart Lane, which is south of the Tlaquepaque Shopping Center in Sedona. Another closed-off road enters the wilderness near the end of Morgan Road. It accesses small canyons that drain the west side of Munds Mountain. The Little Horse Trail begins near the Chapel of the Holy Cross and circles just south of the Church Spires before entering the wilderness. It then takes up Briant Canyon for a little way. In all, this route is about 2 miles in length. A short route circles Bell Rock and nearby Courthouse Rock. Expect to see a lot of people in this area.

Water is scarce in Munds Mountain Wilderness, so pack plenty before setting out. Watch for lightning along the exposed rim areas and mountain tops, especially during frequent summer thundershowers.

18 Woodchute Wilderness

Location: 10 miles W of Jerome
Size: 5,700 acres
Status: Wilderness area (1984)
Terrain: Forested mountain
Elevation: 5,500 feet to 7,834 feet
Management: Prescott NF
Topographic maps: Hickey Mountain, Munds Draw

Although quite small and often overlooked, Woodchute Wilderness offers day hikers some beautiful scenery along with pleasant ponderosa pine forests and interesting

The views from Woodchute Mountain are far-reaching.

geological features. Established in 1984, this 5,700-acre wilderness encompasses the relatively level summit of 7,834-foot Woodchute Mountain.

Seasons
Even though hiking in Woodchute Wilderness might be possible throughout the year, winter generally brings accumulations of snow to the higher reaches of the mountain. Hiking in the summer can be pleasant on most days, although temperatures may occasionally approach the 100-degree mark.

Plants and Wildlife
Although ponderosa pine predominates in this wilderness, stands of pinyon pine and juniper are also common. Some alligator junipers are quite old and gnarled. Various evergreen species of oaks are found here, as well as scattered Gambel oaks. Wildlife includes mule deer, coyotes, mountain lions, and a variety of birds.

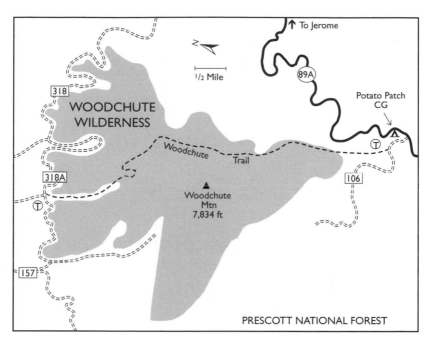

Geology

Woodchute Mountain is a basalt-capped mesa that rises in the northern end of the Black Hills. This basalt resulted from lava flows during the Miocene Epoch, between 5 and 24 million years ago.

ACTIVITIES
Hiking

One trail enters Woodchute Wilderness from a point 8 miles southwest of Jerome, on Arizona Highway 89A. When you reach the top of a saddle there, turn right at Potato Patch Campground and drive 0.3 mile to Forest Road (FR) 106. A new trailhead accesses the Woodchute Trail, although it is possible to drive another 0.7 mile on FR 106 (it soon becomes a rough, high-clearance road) to access the trail farther in. From the forest road, the Woodchute Trail heads north toward the top of its namesake mountain. About 1.25 miles in, the trail reaches an open saddle just south of the summit. From here, it climbs about 400 feet before topping the rim area above. It then continues for another mile before reaching the northern end of the mountaintop. Beyond this point, a much fainter portion of the Woodchute Trail drops off the mountain to reach FR 318A, along the wilderness area's northern boundary. The summit of Woodchute Mountain provides incredible views east toward Sedona, north to the San Francisco Peaks and the Mogollon Rim, and west into Chino Valley.

Water is not available in Woodchute Wilderness, so bring plenty. Watch for lightning when hiking during the summer thunderstorm season.

19 Wet Beaver Wilderness

Location: 17 miles S of Sedona
Size: 6,700 acres
Status: Wilderness area (1984)
Terrain: Canyons and mesa rims
Elevation: 3,800 feet to 6,500 feet
Management: Coconino NF
Topographic maps: Casner Butte, Apache Maid Mountain

Wet Beaver Creek drains into the Verde Valley from the Mogollon Rim. In so doing, it creates a deep and impressive abyss, within which are found riparian areas. While much of this canyon is rugged and untrailed, one easy route enters the canyon from the west. The wilderness boundary mostly follows the rim of the main canyon and its tributaries.

Seasons

Wet Beaver Wilderness offers pleasant hiking any time of the year, although summer temperatures often reach the 100-degree mark. There is only one stream crossing along the main trail, and this can usually be made without getting your feet wet.

Plants and Wildlife

The prime constituents of the riparian community that shades the creek bed are Arizona sycamore, cottonwood, Arizona walnut, and ash. Wild grape and poison ivy add to the tangled growth beneath. Pinyon pine, juniper, pricklypear cactus, and scattered century plant grow out of the reach of the creek. Tucked away in the higher recesses of the canyon are ponderosa pines and Douglas firs. Deer, javelinas, black bears, coyotes, ring-tailed cats, bobcats, and mountain lions reside here. Beaver, great blue herons, wintering bald eagles, trout, round-tailed chubs, Gila Mountain suckers, and black bass are reliant on the watery environs of Wet Beaver Creek.

Geology

Exposed beneath the ever-present cap of dark volcanic basalt are layers of Kaibab Limestone, Toroweap Sandstone, and Coconino Sandstone—all rock types found within the Grand Canyon. Just as the great abyss to the north slices deep into the Colorado Plateau, Wet Beaver Creek has cut into the plateau's southern end.

ACTIVITIES
Hiking

The Bell Trail heads east for 3 miles before reaching Wet Beaver Creek inside the canyon. To find the trailhead, turn off Interstate 17 at the Sedona exit and drive 2 miles southeast on Forest Road (FR) 618. Turn left on FR 618A and drive 0.25 mile to its

Riparian growth along Wet Beaver Creek

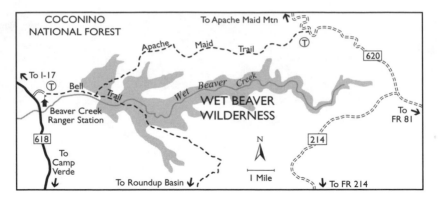

end. For the first 2 miles, the Bell Trail follows an old road that is closed to most vehicles. Along this stretch, the terrain is flat and arid, as the creek itself flows some distance to the south. Near the 2-mile mark, the Bell Trail reaches the start of the Apache Maid Trail, which branches to the left to climb out of Wet Beaver Canyon to the north. This route climbs 2,400 feet in 9.5 miles to reach the vicinity of Apache Maid Mountain. Just beyond this trail junction, the Bell Trail enters Wet Beaver Wilderness, which is marked by a trail register and sign. From here, the route climbs a short distance to reach a bench that runs along the canyon's north wall. About 3 miles in, the Bell Trail drops back into the canyon bottom, where it crosses the creek at Bell Crossing. Eventually, the Bell Trail reaches Roundup Basin, nearly 11 miles from its start. In all, the Bell Trail climbs from 3,820 to 6,270 feet. While it might be possible to follow the canyon along its entire length, the going is very rough and should not be attempted by inexperienced hikers. For further information, check with the U.S. Forest Service.

While water is always available in Wet Beaver Creek, it should be treated before drinking. Be aware that heavy runoff may cause flash flooding along the canyon bottom. Use extreme caution when traveling off established trails.

20 West Clear Creek Wilderness

Location: 11 miles E of Camp Verde
Size: 13,600 acres
Status: Wilderness area (1984)
Terrain: Canyons and mesas
Elevation: 3,700 feet to 6,800 feet
Management: Coconino NF
Topographic maps: Walker Mountain, Buckhorn Mountain, Calloway Butte

Winding for 30 miles, West Clear Creek is the longest drainage that cuts through the Mogollon Rim. Some 2,000 feet deep in spots, this canyon system offers some truly

Ocotillo growing along the West Clear Creek drainage

wild terrain for exploring. Three fairly short routes penetrate the wilderness, but most of the canyon bottom is rugged and trailless. Exposed within this canyon is an interesting array of geologic formations. Because West Clear Creek is a perennial stream, the biotic diversity of the canyon is considerable.

Seasons

It is possible to visit West Clear Creek Wilderness throughout the year, although the many stream crossings are too cold during the winter. Access roads in the higher elevations usually close in the winter because of snow. Spring runoff may render stream crossings impossible at times. During the summer, temperatures can be hot, but the canyon's periodically shady environment tempers that somewhat.

Plants and Wildlife

While pinyon pine, juniper, pricklypear cactus, mesquite, and other upland desert plant species grow among the arid benches and lower canyon slopes, lush riparian communities of Arizona sycamore, cottonwood, walnut, and willow are found along the streambeds. Ponderosa pine, Douglas fir, and white fir are common on ledges in the higher canyon walls. Animal residents include mule deer and white-tailed deer, javelinas, elk,

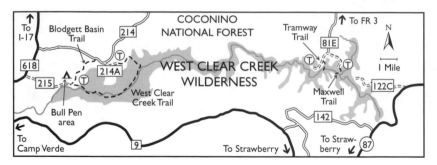

mountain lions, black bears, and ring-tailed cats. Bald eagles frequent the wilderness and two species of trout are a lure for anglers.

Geology

Slicing deep into the Mogollon Rim, West Clear Creek offers an in-depth look at the geology of the Colorado Plateau. The uppermost layer of rock in the canyon consists of dark basalt, which was deposited during a period of volcanic activity. Subsequent layers of Kaibab Limestone, the Toroweap Formation, Coconino Sandstone, and the Supai Formation are also exposed.

ACTIVITIES
Hiking

Entering West Clear Creek Canyon from its mouth, the West Clear Creek Trail offers the easiest access to the drainage system. To reach the trailhead, drive 6 miles southeast from Camp Verde on General Crook Trail (Arizona Highway 260) to Forest Road (FR) 618. Turn north and drive 2.2 miles to FR 215. Follow this dirt road a little more than 3 miles to its end at the Bull Pen dispersed camping area. From this point, the trail heads upcanyon across the old Bull Pen Ranch before continuing up the north bank of the stream. After a little more than a mile, the route encounters the first of four stream crossings. Under normal runoff conditions, these crossings should be easy. Do not attempt to cross them if they are flooding, though. After 5 miles, the West Clear Creek Trail turns north to climb 1,800 feet up a side canyon to FR 214A on the rim above. With a shuttle to pick you up, this 7.7-mile route can be hiked in one long day. Should you wish to return to the Bull Pen trailhead by way of the Blodgett Basin Trail, from the upper end of the West Clear Creek Trail, follow FR 214A and FR 214 to the upper end of the 2.5-mile Blodgett Basin Trail.

While the lower end of the canyon is wide, farther upstream it narrows considerably. Less than a mile long, the Maxwell Trail drops 700 feet from the north rim to reach the creek bottom in the canyon's upper portion. To find this route, drive 7.5 miles south from the U.S. Forest Service Happy Jack Ranger Station on FR 3 to FR 81. Turn right and drive 4 miles to FR 81E. Follow this high-clearance road to its end. Given the considerable grade change in the route, this hike should be considered difficult.

A third route into the canyon from the north rim is the Tramway Trail which, like the Maxwell Trail, drops swiftly to the creek. It is accessed by FR 81E and FR 693, and it, too, is less than a mile in length. The Tramway Trail reaches the canyon bottom just downstream from the Maxwell Trail. For a rewarding trip, consider connecting these two trails with a bushwhack along the stream bottom.

Caution should be used when traveling along trailless sections of the canyon. Water is always available in West Clear Creek, but treat it before drinking. Watch for lightning along the high mesa tops and for occasional flash floods in the canyon bottom.

21 Fossil Springs Wilderness

Location: 10 miles W of Strawberry
Size: 11,550 acres
Status: Wilderness area (1984)
Terrain: Canyons and mesas
Elevation: 3,800 feet to 6,800 feet
Management: Coconino NF
Topographic maps: Strawberry, Pine

Although the combination of perennially flowing water and rugged desert scenery is played out on a number of occasions in Arizona, few areas can match the unique beauty of small, out-of-the-way Fossil Springs Wilderness. Supporting an impressive riparian plant community, Fossil Creek emanates from a series of springs that produces a million gallons of water per hour. Because these springs all bubble up in one short stretch of the canyon, and because the temperature of the water remains a steady 72 degrees, the diversity and lushness of growth surrounding the springs is especially impressive. Add to these natural wonders an historical treasure in the form of a turn-of-the-century flume, and you have a unique backcountry destination.

Seasons

Fossil Springs Wilderness can be visited year-round. Winters may bring occasional snowfall, but the amounts are rarely enough to impede hiking. While summertime temperatures often exceed 100 degrees, shady trees along the way help temper the heat.

Plants and Wildlife

The riparian ecosystem found within this wilderness is what makes it most alluring. Arizona sycamore, cottonwood, Arizona walnut, and alder form a verdant ribbon along the riverbank, while understory growth consists of wild blackberry, columbine, and poisonous hemlock. More than 100 species of birds frequent these lush environs. In

An historic flume leads to the Fossil Springs Wilderness.

contrast, the dry hills support a mixture of pinyon pine and juniper, a variety of oaks, and pricklypear cactus. Wildlife here includes white-tailed and mule deer, javelinas, coyotes, ring-tailed cats, mountain lions, and black bears. In addition, two species of endangered fish inhabit Fossil Creek: the round-tailed chub and the Gila topminnow.

Geology
The word *fossil* in the name Fossil Springs is an incorrect reference to the travertine deposits left on the shoreline, boulders, and such by the heavily mineralized water. Fossils are found, however, in the nearby Redwall Limestone cliff faces. Above the Redwall Limestone is the Supai Formation. It is capped by a layer of volcanic basalt, which covers most of the Mogollon Rim.

History
First noted by cowboys who ran cattle in the area during the 1880s, the generous flow of water from these natural gushers was put to work in 1916 with the construction of a small dam just below the springs and a flume. Channeled nearly 4 miles along the

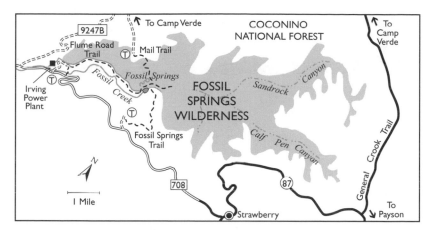

canyon wall, the water then drops to the Irving Power Plant, where it turns generating turbines. Although still in use, the flume is today listed on the National Register of Historic Places.

ACTIVITIES
Hiking
Only one trail penetrates Fossil Springs Wilderness to any degree, while two other backcountry routes approach the Fossil Springs area. The 3.5-mile Flume Road Trail begins along Forest Road (FR) 708, nearly 10 miles west of Strawberry. After making a steep climb to the flume 400 feet above, follow the flume along the adjacent service road. Except for an occasional work truck, the road is closed to all motor vehicles. While walking a road is not exactly a wilderness experience, the historic flume and plenty of outstanding scenery combine to make this an interesting walk just the same.

Just before it reaches Fossil Springs, the Flume Road Trail enters the wilderness, where it connects with the lower end of the Mail Trail. A little more than 3 miles long, this route begins on the rim above and drops 1,300 feet in the process. As the name suggests, the route was once used by riders who carried mail from Camp Verde to Payson. To reach the upper trailhead, drive east from Camp Verde on Arizona Highway 260 to FR 9247B. Turn right and follow this high-clearance 2WD route to the start of the Mail Trail at Stock Tank #2.

Just above the springs, the Mail Trail connects with the lower end of the Fossil Springs Trail. Dropping 1,200 feet in 3 miles, this trail lies mostly outside the wilderness boundary. It nevertheless offers a scenic approach to the springs. The trailhead for this route is found 5 miles west of Strawberry off FR 708.

Caution should be used when traveling off-trail. Water is available, but it should be treated before drinking. Watch for lightning along mesa tops and rims. Be aware of the possibility of flash floods in canyon bottoms.

22 Cedar Bench Wilderness

Location: 25 miles E of Cordes Junction
Size: 14,840 acres
Status: Wilderness area (1984)
Terrain: Mountains and canyons
Elevation: 2,800 feet to 6,678 feet
Management: Prescott NF
Topographic maps: Horner Mountain, Tule Mesa, Arnold Mesa

Located in a remote area of central Arizona, Cedar Bench Wilderness offers backcountry enthusiasts some hiking routes that are memorable for both their interesting scenery and low visitation numbers. Cedar Bench Wilderness stretches across a portion of the Verde Rim, from which the topography drops to the Verde River. The name, Cedar Bench, actually reflects a common misnomer in the Southwest dating back to pioneer times. No cedars grow in the region, but plenty of junipers do.

Seasons

Although winters occasionally bring some snowfall, it is usually not enough to preclude hiking. The problem comes as winter rains render the approach roads impassable. The U.S. Forest Service is especially concerned about the damage to dirt and gravel roads from driving them during wet conditions. Summers may be hot—around 100 degrees on many afternoons—while late spring and autumn months are ideal.

Plants and Wildlife

Thick patches of shrub live oak and manzanita grow across large areas of the lower elevations while pinyon pine and juniper are prevalent on mesa tops, ridges, and in some canyon areas. Two types of junipers (or "cedars," as early settlers erroneously referred to them) grow here: Utah juniper and alligator juniper. Gambel oak is common in these pinyon pine/juniper forests, and agave, or century plant, often grows in open areas and along canyon rims. Riparian areas support Arizona sycamore and Arizona cypress. Wildlife includes mule deer and white-tailed deer, elk, coyotes, mountain lions, black bears, and jackrabbits.

Geology

Taking in a portion of the Black Hills, Cedar Bench Wilderness mostly features dark basaltic rocks and deposits of tuff, both of which resulted from volcanic activity during the Quaternary and Tertiary periods. Erosion has since etched canyons into this landform, and the cutting action of the Verde River has added some interesting relief to the terrain.

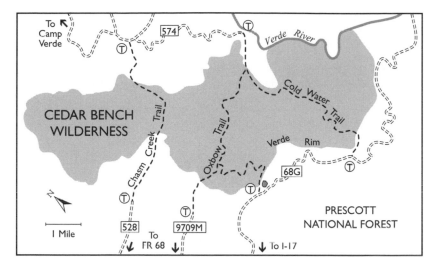

ACTIVITIES
Hiking

Three trails cross Cedar Bench Wilderness. The easiest to get to is the 5.8-mile Oxbow Trail. To reach the trailhead, turn off Interstate 17 at the Dugas exit, a few miles north of Cordes Junction. Drive 11.5 miles east on Forest Road (FR) 68 (Dugas Road), through the small ranching enclave of Dugas. Turn left on FR 68G and continue for another 5 miles to a developed stock pond on the left-hand side of the road. The road is good as far as Dugas, then it becomes a bit rough. FR 68G is rougher still and requires a high-clearance 2WD vehicle. From the stock pond, the Oxbow Trail drops into nearby Gap Creek, then climbs up and over the Verde Rim. It eventually reaches a short access trail that exits the wilderness to meet the end of the 4WD FR 9709M. Turning right at this trail intersection, the Oxbow Trail continues east to eventually drop to a trailhead along FR 574. This end of the trail can be reached by driving south from Camp Verde along the Verde River.

Three miles beyond the Oxbow Trail, along FR 68G, is the southern trailhead for the Cold Water Trail. Along its 5.7-mile length, the Cold Water Trail heads north to reach the Oxbow Trail about a mile from FR 574. Originally, the Cold Water Trail was used by army troops traveling from Fort McDowell to Camp Verde. An overall elevation change of 2,500 feet, along with faded sections of tread, makes this a difficult hike. It is possible to complete an 11-mile loop hike by following the Oxbow and Cold Water Trails, but to do so, you will have to walk a 3-mile stretch of FR 68G.

The third trail within Cedar Bench Wilderness is the 6.1-mile Chasm Creek Trail. It crosses the northern third of the wilderness, heading eastward from FR 528 to FR 574. Although only a third of this route falls within the wilderness, the trail's entire length is remote and interesting. Like the Oxbow and Cold Water Trails, the Chasm

Creek Trail is difficult due to stiff elevation changes (2,000 feet in all) and rough, faded sections of trail.

Water is available at scattered springs, tanks, and perennial streams, but it should be treated before drinking. Consider carrying your own water, since there are long stretches of hot and dry hiking in between. Watch for lightning on exposed mesa tops.

23 Pine Mountain Wilderness

Location: 25 miles E of Cordes Junction
Size: 20,100 acres
Status: Wilderness area (1972)
Terrain: Forested mountains
Elevation: 3,800 feet to 6,814 feet
Management: Prescott NF and Tonto NF
Topographic maps: Tule Mesa, Verde Hot Springs

Located far from the nearest paved road, Pine Mountain Wilderness offers plenty of solitude in a scenic area of the state. Encompassing a portion of the Verde Rim, much of the wilderness is characterized by cool ponderosa pine forests. Its eastern slope, however, features tangled chaparral. A network of hiking trails accesses the summit of Pine Mountain and the northwestern section of the wilderness.

Seasons
Access to Pine Mountain Wilderness is possible year-round. Winter rains and occasional snow, however, can turn approach roads into a muddy mess. Trails in the highest reaches of the wilderness may also be snowed in for brief periods. Summers can bring temperatures above 100 degrees, while spring and fall provide the best weather for visiting the wilderness.

Plants and Wildlife
Much of the western slope of the wilderness includes stands of ponderosa pine and Gambel oak. Scattered pinyon pines and junipers are also common. Along the area's drainage bottoms are found some old sycamore trees, a few aspen trees, and bigtooth maples. Dropping off the eastern face of Pine Mountain is a more arid terrain that features impassable thickets of shrub live oak and mountain mahogany. Wildlife in Pine Mountain Wilderness includes mule deer and white-tailed deer, occasional elk, javelinas, black bears, coyotes, and mountain lions.

Geology
Pine Mountain Wilderness is divided into two distinct topographical sections. The first lies west of the Verde Rim and mostly features basalt rock and tuff that originated during

Detail of juniper bark

relatively recent volcanic activity. The more rugged eastern side of the wilderness breaks away abruptly, dropping from the Verde Rim into the Verde River drainage. Erosion has been the key influence in this portion.

ACTIVITIES
Hiking

All trails within Pine Mountain Wilderness are found west of the Verde Rim, in the Prescott National Forest portion of the wilderness. The handiest access point for these routes is the Salt Flat dispersed camping area. To reach it, turn off of Interstate 17 at the Dugas exit and follow Forest Road (FR) 68 (Dugas Road) 19 miles east to its end. The last 8 miles of this road may require a high-clearance 2WD vehicle. From the Salt Flat trailhead, the 8.5-mile Nelson Trail follows Sycamore Creek a short distance to Nelson Place—a long-abandoned homestead. Beyond Nelson Place, the Nelson Trail continues upcanyon to eventually reach Willow Spring, about 2 miles from the trail-head. At this point, the Nelson Trail turns right to climb out of Sycamore Canyon and continue southwest across the wilderness, before finally reaching the end of FR 677A. This high-clearance 2WD route may be reached by turning right on FR 677, just west of Dugas. Turning right off the Nelson Trail at Nelson Place is the 3.2-mile Pine Flat Trail. After following Beehouse Canyon for a way, the Pine Flat Trail eventually con-nects back up with the Nelson Trail to create a 9.3-mile loop. The Pine Flat Trail may be obscured by growth, fallen pine needles, and other material in places.

Continuing up Sycamore Creek from where the Nelson Trail turns southwest is the 1.6-mile Willow Spring Trail. It climbs an easy to moderate grade, to eventually reach the Verde Rim and the 5.3-mile Verde Rim Trail. From the head of the Sycamore Creek drainage, the Verde Rim Trail continues north for 2.1 miles before reaching the

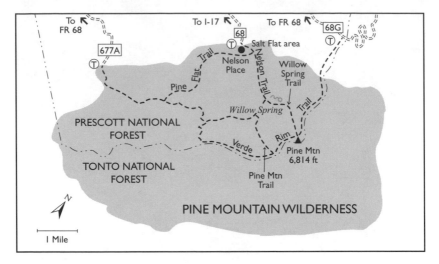

4WD FR 68G. FR 68G turns off FR 68 east of Dugas. Heading south from the upper end of the Willow Springs Trail, the Verde Rim Trail climbs less than a mile before reaching the summit of 6,814-foot Pine Mountain. The top is actually 0.25 mile east of the trail. Beyond Pine Mountain, the Verde Rim Trail intersects the upper end of the 1.2-mile Pine Mountain Trail, which provides a shortcut to the above-mentioned Nelson Trail. The Verde Rim Trail ends at the Nelson Trail, 3.6 miles southwest of the head of Sycamore Creek. This intersection is located 1.8 miles south of Willow Spring. The interconnected trails afford some nice loop hikes.

Water is available in springs and some streambeds, but it should be treated before drinking. Watch for lightning when hiking along the Verde Rim.

24 Granite Mountain Wilderness

Location: 7 miles N of Prescott
Size: 9,700 acres
Status: Wilderness area (1984)
Terrain: Mountains
Elevation: 5,000 feet to 7,626 feet
Management: Prescott NF
Topographic maps: Iron Springs, Jerome Canyon

A noted landmark in the Prescott area, Granite Mountain is the focal point of the interesting little wilderness of the same name. This wilderness features an attractive collection of granite outcrops, cliff faces, and other landforms. One trail accesses the top of Granite Mountain, while others run adjacent to various boundaries of the wilderness.

Seasons

The lower portions of Granite Mountain Wilderness are accessible year-round, but the upper reaches of Granite Mountain may be snow-covered during the months of December, January, and February. Summers may also prove uncomfortably hot.

Plants and Wildlife

In the lowest elevations, pinyon pine and alligator juniper predominate. Manzanita and a variety of desert oaks are also common, as are small stands of ponderosa pine. As the terrain climbs toward the summit of Granite Mountain, drier slopes become entangled with shrub live oak. An occasional agave may also be spotted. Ponderosa pine grows in prodigious numbers on the broad summit of the mountain. You may even see an isolated colony of aspen tucked in among the granite boulders. Mule deer

The view from Granite Mountain

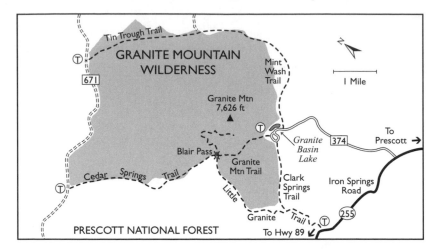

and coyotes are common residents of the wilderness, along with both Abert and gray squirrels. A variety of songbirds live here, and endangered peregrine falcons nest in ledges on Granite Mountain's rugged cliff faces. Because of the falcons' nesting activities, the Forest Service prohibits climbing in these areas from February to July.

Geology
The granite outcrops that characterize much of Granite Mountain Wilderness are thought to be nearly 2 billion years old. Subsequently broken into blocks by vertical joints, or fractures, these formations were then rounded off by water and wind erosion. The resulting unusual rock gardens are coveted by both technical climbers and less intrepid explorers alike.

ACTIVITIES
Hiking
Only one trail—the 4.1-mile Granite Mountain Trail—enters Granite Mountain Wilderness for any length. Beginning at a trailhead just beyond Granite Basin Lake, this popular route climbs gently for a little more than a mile to Blair Pass. From the pass, the Granite Mountain Trail turns north to begin a somewhat steeper climb to Granite Mountain Saddle. In 1.3 miles, this section of the route climbs about 800 feet. From the saddle, the trail then heads south for 1.5 miles to a vista point along the southern edge of the mountain. The actual summit of Granite Mountain rises 0.5 mile to the east. To reach the trailhead, drive 3 miles west from Prescott on Iron Springs Road to Forest Road (FR) 374. Drive 4 miles north on this road to its end.

A number of other trails circumnavigate the wilderness boundaries. From Blair Pass, the 2.7-mile Cedar Springs Trail heads northwest along the wilderness boundary to FR 671, the 3.3-mile Little Granite Trail drops from Blair Pass to Iron Springs

Road. The Clark Springs Trail follows along the southern boundary of the wilderness. The Mint Wash Trail follows the southeastern boundary, and the Tin Trough Trail runs closely along the northeastern boundary. Because portions of these routes lie outside the wilderness area, they may be open to mountain bikes.

Water is not available in Granite Mountain Wilderness. Watch for lightning in exposed locales.

Rock Climbing

Given the plentiful supply of solid granite, Granite Mountain Wilderness is a delight for technical rock climbers. Especially challenging routes are found along the precipitous south face of Granite Mountain. Keep in mind that these cliffs are closed between February to July, as they constitute an active nesting area for endangered peregrine falcons.

2.5 Apache Creek Wilderness

Location: 40 miles NW of Prescott
Size: 5,420 acres
Status: Wilderness area (1984)
Terrain: Forested canyons and ridges
Elevation: 5,200 feet to 7,200 feet
Management: Prescott NF
Topographic maps: Juniper Mountain, Campwood

Barely tipping the size requirement for wilderness status, Apache Creek Wilderness is a rarely visited concoction of timbered drainages and ridges. Unfortunately for hikers, it includes only one very short, hard-to-reach trail. While its northern boundary is less than 0.5 mile from a major road, access is blocked by private lands. For those willing to travel cross-country, however, this area is a real treat. For inexperienced hikers, it is not the best of choices.

Seasons

This wilderness sees some snow and cold temperatures in the winter, while summer afternoons may be hot. The best times for an excursion are in spring and fall.

Plants and Wildlife

Apache Creek Wilderness supports a mixture of ponderosa pine, Douglas fir, alligator juniper, pinyon pine, Gambel oak, manzanita, mountain mahogany, and some riparian species such as cottonwood. Wildlife includes deer, elk, coyotes, mountain lions, and bobcats, among other species.

A gnarled tree trunk near Apache Springs

Geology

Much of the wilderness features well-eroded boulders and Precambrian granite out-crops. These formations are similar to those found north of Prescott in the Granite Mountain area. Stream erosion has shaped the land significantly, dissecting it into many drainages.

ACTIVITIES
Hiking

Although a trail once entered the wilderness from the north, the lack of legal access has led to the route's discontinued status. Cross-country access to the lower reaches of the wilderness is possible, however, from Forest Road (FR) 95A. FR 95A branches off FR 95 a couple of miles south of the Walnut Creek Center, a U.S. Forest Service work station reached by driving 36 miles north from Prescott on Williamson Valley Road. Turn left on FR 95 and drive 1.5 miles. Considerable skill in reading topographic maps and using a compass is required for any cross-country approach to the wilderness.

One trail that does penetrate Apache Creek Wilderness for a short way can be

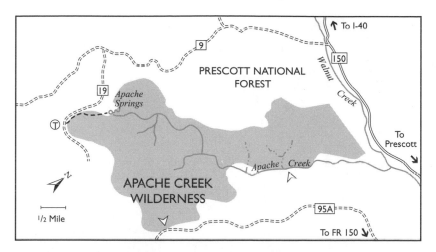

reached by driving about 4 miles west from the Walnut Creek Center to FR 9. Turn south on this rough 2WD road and drive 5.6 miles to the 4WD FR 19. Drive 2 miles to where the road reaches a saddle. From here, an old trail heads south into the head of Apache Creek for 1 mile to reach Apache Springs. An Apache Creek Wilderness sign is located a short distance from the road. Some Arizona walnut trees, along with other broad-leafed trees, cattails, and other greenery add to the allure of these springs. Experienced cross-country hikers can continue downstream along Apache Creek. Be warned, however, that boulder chokes and thick growth make the going slow.

Water is available along the perennial Apache Creek, but it should be treated before drinking. With the exception of the short route to Apache Springs, hiking within this wilderness is only for those who are very experienced in backcountry orientation and travel.

26 Juniper Mesa Wilderness

Location: 40 miles N of Prescott
Size: 7,640 acres
Status: Wilderness area (1984)
Terrain: Timbered mesa
Elevation: 5,400 feet to 7,081 feet
Management: Prescott NF
Topographic maps: Juniper Mesa, Indian Peak

This small wilderness includes a trio of trails that access the mostly flat top of its name-sake landform. Juniper Mesa is characterized by ubiquitous pinyon pine and juniper forests. Some fine vistas are to be had from this high tableland.

A ponderosa pine near the summit of Juniper Mesa

Seasons

Although it is possible to visit Juniper Mesa Wilderness any month of the year, winter often brings some snow to the area, rendering the trails impassable at worst and making the roads somewhat sloppy at least. Because summers see temperatures occasionally above the 100-degree mark, spring and autumn are best.

Plants and Wildlife

As the name suggests, this wilderness is home to plenty of juniper, which mingles with pinyon pine and ponderosa pine. Shrub live oak and Gambel oak are just two of several oak species found here. Beargrass, mountain mahogany, pricklypear cactus, and agave also grow in the wilderness. Animal residents include mule deer, elk, black bears, coyotes, bobcats, and Abert squirrels.

Geology

Juniper Mesa features a variety of sedimentary rocks similar to those found in the upper reaches of the Grand Canyon. These formations include Tapeats Sandstone, Bright Angel Shale, the Martin Formation, and the Redwall Formation. Dating back to the Paleozoic era, many of these rocks are studded with fossils of mollusks, coral, and other primitive life forms.

ACTIVITIES
Hiking

Of the four trails that enter Juniper Mesa Wilderness, the Bull Spring Trail is probably the most accessible. To reach the trailhead, drive 36 miles north of Prescott on Williamson Valley Road to Forest Road (FR) 95. Turn left and drive 1.5 miles to the Walnut Creek Center, a U.S. Forest Service Work Station. Turn right onto FR 150 and continue about 6 miles to the signed trailhead. These roads are passable to all vehicles.

A mile or so from the trailhead, the Bull Spring Trail connects with the Juniper Mesa Trail. Offering the best views within the wilderness, the 6.5-mile Juniper Mesa Trail follows the rim of the mesa. It begins along 4WD FR 9867A near Juniper Spring, east of the wilderness. It soon climbs some 800 feet to top the mesa rim. Eventually, the Juniper Mesa Trail terminates along the Oaks and Willows Trail, which begins a short distance beyond the Bull Spring trailhead. The Oaks and Willows Trail traverses the western section of the wilderness and enters George Woods Canyon, where it begins to climb up the south face of Juniper Mesa. The route is steep in places, but the going is mostly easy. Some very old alligator junipers are the hike's main attractions. Eventually topping out on the mesa, the Oaks and Willows Trail then turns east to drop slightly over the next 3 miles. The trail finally reaches the Pine Spring trailhead 6.6 miles

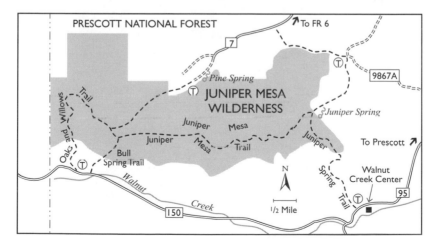

from the start. Pine Spring is located north of the wilderness at the end of FR 7.

Offering access to the Juniper Mesa Trail from the vicinity of the Walnut Creek Center is the Juniper Spring Trail. This 3.7-mile route continues for 2.5 miles to the wilderness boundary, where it then crosses the southeastern corner of the wilderness area. It ends at the Juniper Spring trailhead and the eastern section of the Juniper Mesa Trail. Difficult to follow at times, the Juniper Spring Trail climbs more than 1,000 feet to access the rim of Juniper Mesa.

Water is scarce within the wilderness. Although some springs are found in the vicinity, they are not reliable during dry periods. It is best to bring all that you will need. Watch for lightning in higher, exposed areas.

27 Castle Creek Wilderness

Location: 35 miles S of Prescott
Size: 29,770 acres
Status: Wilderness area (1984)
Terrain: Mountains and canyons
Elevation: 2,800 feet to 7,000 feet
Management: Prescott NF
Topographic maps: Crown King, Bumble Bee, Battle Flat, Cleator

Rising abruptly out of the desert, the Bradshaw Mountains are one of the more dramatic mountain ranges in Arizona. Nowhere is this more evident than along the range's eastern slope, where the terrain shoots up more than 4,000 feet. Encompassing the impressive east side of the Bradshaw Mountains is the nearly 30,000-acre Castle Creek Wilderness. Thanks to its broad range of elevations, this wilderness offers both stunning scenery and a wide array of plant communities.

Seasons
Visitors will find year-round hiking in Castle Creek Wilderness, thanks to its range of elevations. Winter and spring are the best seasons for a visit to the lower elevations, along the area's east side, while late spring, summer, and autumn are the times to hike its upper reaches. The nearby town of Crown King is a popular summertime retreat for many folks from Phoenix.

Plants and Wildlife
Growing at the lowest elevations of the wilderness are saguaro cactus, paloverde, mesquite, creosote bush, cholla, pricklypear cactus, and ocotillo. Moving up in elevation, plant species include shrub live oak, manzanita, Arizona white oak, and alligator juniper. In the uppermost reaches of the wilderness, where there is more moisture, you'll find ponderosa pine, Gambel oak, and the occasional Douglas fir. Wildlife includes mule

A flowering agave plant in the Castle Creek Wilderness

deer, javelinas, coyotes, mountain lions, black bears, a variety of rodents, and many different species of birds.

Geology

The Bradshaw Range consists mostly of Precambrian granite, although some Precambrian schist is found along a narrow strip on the east side of the range. Dark volcanic rocks that resulted from lava flows during the Tertiary period are common at the southern end of the mountains.

History

The Bradshaws have a century-long history of mining for gold and other precious metals. Within the wilderness, this is best illustrated by the Algonquin Mine, which dates back to the turn of the century. Located along the Algonquin Trail, the mine is today little more than a collapsed mineshaft, some old rails, and the dilapidated remains of a few structures. Lone prospectors still work claims in other parts of the Bradshaws, however.

ACTIVITIES
Hiking

Accessing the western section of Castle Creek Wilderness is the 5-mile Algonquin Trail, which drops more than 2,000 feet into Horsethief Canyon. There it encounters the Algonquin Mine. In the vicinity of the mine, the Algonquin Trail intersects the lower end of the Horsethief Canyon Trail. From the mine area, the Horsethief Canyon Trail climbs about 2,000 feet in a little more than 2 miles. The northern end of the Algonquin Trail is reached by driving 26 miles on Forest Road (FR) 259 (Crown King Road) from the Bumble Bee interchange on Interstate 17, or a few miles northeast from the town of Crown King on FR 259. Its southern end is located a few miles beyond Crown King on FR 52. The upper end of the Horsethief Canyon Trail is found at the Turkey Gulch Campground, which is farther up FR 52.

In the lower eastern section of the wilderness, the 6.7-mile Castle Creek Trail can be accessed near its midpoint by way of a 1-mile spur trail. This short access trail climbs 1,000 feet from a trailhead located near the end of FR 684. A rough 2WD route, FR 684 can be reached by driving north from Phoenix on Interstate 17 to the Bumble Bee interchange. Drive about 5 miles north on Crown King Road (a good gravel route) to the signed turnoff for FR 684. From this spur trail, the Castle Creek Trail heads west for 4 miles to climb 2,200 feet before reaching a trailhead near Kentuck Springs in Horsethief Basin. Horsethief Basin is a high area located southwest of the wilderness. It may be reached by driving 7 miles south on FR 52 from the small community of Crown King.

Continuing north from the spur trail intersection, the Castle Creek Trail continues for nearly 3 miles before intersecting the Twin Peaks Trail. The Twin Peaks Trail also begins at Horsethief Basin, but it continues northeast across the wilderness before

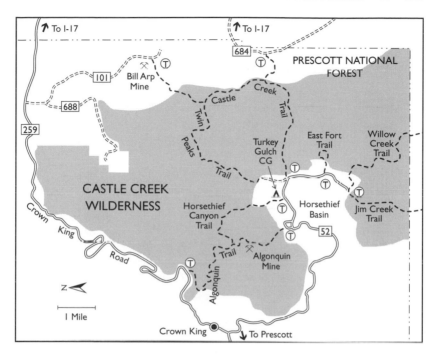

reaching the 4WD FR 101 at the Bill Arp Mine. Along its 7.75-mile length, the Twin Peaks Trail descends some 2,700 feet from a peak elevation of 6,720 feet. While hiking one way on the Twin Peaks Trail requires a shuttle, it is possible to enjoy an 11-mile loop by following the length of the Castle Creek Trail, then turning left on the Twin Peaks Trail. The two trailheads for this loop are separated by less than 2 miles of road in the Horsethief Basin area.

The very short, 0.8-mile-long East Fort Trail penetrates Castle Creek Wilderness from Horsethief Basin to reach its namesake, the East Fort Ruin. East Fort is an old army post built during the Indian wars of the late 1800s. A very easy route, the East Fort Trail changes very little in elevation.

A pair of trails also heads south from Horsethief Basin. These are the Jim Creek Trail, which continues 1.8 miles before exiting the wilderness to enter BLM land beyond, and the 4.1-mile-long Willow Creek Trail, which loops south into the Willow Creek drainage. A secondary route branches off the Willow Creek Trail to head south out of the wilderness and onto state lands. Both of these routes receive very little use and are difficult to follow. Also, because they drop significantly, they are very rough in places.

Water is available within the wilderness in the form of scattered springs. Be sure to treat all surface water before drinking. Watch for lightning in the higher terrain and for flash floods along streambeds.

28 Agua Fria National Monument

Location: 40 miles N of Phoenix
Size: 71,100 acres
Status: National monument (2000)
Terrain: Mesas and canyons
Elevation: 900 feet to 1,300 feet
Management: Agua Fria NM, BLM (Phoenix Field Office)
Topographic maps: Cordes Junction, Joes Hill

Established in January of 2000 by then president, Bill Clinton, Agua Fria National Monument encompasses two principal mesas—Black and Perry—and a scenic canyon system in between. Typified by expansive grasslands that stretch across the fairly flat mesa tops and by rugged drainages formed by the Agua Fria River and various perennial side streams, this 71,100-acre parcel of land is scenic in its own right. The primary reason for its recognition, however, lies in the numerous archeological sites

Cacti are plentiful in Agua Fria National Monument.

that dot the land. For backcountry explorers, no established trails exist, but drainage bottoms and open grasslands do lend themselves well to backcountry travel.

Seasons

Although slightly higher in elevation than the Phoenix area to the south, Agua Fria National Monument typically experiences hot summertime temperatures. Late spring and early fall may prove quite uncomfortable as well. Winter is typically snow-free and the hiking can be good. Cool fall days are nice and springtime brings a plethora of wildflowers.

Plants and Wildlife

Within the canyon bottoms, especially where there is a live stream, expect to find cottonwoods, Arizona sycamores, willows, tamarisks, and the like. A bit too high for saguaro cactus, the upper reaches of the monument most often feature open grasslands that are dotted with yuccas, pricklypear cactus, mesquite, and junipers. Wildlife of the monument includes deer, javelinas, badgers, coyotes, and mountain lions.

Geology

The dark complexion of rimrock in the monument is indicative of past volcanic activity. These basalt-covered mesas, in fact, resulted from lava flows during the Quaternary and Tertiary periods. Stream erosion has since etched the beautiful canyon systems of the area.

History

Archaeologists have identified nearly 500 different prehistoric sites, some of which are small, fortresslike structures among the canyon rims while others are full-blown pueblo villages. It is believed that the area was inhabited between A.D. 1250 and 1450. Further evidence of past habitation is found in the many petroglyphs etched into the dark basaltic rock. All of these archaeological sites are fully protected by federal law, and visitors should take care not to damage them by walking on stone walls or digging for or removing artifacts.

ACTIVITIES
Hiking

No established trails exist in the Agua Fria National Monument, but a trailhead has been established for those hikers who want to follow a side canyon of the Agua Fria River. From Phoenix, drive north on Interstate 17 to the Badger Springs Wash exit (exit 256), which is nearly 3 miles north of the Sunset Point rest area. Upon exiting, drive east for less than a mile to the signed trailhead. A number of roads braid the area leading toward Badger Springs Wash, some of which are in better shape than others. A high-clearance 2WD vehicle may be required to reach the trailhead. From there, drop directly south to the Badger Springs Wash bottom a short distance away. This drainage is easy to follow as it drops gently for about a mile before emptying into the

Agua Fria River. From this point, it would be possible to follow the river upstream or down for several miles. Unfortunately, access to the Agua Fria River from the downstream end is blocked by private land directly south of the monument boundary.

Offering ready access to the central portion of the monument is the Bloody Basin Road, which crosses the monument to reach the Tonto National Forest beyond. Exiting

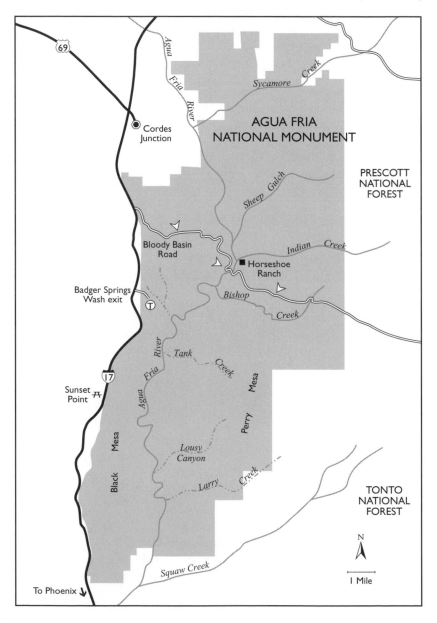

Interstate 17 a few miles north of the Badger Springs Wash exit, the Bloody Basin Road can be rough in spots and washboarded, but it is passable to most passenger vehicles (not so during or after heavy rains, however). From this route, it is possible to hike cross-country along the mostly open mesa tops and gentle ridges. Watch for rattlesnakes during the warmer months, however, and respect private property signs denoting the boundaries of the Horseshoe Ranch, which is located within the monument along the Agua Fria River.

Other backcountry roads access other portions of the monument and several old jeep routes (now closed to vehicular traffic) can make for some fine hiking routes. For information on these, check with the BLM at the Phoenix Field Office.

29 Mazatzal Wilderness

Location: 25 miles NE of Carefree
Size: 252,500 acres
Status: Wilderness area (1964)
Terrain: Deserts and mountains
Elevation: 1,600 feet to 7,904 feet
Management: Tonto NF
Topographic maps: Mazatzal Peak, North Peak, Cypress Butte, Table Mountain, Horseshoe Dam, Lion Mountain, Reno Pass, Chalk Mountain, Wet Bottom Mesa, Verde Hot Springs, Cane Springs Mountain, Buckhead Mesa

Covering a quarter-million acres, Mazatzal Wilderness is a crown jewel among Arizona wilderness areas. Because it spans 6,000 vertical feet, the array of plant communities in the wilderness is considerable, featuring everything from Lower Sonoran desert life to Transition Zone evergreen forests. The scenery is superb throughout, thanks to the rugged topography of the Mazatzal Mountains. And, because the wilderness contains nearly 150 miles of trails, the hiking possibilities are considerable.

Seasons
Mazatzal Wilderness is suitable for hiking year-round, due to the wide array of elevations found within. Hiking at the highest elevations can be hot during the summer months. Late spring and early fall are the best times. Winter occasionally brings snow and cold temperatures to these areas. At the lower elevations, daytime temperatures are generally comfortable from late fall through early spring. Summers are far too hot in these areas to be suitable for hiking.

Plants and Wildlife
Across the lowest elevations in the western portion of the wilderness are stands of saguaro cactus interspersed with cholla, ocotillo, paloverde trees, and a variety of other

Along the Barnhardt Trail in the Mazatzal Wilderness

desert plants. Moving up in elevation, a tangle of shrubs—various evergreen oaks, manzanita, and such—become common. Midlevel elevations feature pinyon pine and juniper. In the highest elevations, ponderosa pine and Douglas fir enjoy moister conditions, and along perennial streams and canyon bottoms grow riparian communities of velvet ash, cottonwood, Arizona sycamore, and Arizona walnut. Wildlife includes deer, javelinas, coyotes, bobcats, mountain lions, black bears, golden eagles, and bald eagles.

Geology

Encompassing the northern portion of the rugged Mazatzal Mountains, Mazatzal Wilderness includes exposures of Precambrian Mazatzal quartzite, Deadman quartzite, and Maverick shale. Rhyolite, which was formed during more recent volcanic activity, is also present. In the western portion of the wilderness are found ancient lava flows and outcrops of volcanic tuffs. The Mazatzals are the largest mountain range within the central Arizona highlands.

History

The Mazatzal Mountains won recognition as a designated primitive area in 1938. In 1964, passage of the Wilderness Act led to the establishment of Mazatzal Wilderness, then, in 1984, the Arizona Wilderness Act added some 35,000 acres to the area, bringing its total up to the present 252,500 acres. Prior to these moves toward preservation, the Mazatzal Mountains were home to the prehistoric Salado and Hohokom Indians. Later, the Yavapai and Apache roamed these mountains on hunting and food gathering trips. Anglo-American trappers first explored the range in the early 1800s. Miners poked around in the late nineteenth century and ranchers soon followed. The word *mazatzal* is Aztec for "place inhabited by deer," but it is not clear how this central Arizona mountain range earned the name.

ACTIVITIES
Hiking

One of the most heavily used access points is the Barnhardt trailhead, which is located on the eastern edge of the wilderness. It can be reached by driving 14.5 miles south from Payson on Arizona Highway 87 to Forest Road (FR) 419. Turn west and drive 5 miles to its end. From the trailhead, most hikers climb up the Barnhardt Trail in order to access the area around Mazatzal Peak—the 7,904-foot-high point of the wilderness. Along its 6.2-mile length, the Barnhardt Trail climbs nearly 2,000 feet before reaching the Mazatzal Divide Trail. To complete a 17-mile loop hike around Mazatzal Peak (this hike does not actually go all the way to the top of the rugged peak), turn left on the Mazatzal Divide Trail and continue a few miles south to its intersection with the 7-mile-long Y Bar Basin Trail. Turn left on this route and follow it northeast to return to the Barnhardt trailhead. There are a number of suitable camping spots along this loop and, of course, the scenery is spectacular throughout.

In addition to the Barnhardt and Y Bar Basin Trails, the Barnhardt trailhead also provides access to the 4.5-mile-long Half Moon Trail. This relatively new trail traverses the eastern foothills, maintaining a mostly level grade the entire way. Upon reaching the end of the high-clearance, 2WD FR 442, the Half Moon Trail connects with the far steeper Rock Creek Trail. A little more than 3.5 miles in length, the Rock Creek Trail climbs more than 3,000 feet to reach the Mazatzal Divide Trail near the head of Deadman Creek.

A second popular access point along the wilderness area's eastern side is the Deer Creek trailhead, which lies just off Arizona Highway 87, adjacent to the Highway 87 and Highway 188 junction. This trailhead accesses two trails that enter the wilderness: the 8.8-mile Deer Creek Trail, which follows the north fork of Deer Creek to its headwaters and FR 201, and the 6.4 mile South Fork Trail, which follows the south fork of Deer Creek to also reach FR 201. These trails gain 2,200 feet and 2,600 feet, respectively, and both access interesting canyons with nice riparian growth. FR 201 turns north from Arizona Highway 87 at the Slate Creek Divide.

Traversing the east-central portion of the wilderness from north to south, the above-mentioned Mazatzal Divide Trail covers 29 miles in all. Its northern trailhead is

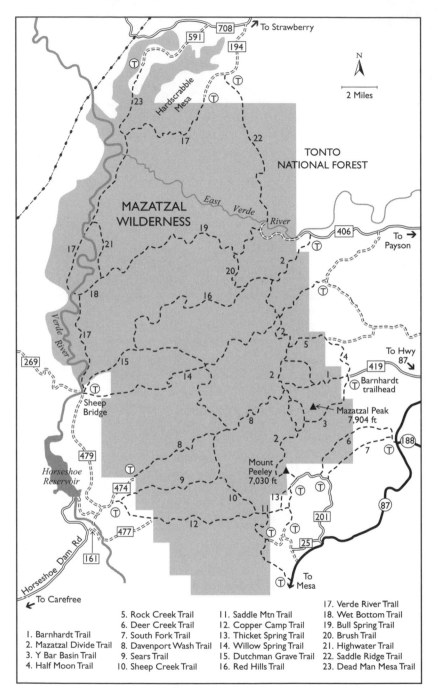

To Strawberry

708
591
194

⊤
⊤
23

Hardscrabble Mesa

17

22

TONTO
NATIONAL FOREST

N
2 Miles

MAZATZAL
WILDERNESS

East Verde River

406
To Payson

19

⊤

17
21
20

2

16

2

5

4

17

18

To Hwy
87

419

2

1

⊤ Barnhardt
trailhead

15

14

Verde River

269

⊤

Sheep
Bridge

8

▲ Mazatzal Peak
7,904 ft

3

479

8

2

6

7

⊤

188

Horseshoe
Reservoir

9

Mount
Peeley ▲
7,030 ft

⊤ ⊤

474

⊤

10

13 1

11

⊤

87

477

⊤

12

⊤

201

161

25

To Mesa

Horseshoe Dam Rd

To Carefree

⊤

5. Rock Creek Trail
6. Deer Creek Trail
7. South Fork Trail
8. Davenport Wash Trail
9. Sears Trail
10. Sheep Creek Trail

11. Saddle Mtn Trail
12. Copper Camp Trail
13. Thicket Spring Trail
14. Willow Spring Trail
15. Dutchman Grave Trail
16. Red Hills Trail

17. Verde River Trail
18. Wet Bottom Trail
19. Bull Spring Trail
20. Brush Trail
21. Highwater Trail
22. Saddle Ridge Trail
23. Dead Man Mesa Trail

1. Barnhardt Trail
2. Mazatzal Divide Trail
3. Y Bar Basin Trail
4. Half Moon Trail

located west of Payson, along FR 406 (a poorly maintained graveled road); its southern trailhead is found along FR 201. Elevations range from 3,500 feet to 7,180 feet, and the trail is not difficult to follow. Given the number of trails that intersect the route along the way, several long-distance hikes are possible. If you have access to a shuttle, you might consider hiking the length of the Mazatzal Divide Trail in either direction.

Just as the Mazatzal Divide Trail traverses the eastern portion of Mazatzal Wilderness, a number of trails cross the wilderness from west to east. One of these routes, the 15-mile Davenport Wash Trail, runs between the Mazatzal Divide Trail and a trailhead southwest of the wilderness. Because this route climbs 3,600 feet, parts of the trail are steep, but the interesting terrain along the way makes it a particularly worthwhile route. Unfortunately, access to the western trailhead is somewhat difficult because of the Verde River. It was once possible to drive to the start of the Davenport Wash Trail from Carefree, by way of Cave Creek and Horseshoe Dam Roads, but officials have since closed the Horseshoe Dam to vehicles. The trailhead must now be reached by fording the river by 4WD vehicle. The crossing point is located on FR 161, which turns right about 3 miles south of the dam. Once across the river, follow FR 479 to FR 474, turn right and continue to the road's end.

Another trailhead found along the above-mentioned FR 474 accesses the western section of the 6.9-mile Sears Trail, which climbs about 2,000 feet before intersecting the midway point of the Sheep Creek Trail. The Sheep Creek Trail runs for 10 miles between the Davenport Wash Trail to the north and the Saddle Mountain Trail to the south. As the Sheep Creek Trail approaches the Saddle Mountain Trail, it also intersects the eastern section of the 7.2-mile Copper Camp Trail, which heads west to intersect the above-mentioned Sears Trail near FR 474. These interconnected trails make for some interesting loop hikes through the southern portion of Mazatzal Wilderness. As this is a very remote section of the wilderness, and because trail conditions are not always ideal, only experienced hikers should attempt these routes.

The Sheep Creek Trail can also be hiked in connection with portions of the Mazatzal Divide and Davenport Wash Trails, the 2.6-mile Thicket Spring Trail, and the last mile of the above-mentioned FR 201. This lengthy loop hike takes in the western slope of Mazatzal Peak, Mount Catherine, and Mount Peeley, as well as portions of several westward-flowing drainages. Again, such a hike should be attempted only by experienced backpackers.

A second access point along the wilderness area's western boundary is located at Sheep Bridge, which is upstream from the Horseshoe Reservoir. From Carefree, drive 35 miles north on Cave Creek Road to FR 269. Turn right and drive 12 miles to the trailhead. From Sheep Bridge, two trails head east to access the west-central portion of the wilderness. The 16-mile-long Willow Spring Trail climbs some 4,000 feet before connecting with the Mazatzal Divide Trail, north of Mazatzal Peak. The second route to head east from Sheep Bridge is the 12-mile Dutchman Grave Trail. After heading northeast from the bridge, this trail connects with the 14.5-mile Red Hills Trail which, like the Willow Spring Trail, connects with the Mazatzal Divide Trail. The Dutchman

Grave Trail eventually connects with the Willow Spring Trail near Mountain Spring. By following the Willow Spring Trail, a portion of the Mazatzal Divide Trail, the Red Hills Trail, and the lower portion of the Dutchman Grave Trail, intrepid hikers can occupy themselves for a week or more. A shorter loop of about 25 miles follows the Willow Spring Trail east to the far end of the Dutchman Grave Trail, then returns by the latter route.

North of Sheep Bridge, the wilderness boundary bulges westward to take in a section of the Verde River that has been designated as a Wild and Scenic River. Hikers interested in exploring the river bottom north of Sheep Bridge should consider taking the 28-mile Verde River Trail, which begins at Sheep Bridge and continues north, paralleling the river much of the way. Two river crossings impede foot travel during periods of high water—cross at your own risk! In the last 10 miles, the Verde River Trail leaves the river bottom to climb Hardscrabble Mesa, where it reaches FR 194. FR 194 heads south from the small town of Strawberry.

Turning east from the Verde River Trail, 7 miles north of Sheep Bridge, is the 9.4-mile Wet Bottom Trail. After climbing 2,500 feet, this route connects with the Bull Spring Trail, which heads east for 10 miles to reach FR 406. The Bull Spring route, in turn, connects with the 3.5-mile Brush Trail, which heads south to intersect the above-mentioned Red Hills Trail. The Wet Bottom Trail also connects with the 4.4-mile Highwater Trail. Because the Wet Bottom Trail turns off the Verde River just prior to

Majestic sycamore trees grace many riparian areas in the Mazatzal Wilderness.

the first crossing, and the Highwater Trail connects back up with the Verde River Trail after the second crossing, these trails provide a dry route during times of high water.

In the northernmost portion of Mazatzal Wilderness, two trails enter from the north. The 9-mile Saddle Ridge Trail begins along the above-mentioned FR 194 on Hardscrabble Mesa and continues south to FR 406. The southern trailhead is located near the L.F. Ranch, a private parcel of land located within the wilderness. The last few miles of FR 406 are still used for vehicle access to the ranch, but it is closed to public vehicles. In the extreme northern tip of the wilderness is the Dead Man Mesa Trail, which climbs 2,300 feet in 4 miles to the top of its namesake. Very rough and located mostly outside the wilderness, the Dead Man Mesa Trail begins at the end of the 4WD FR 591, west of Strawberry.

Water is found in some springs in the wilderness, but it should be treated before drinking. Watch for lightning in the higher elevations, and be wary of flash floods in the canyon bottoms after heavy rains.

River Running

While high water may preclude hiker access to certain trailheads in the western portion of Mazatzal Wilderness, it nevertheless provides ideal boating conditions on the Verde River itself. The Verde River is not usually prodigious enough for river running, but during spring runoff there is often sufficient flow to sweep kayaks and rafts downstream. Rapids along the way are not overly difficult, but they are challenging enough to make travel by canoe difficult. To begin the 59-mile float trip, put in at Camp Verde; the takeout is at Sheep Bridge. The best time of year for floating the Verde is between January and April. A wet suit is suggested.

30 Hellsgate Wilderness

Location: 18 miles E of Payson
Size: 36,780 acres
Status: Wilderness area (1984)
Terrain: Canyons and mountains
Elevation: 3,960 feet to 6,440 feet
Management: Tonto NF
Topographic maps: Diamond Butte, McDonald Mountain, Sheep Basin Mountain, Buzzard Roost Mesa, Payson South, Gisela

True to its name, the central features of Hellsgate Wilderness are several rugged canyons. Carved by Tonto Creek and its tributaries, this canyon system includes sheer walls of rock, boulder chokes, and deep pools of water. A few steep trails access the wilderness, making for relatively straightforward explorations of the area, while more intrepid hikers may want to try following the canyon bottoms themselves.

Seasons

It is possible to visit Hellsgate Wilderness any time of year, but stream crossings may be very cold during the winter. Winter also brings subfreezing nighttime temperatures and occasional snow to the higher terrain. Spring runoff may lead to water levels too high for safe canyon traverses. Summers can be quite hot, which becomes especially uncomfortable when you are hiking away from the creek bottom.

Plants and Wildlife

At the lowest elevations, near the canyon's mouth, grow a few saguaro cactus, ocotillo, cholla, and other desert plants. Moving up in elevation, abundant chaparral, consisting of a mixture of shrub live oak, manzanita, and the like, is much in evidence. Alligator juniper, pinyon pine, and various species of evergreen oaks also grow here. In the highest portions of the wilderness are found forests of ponderosa pine and Douglas fir. Along the creek beds, riparian communities of sycamore, willow, and cottonwood are abundant. Wildlife of the wilderness includes deer, black bears, coyotes, mountain lions, bobcats, javelinas, beavers, and two varieties of trout.

Geology

Two perennial streams—Tonto and Haigler Creeks—have carved deeply into the rugged terrain below the Mogollon Rim (as much as 1,000 feet in places). Within much of this canyon system are exposed formations of Precambrian granite, gneiss, and schist.

Pine forest in the Hellsgate Wilderness

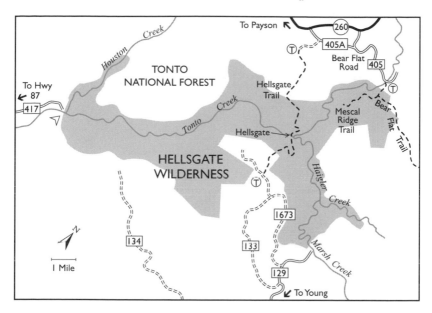

ACTIVITIES
Hiking

The most promising of the three trails to enter the wilderness is the Hellsgate Trail, which accesses its namesake, a scenic corridor of the canyon where the Tonto and Haigler Creeks meet. Traversing the wilderness from south to north, this 11-mile trail is quite strenuous, as it drops more than 1,600 feet in a very short distance. Uncertain footing and rocky terrain also add to the difficulties of this hike. For those who make the hike in, beautiful pools of water, sheer rock walls, and shady streamside rest spots offer ample reward for the effort. There is only one camping spot at Hellsgate. To access the Hellsgate Trail from the community of Young, drive west along Forest Road (FR) 129 for 7.5 miles to the 4WD FR 133. Turn left and drive about 8 miles to the southern terminus of the trail. From the north, the Hellsgate Trail can be reached by driving Arizona Highway 260 east from Payson about 11 miles to the turnoff for FR 405A. Turn right and drive 0.5 mile to FR 893. You may want to park here, although 4WD vehicles can drive a bit farther on FR 893. The trail continues south from this point to the canyon rim and beyond.

Another interesting trail is the 9.25 mile Bear Flat Trail. It begins at Tonto Creek, just upstream from the wilderness. From Payson, drive 14 miles east on Arizona Highway 260 to FR 405. Turn south and drive 4.5 miles to where the road crosses the creek. Park west of the creek and wade across to find the start of the trail. Climbing steeply at first, the Bear Flat Trail soon levels off to continue east. The route leaves the wilderness after a mile or so, but it is still very scenic. Within the first mile, the Bear Flat Trail intersects the 3-mile Mescal Ridge Trail, which heads southwest into the wilderness along its scenic namesake.

In addition to the above-mentioned trails, it is also possible to hike cross-country along Tonto and Haigler Creeks. These canyon bottoms may be accessed from either the Hellsgate Trail or from Bear Flat Trail. North of the small community of Gisela (which is south of Payson), you can also park outside some private land and walk around to enter the lower west end of the wilderness, along Tonto Creek. The going is slow along drainage bottoms due to boulder chokes, pools that require swimming, and such. Such an adventure should be attempted only by very experienced hikers.

While water is available along some drainages within Hellsgate Wilderness, it should be treated before drinking. Watch for flash floods in the canyon bottoms after heavy rains.

31 Salome Wilderness

Location: 40 miles NW of Globe
Size: 18,530 acres
Status: Wilderness area (1984)
Terrain: Canyons and mountains
Elevation: 2,500 feet to 6,543 feet
Management: Tonto NF
Topographic maps: Copper Mountain, Armer Mountain, Windy Hill, Greenback Creek, McFadden Peak

Characterized by a deep canyon system, Salome Wilderness offers hikers an opportunity to find solitude in a wild and natural setting. Because it is not as big as the nearby Mazatzal and Superstition Wildernesses, and because it is a bit harder to reach, this area is often overlooked by the throngs of hikers that pour out of Phoenix on the weekends.

Seasons

In the lowest reaches of Salome Wilderness, summertime temperatures often top 100 degrees, while winter evenings typically bring subfreezing temperatures (and occasionally snow) to the higher terrain. The best times for a visit to Salome Wilderness are in the spring and fall.

Plants and Wildlife

Growing in the lower reaches of the wilderness are a few saguaro cactus, ocotillo, cholla, pricklypear cactus, and other desert plants. Higher up are stands of pinyon pine, alligator juniper, and a variety of evergreen oaks. Douglas fir grows on ledges in north-facing canyon walls, and ponderosa pine is typical in the highest reaches of the wilderness, where more moisture is available. Along the perennial Salome and Workman Creeks

Opposite: *Workman Creek in the Salome Wilderness*

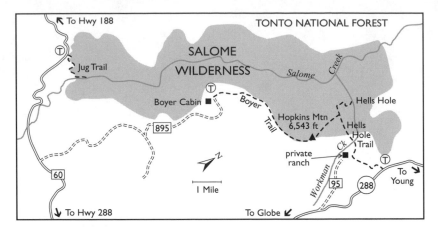

are beautiful riparian communities of Arizona sycamore, birch, maple, and other water-loving deciduous trees. Wildlife includes mule deer and white-tailed deer, coyotes,
mountain lions, bobcats, javelinas, and a variety of birds. Trout are also found in Salome
and Workman Creeks.

Geology

Most of the rocks exposed within Salome Wilderness are sedimentary in origin, although some Precambrian granite may be found in the deepest sections of the canyons. Erosion by Salome Creek and its tributaries has dissected the terrain into a
complex of canyons.

ACTIVITIES
Hiking

Of the two trails that access Salome Wilderness, the most readily accessible is the 5.3-
mile Hells Hole Trail, which begins along Arizona Highway 288 at the Reynolds trailhead, 27 miles north of Arizona Highway 88. From the trailhead, the Hells Hole Trail
climbs a short distance and then drops into the Workman Creek drainage. About a
mile in, the trail passes a private ranch. It then crosses Workman Creek, after which it
gains the top of a plateau to the east. Finally, it drops into its namesake—a particularly
rugged portion of the Workman Creek drainage. Elevations along the Hells Hole Trail
range from 3,920 feet to 5,480 feet.

On top of the above-mentioned plateau, a second route—the 5-mile-long Boyer
Trail—branches south to follow the rim above Salome Creek. It eventually drops
into Boyer Creek and follows the creek for a ways. The route reaches the Boyer trailhead at Boyer Cabin, along the 4WD Forest Road (FR) 895. FR 895 is reached by
driving 13 miles north on Arizona Highway 288 from Arizona Highway 88. Turn
west on FR 60 and drive 9 miles to the turnoff for FR 895. The Boyer Trail includes
an elevation change of about 1,600 feet and is considered difficult in places.

A third route, which runs along the wilderness's southern boundary, is the 2-mile Jug Trail. This short but interesting route winds its way among chaparral-covered hills before dropping into the Salome Creek drainage. Elevation changes are not great, although some steep pitches along the way can be expected.

While water is found within Salome Wilderness, especially along Salome and Workman Creeks, it should be treated before drinking. Watch for flash floods in the canyon bottoms after heavy rains.

32 Sierra Ancha Wilderness

Location: 45 miles NW of Globe
Size: 20,850 acres
Status: Wilderness area (1964)
Terrain: Mountains and canyons
Elevation: 2,800 feet to 7,748 feet
Management: Tonto NF
Topographic maps: Aztec Peak, McFadden Peak, Meddler Wash, Sombrero Peak

Defined by soaring cliffs to the south and east, Sierra Ancha Wilderness offers some of the most scenic hiking in central Arizona, as well as a variety of vegetation. Undoubtedly, it was these natural wonders that helped win preservation status for the area in 1933, when Sierra Ancha Primitive Area was designated. A massive wildfire in spring 2000 charred much of the wilderness, changing the complexion of the land for generations to come.

Seasons

Although it is possible to visit Sierra Ancha Wilderness throughout the year, some seasons are better than others for hiking. Winters occasionally bring snow to the higher reaches and rain to all portions. This often makes the approach roads impassable. Spring is pleasant throughout the wilderness, as is much of autumn. The summer months are hot in the lower elevations but nicer in the higher terrain.

Plants and Wildlife

Plant communities found here range from desert shrub and grasslands in the lower reaches to a mixture of oak and mountain mahogany in the middle elevations, and to ponderosa pine and Douglas fir in the highest portions. Stands of pinyon pine and juniper are also common. Wildlife includes deer, elk, javelinas, coyotes, bobcats, mountain lions, black bears, various birds of prey, and turkeys. Within the 10,000 acres that burned during the Coon Creek Fire in April and May of 2000, a variety of successional plant communities exist.

Geology

Encompassing the eastern end of the Sierra Ancha Mountains, Sierra Ancha Wilderness includes exposures of Pinal schist, and quartzites, shales, and limestones that are collectively known as the Apache series. Considerable faulting has occurred in the area, as evidenced by the massive cliffs that define the eastern and southern portions of the wilderness. In the 1950s, miners prospected within the wilderness in hopes of finding uranium. The boom did not last, however.

ACTIVITIES
Hiking

As the high point of the wilderness, Aztec Peak is also home to an active fire lookout and may be reached by a primitive road. This makes it possible to reach the uppermost portions of the wilderness in short order. A number of interesting trails may be accessed from the vicinity of Aztec Peak. One of these is the Rim Trail, which runs for 7.6 miles along the crest of the cliffs that ring Aztec Peak. To reach the Rim Trail, drive 25.5 miles north on Arizona Highway 288 from Arizona Highway 88 to Forest Road (FR) 487. Turn right and drive 4 miles (this road may require a 4WD vehicle) to the trailhead. FR 487 is closed from December through March because of snow. From the trailhead, follow the Parker Creek Trail for a short way to reach the start of the Rim Trail. The

A trail sign in the Sierra Ancha Wilderness

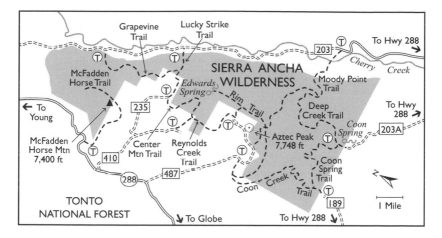

Rim Trail then continues north until it dead-ends at Edwards Spring. The trail is in good condition and is considered easy. The Parker Creek Trail heads southwest from the trailhead, away from the wilderness boundary.

Also accessed by way of the Parker Creek Trail is the 4.4-mile Coon Creek Trail. Following its namesake drainage, this route drops some 2,400 feet to reach a trailhead south of the wilderness. You'll probably need to set up a shuttle to meet you at the other end of this trail. The lower trailhead is located at the end of the high-clearance 2WD FR 189, which branches east from Arizona Highway 288 about 15 miles north of Arizona Highway 88. Because the Coon Creek Trail was greatly impacted by the Coon Creek Fire in 2000, travel along it may be at best, inconvenient, and at worst, dangerous, due to falling timber.

Beginning along the Coon Creek Trail, near the end of FR 189, is the 4-mile Coon Spring Trail. It drops into the lower portion of the Coon Creek drainage, where it encounters Coon Spring before reaching the Deep Creek Trail. The 5-mile Deep Creek Trail heads north from the high-clearance 2WD FR 203A, following an old road most of the way. Maintaining an elevation of around 5,000 feet, the Deep Creek Trail ends at its intersection with the considerably rougher Moody Point Trail.

Covering 8.5 miles and dropping 4,200 feet, the Moody Point Trail traverses the wilderness west to east. Portions of the trail may be difficult to find, and Cherry Creek may not be safely crossed during periods of high water. The dividends of this trail include great scenery and its remote terrain. The trail's upper trailhead is reached by driving about 5 miles east on FR 487. Its downhill end is nearly 19 miles northeast on FR 203 (Cherry Creek Road) from State Highway 288.

The narrow northern portion of Sierra Ancha Wilderness is accessed by some short and interesting trails. Offering access to three of these are the 4WD FR 410 and FR 235. From the end of FR 410, the 3.7-mile Reynolds Creek Trail climbs the switchbacks, then crosses a small western extension of the wilderness, before finally reaching the privately owned Murphy Ranch. Steep and hard to find in places, the Reynolds Creek

Trail is considered difficult. FR 410 turns off Arizona Highway 288 approximately 28 miles north of Arizona Highway 88. The trailhead is located 4 miles up FR 410.

FR 235 turns off FR 410 about 2.5 miles east from Arizona Highway 288, then continues 2.5 miles before ending at the crest of the mountains. From this point, the 4.7-mile Lucky Strike Trail drops 2,800 feet to reach Cherry Creek Road. Because it follows an old jeep road, it is easy to hike. Along the way, it passes some old mines and intersects the southern end of the 5-mile-long Grapevine Trail. Also an old vehicle road, this trail offers easy, low-elevation hiking. It eventually ends at FR 203, some 32 miles northeast of Arizona Highway 288. The eastern trailhead for the Lucky Strike Trail is located nearly 27 miles up FR 203.

Also heading out from the end of FR 235 is the Center Mountain Trail. This 2.5-mile route heads south over its namesake, where it eventually ends. There are nice views along portions of the trail. Attractive stands of ponderosa pine provide a cool hiking environment in summer. The Center Mountain Trail climbs 800 feet in all.

One additional trail that penetrates the northernmost portion of Sierra Ancha Wilderness is the McFadden Horse Trail. From a trailhead along Arizona Highway 288, this 3.3-mile route climbs McFadden Horse Mountain to offer some nice views. It gains 1,200 feet in all and is steep in places.

Because of the Coon Creek Fire, hikers should use caution in all burn areas. The fire engulfed much of the western half of the wilderness. Water is available at a handful of springs and in some streams, but it should be treated before drinking. Watch for lightning along exposed terrain such as that found along the Rim Trail.

33 Salt River Canyon Wilderness

Location: 17 miles N of Globe
Size: 32,100 acres
Status: Wilderness area (1984)
Terrain: River canyon and desert mountains
Elevation: 2,200 feet to 4,200 feet
Management: Tonto NF
Topographic maps: Salt River Peak, Medlee Wash, Dagger Peak, Rockinstraw Mountain, Haystack Butte

Although often siphoned dry by the time it reaches Phoenix, the Salt River is one of the important rivers of the Southwest. Rising in the White Mountains of east-central Arizona, this waterway usually gathers sufficient strength to allow the upper portions of it to be rafted in springtime. As it flows west into the central desert basins of the state, it drops fairly swiftly (an average of 25 feet per mile compared with 8 feet per mile in the Grand Canyon) through a spectacular canyon many miles long. A portion of the river falls within Salt River Canyon Wilderness.

The mouth of the Salt River Canyon

Seasons
While Salt River Canyon Wilderness may be visited throughout the year, the river-running season typically falls between March and May, depending on the snowpack upstream and the rate of melt. The rest of the year, water levels are too low for successful float trips.

Plants and Wildlife
Much of the lower portion of Salt River Canyon Wilderness is characterized by plants typical of the Sonoran Desert, such as saguaro, barrel cactus, cholla, ocotillo, paloverde, and creosote bush. The upper elevations support a mixture of shrub live oak, manzanita, and other plants. Javelinas, mule deer, coyotes, bobcats, and mountain lions call the area home. The river has its own denizens. These include river otters, beavers, and a variety of fish species, including catfish and chub.

Geology
Salt River Canyon reveals a number of rock types, including Precambrian granite, gneiss, schist, and quartzite, as well as sedimentary layers such as limestones and

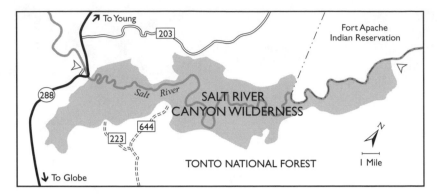

conglomerates. Occasional sills formed when molten magma was injected into the Precambrian bedrock. Water erosion has played the biggest role in creating today's landscape in the Salt River Canyon.

History

While the early Spanish explorer Coronado was the first European to visit the Salt River in 1540, the river was named in 1699 by a Jesuit missionary named Father Kino. Of course, this waterway was known to the Apache Indians for as long as they have inhabited the White Mountains. In 1826, trapper James Ohio Pattie traveled the length of the upper Salt River. In more recent times, recreational river runners have enjoyed the river's wild ride. Of the numerous rapids that enthrall boaters along the Salt, one impediment—Quartzite Falls—had forced boaters to portage their crafts. Unfortunately, a disgruntled rafting guide from Phoenix, along with some friends, leveled the Class 6 rapid with explosives in 1994. Not only did this action irrevocably change the river but it also has opened its upper portions to nonnative species of fish.

ACTIVITIES
River Running

There are no hiking routes in this wilderness, but rafters will find one of the most exciting float trips in the American Southwest. In all, the trip covers 52 river miles and takes 3 days or longer. River parties typically put in where US Highway 60 crosses the Salt River Canyon, about midway between the towns of Show Low and Globe. Because the first 3 miles of the float fall within two Apache Indian reservations, a tribal permit must first be obtained (a small fee is charged). It is possible to put in along Cibeque Road, which cuts up to 10 miles off the trip. Dropping 1,234 feet along its length, this float trip accesses such colorfully named rapids as Maytag Rapid, Overboard Rapid, Exhibition Rapid, Sluicebox Rapid, Tomato Juice Rapid, Rat Trap Rapid, Eye of the Needle, and Corkscrew Rapid. While the last 32 miles of the float falls within the wilderness area, the entire trip is scenic and wild. A Forest Service permit is required to float the wilderness section of the river corridor.

Four Peaks Wilderness

Location: 25 miles NE of Mesa
Size: 60,740 acres
Status: Wilderness area (1984)
Terrain: Deserts and mountains
Elevation: 1,600 feet to 7,657 feet
Management: Tonto NF
Topographic maps: Four Peaks, Theodore Roosevelt Dam, Horse Mesa Dam, Mormon Flat Dam, Tonto Basin, Mine Mountain

Encompassing the southern end of the Mazatzal Mountains, Four Peaks Wilderness offers hikers some wonderful possibilities. The area's namesakes—a cluster of rugged peaks—serve as a landmark that can be seen throughout central Arizona. Ecologically, few other areas in the state can equal the biodiversity found in this wilderness. Several trails form a network of routes that offer both day-long and overnight hikes. Due to the 63,000-acre Lone Fire in 1996, however, visitors should first check with the Forest Service concerning the condition of trails in the area.

Seasons

Snow is fairly common in the higher reaches of Four Peaks Wilderness during the winter months. The terrain is high enough, though, that summer hiking can be pleasant. Lower elevations offer good hiking from November through March, and midlevel elevations are best visited during spring and fall.

Plants and Wildlife

At the lowest elevations, plants are typical of the Sonoran Desert, including saguaro cactus, cholla, ocotillo, and paloverde. Higher up, cooler conditions allow ponderosa pine, Douglas fir, and Gambel oak to gain a foothold. Aspen trees are even found on the northern slope of Browns Peak. There are also plenty of evergreen oaks, manzanita, pinyon pine, and juniper. Along canyon bottoms and adjacent to springs, riparian communities of cottonwood and Arizona sycamore line the banks. The wilderness has a large population of black bears. Other residents include mule deer and white-tailed deer, javelinas, coyotes, bobcats, mountain lions, and desert bighorn sheep.

Geology

Although much of Four Peaks Wilderness consists of Precambrian granite and schist, other formations are also found here. The Four Peaks themselves actually formed as roof pendants, or upward protrusions of magma. The sheer faces of the peaks are composed of shales and Mazatzal quartzite that date back to Precambrian times. In the

One of the namesake summits of the Four Peaks Wilderness

southern portion of the wilderness, a formation known as the Painted Cliffs resulted from volcanic activity that occurred during the Tertiary period.

ACTIVITIES
Hiking

The Four Peaks Wilderness high country is some 5,000 feet higher than the surrounding terrain, but is, nevertheless, readily accessible. One trailhead in this area is located at Lone Pine Saddle, just north of the wilderness boundary. To reach the saddle, drive about 30 miles north from Mesa on Arizona Highway 87 to Forest Road (FR) 143.

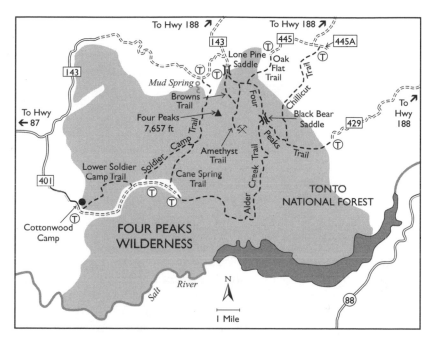

Turn right and drive 19 miles to El Oso Divide. Turn south onto FR 648 and drive 1.3 miles to the trailhead, which is located at road's end. A second approach to the Lone Pine Saddle begins along Arizona Highway 188, about 8 miles south of Punkin Center. Turn west and follow FR 143 for 9 miles to El Oso Divide. From either end, FR 143 is steep and twisted and may require a high-clearance 2WD vehicle. Heading south from the Lone Pine Saddle trailhead, the 10-mile-long Four Peaks Trail passes below its namesakes before picking up Buckhorn Ridge, which extends south from the peaks. In its first few miles, the Four Peaks Trail is easy to follow. As it drops along Buckhorn Ridge, however, the trail is steep and rugged in places. The route's southern end is located along the 4WD FR 429, which turns off Arizona Highway 188 near Roosevelt Lake.

A second trail to head south from Lone Pine Saddle is the 2-mile-long Browns Trail. This route connects with the Amethyst Trail near Browns Saddle. The 3-mile Amethyst Trail, in turn, runs from the Four Peaks Trail to the Amethyst Mine, which is located on the western slope of the Four Peaks. The mine is privately owned, and permission must be obtained before entering. Both the Browns and Amethyst Trails climb about 1,000 feet along their lengths. A nice loop of about 4 miles can be enjoyed by following the Browns, Amethyst, and Four Peaks Trails.

Three other trails also branch off the Four Peaks Trail. The eroded Oak Flat Trail descends from an elevation of 5,400 feet to 3,680 feet in 1.8 miles, to reach the end of FR 445. This 4WD road turns off Arizona Highway 188 near the Roosevelt Dam. The 7-mile-long Chillicut Trail drops north from the Four Peaks Trail near Buckhorn Mountain to reach FR 445A, a branch of FR 445. The Chillicut Trail has an elevation change of about 3,600 feet and is steep in places. Intersecting the Four Peaks Trail at Black Bear Saddle, the Alder Creek Trail follows its namesake drainage south to within a mile of Apache Lake. It then turns west and cuts across the lower foothills to reach the end of FR 401. In all, the Alder Creek Trail is 12 miles long and spans elevations from 2,280 to 5,560 feet. FR 401 turns off the above-mentioned FR 143 about 2.5 miles east of Arizona Highway 87. The last 6 miles of FR 143's 10-mile length are rugged and require a 4WD vehicle.

FR 401 also accesses the 8-mile-long Soldier Camp Trail, which traverses lower elevations west of the Four Peaks before climbing to Mud Spring. Mud Spring is located along FR 143, about 16 miles east of Arizona Highway 87. The trail climbs 2,100 feet and is considered difficult in places. Because the Soldier Camp Trail begins approximately 8 miles up FR 401, some 3 miles of 4WD road must be driven to access the trailhead. Offering a partial alternative to this rugged vehicle way is the 2-mile-long Lower Soldier Camp Trail, which begins at Cottonwood Camp (located where FR 401 turns into 4WD) and ends back on FR 401, less than 1 mile west of the start of the Soldier Camp Trail. This trail is steep in spots.

One additional route to connect up to the Soldier Camp Trail is the 2.3-mile Cane Spring Trail, which begins near the end of FR 401 and continues north to where it intersects the Soldier Camp Trail. It is considered difficult, as it is poorly defined in places. For serious backpackers, a lengthy loop hike of about 30 miles might take you along the Soldier Camp Trail, a few miles of FR 143, the Four Peaks Trail, and the Alder Creek Trail.

Watch for lightning in exposed terrain and for flash floods along canyon bottoms. Water is available at springs and creeks in the wilderness, but it should be treated before drinking.

35   Superstition Wilderness

Location: 7 miles E of Apache Junction
Size: 160,200 acres
Status: Wilderness area (1964)
Terrain: Desert mountains
Elevation: 2,000 feet to 6,265 feet
Management: Tonto NF
Topographic maps: Weavers Needle, Goldfield, Mormon Flat Dam, Horse Mesa Dam, Iron Mountain, Haunted Canyon, Pinyon Mountain, Two Bar Mountain

Steeped in folklore, the Superstition Mountains have captured the imagination of many a would-be treasure hunter. As the story goes, the Lost Dutchman Mine—purportedly located somewhere within the shadow of the fabled Weavers Needle—contains untold amounts of gold, left behind by a German immigrant whom nineteenth-century

A cholla cactus forest on Black Mesa

Arizonans tagged as a Dutchman. Whether or not such a treasure exists, the Superstitions are rich in natural wonders. From saguaro cactus forests, deep canyons, and volcanic plugs in the western portion of the wilderness, to forested mountains in the east, this range is a real treat for hikers of all abilities. Due to its proximity to Phoenix, this wilderness area receives heavy use. But, because it includes some three dozen trails, there is something for everyone here.

Seasons
Summers in the Superstition Mountains are scorching, especially in the lower western portion, while winters may bring snow and cold temperatures to the higher elevations. The best times to hike here are during the months of February, March, April, October, and November. Depending on winter rainfall, late March is often a prime time to view sweeping carpets of wildflowers, which enliven the desert.

Plants and Wildlife
The lower western portion of the wilderness supports typical desert vegetation, including saguaro cactus, ocotillo, cholla, and paloverde. Spring bloomers include Mexican golden poppies, Indian paintbrush, and brittlebush. Higher up, a number of species

of oak—Emory and Arizona white among them—grow in thick patches. Manzanita, alligator juniper, and pinyon pine are common. In a few isolated locales are found stands of ponderosa pine. Riparian vegetation includes Arizona sycamore, Arizona walnut, and velvet ash. Mule deer and white-tailed deer, javelinas, coyotes, mountain lions, and bobcats are among the creatures that call the wilderness home.

Geology

The rugged, angular Superstition Mountains are the result of a complex and lengthy geological metamorphosis. The high, sharp profiles of these mountains comes from their relatively recent volcanic history. Composed of colorful tuff, volcanic plugs, and dark volcanic rock, much of this topography resulted from a fiery period of volcanic eruptions between 15 and 35 million years ago. Five calderas formed when magma chambers collapsed within the Superstitions. It is thought that these volcanic rocks were deposited on top of a preexisting base of Precambrian granite and schist. Despite their colorful history, the Superstitions are not heavily mineralized, and the chances of finding large deposits of gold and other metals is low.

History

The legend of Lost Dutchman Mine began in 1845 with Don Miguel Peralta, who reportedly discovered a large deposit of gold. Peralta died at the hands of Apache warriors soon after the discovery, but one member of his party did survive to relate the story to a German immigrant by the name of Jacob Waltz, three decades later. Known as The Dutchman, Waltz took the information about the location of Peralta's mine to his grave in 1891. In the years since, hundreds have searched for the fabled hole, all to no avail. Other episodes in the history of the Superstitions are based more on fact than fancy. The Salado people occupied the area some 700 years ago, leaving behind a handful of cliff dwellings. It goes without saying that such relics are protected by law. Ranching has taken place in the vicinity since the late 1800s. At that time, a rancher by the name of Elisha Reavis settled in a secluded valley in the eastern portion of the range, where he raised cattle and grew vegetables and fruit.

ACTIVITIES
Hiking

Of the several trailheads that access the area's widespread network of trails, a good place to begin is at the First Water trailhead, in the northwestern corner of the wilderness. To reach it, drive 5 miles north from Apache Junction on Arizona Highway 88 (the Apache Trail) to Forest Road (FR) 78. Turn right and continue 2.6 miles to its end. Camping is prohibited along this gravel road and a $4.00/vehicle/day use fee (as of summer 2002) is charged from October 1 to April 30. From the First Water trailhead, the 18.2-mile Dutchman's Trail sets off toward the southeast to cross the western end of the wilderness. (This popular route eventually ends at the Peralta trailhead,

Opposite: *Fish Creek Canyon in the Superstition Wilderness is deep and highly scenic.*

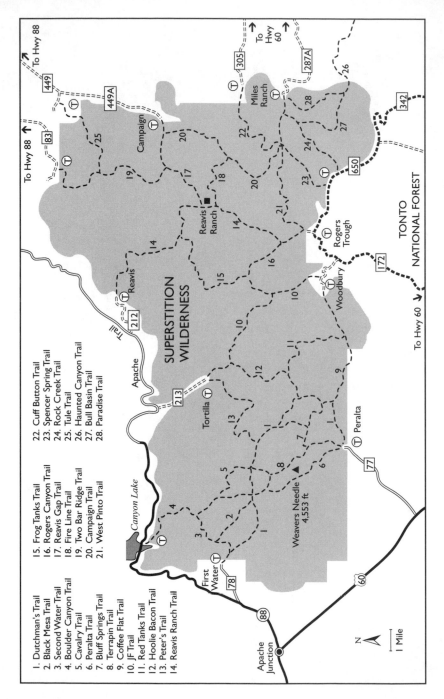

which is discussed below.) Crossing from drainage to drainage, the Dutchman's Trail intersects many other trails, making it an ideal corridor for longer trips. If a day hike is what you are after, you may want to follow the Dutchman's Trail 3.5 miles to the Black Mesa Trail, then turn left and walk 3 miles over Black Mesa, before dropping into Garden Valley. Once there, turn left on the Second Water Trail and continue back to the Dutchman's Trail. The entire loop is 8 miles long and considered moderately difficult.

A little more than 3 miles long, the Second Water Trail runs northeast from Garden Valley to the Boulder Canyon Trail. Boulder Canyon is a narrow chasm that eventually drains into the similarly interesting La Barge Creek. The Boulder Canyon Trail begins at Canyon Lake (15.5 miles north of Apache Junction, on Arizona Highway 88) and travels south along La Barge Creek, and then along Boulder Creek itself. After 7.3 miles, this sometimes rugged route ends on the Dutchman's Trail, near the start of the above-mentioned Black Mesa Trail. Adding to this network of trails is the 3.1-mile Cavalry Trail, which branches east from the Boulder Canyon Trail to eventually connect with the Dutchman's Trail.

As mentioned above, the Dutchman's Trail can also be reached from the extremely popular Peralta trailhead, which is located along the southwestern border of the wilderness. A $4.00/vehicle/day use fee (as of summer 2002) is charged from October 1 to April 30. To reach the Peralta trailhead, drive 8.5 miles southeast from Apache Junction on US Highway 60-89 to the signed turnoff. Follow this good gravel road (FR 77) for 8 miles to its end. The 6.3-mile Peralta Trail climbs 1,300 feet in 2 miles to reach Fremont Saddle, from which there is an impressive view of Weavers Needle. The Peralta Trail then drops down East Boulder Canyon, before terminating along the Dutchman's Trail, 5 miles from the First Water trailhead. By turning right on the Dutchman's Trail, an extended loop hike of nearly 20 miles will return you to the Peralta trailhead.

A number of return routes are possible for hikers following the Dutchman's Trail from the Peralta trailhead. About 4 miles in, you may return to your car by way of the 3.4-mile Bluff Springs Trail. The Terrapin Trail heads north from the Bluff Springs route for 2.9 miles, before reaching the Dutchman's Trail near its halfway point. It may also be used as a return route for those following the Peralta Trail for its entire length. This suggested loop trip covers approximately 12 miles.

The Dutchman's Trail also hooks up with a handful of trails that cross into the eastern portion of Superstition Wilderness. One of these is the 7.9-mile Coffee Flat Trail, which branches off the Dutchman's Trail within 2 miles of the Peralta trailhead. Running due east, this rugged route crosses Coffee Flat, near the southern boundary, before dropping into Fraser Canyon. It ends at FR 172. Located about a mile east on this road, the Woodbury trailhead marks the start of the 8.9-mile JF Trail described below. To reach this access point, drive 2 miles east on US Highway 60 from Florence Junction to Queen Valley Road. Turn left and drive another 2 miles to FR 357. Turn right and continue 3 miles to the start of FR 172. Turn north and drive 10 miles to the trailhead near the road's end.

A second route to head east from the Dutchman's Trail is the 9.1-mile Red Tanks Trail. Intersecting the Dutchman's Trail at La Barge Spring, this often difficult route follows La Barge Creek upstream through the Upper La Barge Box, a narrow corridor. After crossing Red Tanks Divide, the route drops down Red Tanks Canyon to meet up with the Coffee Flat Trail. Similarly difficult, the 4.6-mile Hoolie Bacon Trail heads north from the Red Tanks Trail to eventually reach the Tortilla trailhead, just north of the wilderness. To reach this access point, drive 22 miles northeast from Apache Junction on Arizona Highway 88 to FR 213. Turn there and follow the 4WD road 2 miles to the wilderness boundary. Two other trails accessed by the Tortilla trailhead are the above-mentioned JF Trail and Peter's Trail. Running 8.9 miles north from the Woodbury trailhead to the Tortilla trailhead, the JF Trail accesses the central portion of the wilderness. The 7.2-mile Peter's Trail travels southwest through some rugged terrain to reach the Dutchman's Trail near Charlebois Spring.

Farther east, another lengthy trail crosses the wilderness from north to south. The 15.3-mile Reavis Ranch Trail begins at the Reavis trailhead (reached by driving 28 miles from Apache Junction on Arizona Highway 88 and then 3 miles on FR 212, a high-clearance 2WD road). The route heads south over Windy Pass, then drops into the Reavis Creek drainage, the site of the historic Reavis Ranch. The trail continues up Reavis Creek before crossing into Grove Canyon. It then feeds into the upper reaches of Rogers Canyon, which it follows upstream to the Rogers Trough trailhead. Rogers Trough is reached by driving 9 miles north on the above-mentioned FR 172, then 4 miles on the 4WD FR 172A.

Prehistoric cliff dwelling in the Superstition Wilderness

Along the way, the Reavis Ranch Trail connects with many other trails to offer some nice overnight loop-hike possibilities. The rugged and seldom-used 6.8-mile Frog Tanks Trail turns west to access Angel Basin, where it intersects the midpoint of the 4.5-mile Rogers Canyon Trail. A left turn here heads up Rogers Canyon to the southern end of the Reavis Ranch Trail, a round trip of about 18 miles. A right turn at Angel Basin takes you up to Tortilla Pass and the northern end of the above-mentioned JF Trail. At this point, the Woodbury trailhead is just 2 miles to the south.

From the vicinity of Reavis Ranch, the 5.5-mile Reavis Gap Trail heads northeast over its namesake to reach the Campaign trailhead. This remote trailhead is accessed by 4WD FR 449A from Arizona Highway 88. The 8-mile-long Two Bar Ridge Trail heads north from the Reavis Gap Trail across the least-visited portion of the wilderness. This scenic route eventually ends at FR 83, which is reached from Arizona Highway 88. The Tule Trail branches off the Two Bar Ridge Trail to reach FR 449. The 3.6-mile Fire Line Trail begins near Reavis Ranch and continues past Whiskey Spring. It then drops steeply to its intersection with the 10.2-mile Campaign Trail.

Beginning at the Miles Ranch trailhead (at the end of FR 287A), the West Pinto Trail runs west along the West Fork of Pinto Creek to Oak Flat. In addition to connecting with the West Pinto Trail, the Campaign Trail also picks up the southern end of the 3-mile Cuff Button Trail to end at FR 305. Reaching the West Pinto Trail near Oak Flat, from the south, is the 4.6-mile Spencer Spring Trail. Beginning along FR 650, this rugged route follows the Spring Creek drainage for most of the way. By following FR 650 southeast for a little more than a mile, the Spencer Spring Trail may be used in conjunction with the 4.8-mile Rock Creek Trail, which drops down its namesake drainage to the West Pinto Trail, 0.25 mile from the Miles Ranch trailhead. West of Oak Flat, the West Pinto Trail reaches the southern end of the Reavis Ranch Trail just north of the Rogers Trough trailhead. The Bull Basin Trail intersects the Rock Creek Trail at Yellow Jacket Spring and heads southeast to meet the Haunted Canyon Trail near the wilderness boundary. The Haunted Canyon Trail follows its namesake before reaching FR 287A. The Paradise Trail also branches off the Haunted Canyon Trail. The Miles Ranch trailhead is accessed by turning north on FR 287, a few miles west of Miami, on US Highway 60. Follow it 6.5 miles to a left turn onto FR 287A. Continue on this high-clearance 2WD road for 5.5 miles, until you reach the end. A lengthy 4WD route, FR 650 is reached from FR 8, which turns off US Highway 60 just west of Superior.

Water is available at many streams and at some springs, but it should be treated before drinking. Watch for lightning in the higher elevations and flash floods along narrow canyon bottoms. Orientation is easy in this wilderness, as long as you bring along a good map, but some areas are quite remote. Take care when hiking in these areas.

Rock Climbing

The many volcanic cliffs, buttes, and plugs of the western end of Superstition Wilderness offer some great climbing challenges. Among these is Weavers Needle. Climbers will find a number of pitches on this monolith to choose from, all of them involving near-perpendicular faces. Be aware that Weavers Needle can be crowded on weekends. Tonto National Forest policy prohibits the installation of permanent fixtures such as pitons or bolts.

36 Mount Baldy Wilderness

Location: 30 miles SW of Springerville
Size: 7,079 acres
Status: Wilderness area (1970)
Terrain: Forested mountains
Elevation: 9,200 feet to 11,403 feet
Management: Apache–Sitgreaves NF
Topographic map: Mount Baldy

As the highest summit in the White Mountains of eastern Arizona, Mount Baldy and its namesake wilderness offer some memorable hiking. Pristine forests, open meadows, beautiful trout streams, and twisted *krummholz* forests are but four of its natural treasures. One thing to keep in mind, however, is that the actual summit of Mount Baldy is located just outside national forest land on the Fort Apache Indian Reservation and is off limits to hikers.

Seasons
Given the high elevation of Mount Baldy Wilderness, the normal season for visiting is from June to October. The months of July and August are best for wildflowers.

Plants and Wildlife
Forests of ponderosa pine, white fir, corkbark fir, and Engelmann spruce are found in Mount Baldy Wilderness. There are patches of aspen in places, and Colorado blue spruce grows along forest edges. A handful of natural meadows offer promising places to spot elk and deer, especially in the early morning. Black bears and mountain lions inhabit the area, as do wild turkeys and blue grouse. While the West Fork of the Little Colorado has long harbored trout, its fish habitat has been enhanced by the placement of simple log dams.

Geology
Mount Baldy is an extinct volcano that last erupted about 10 million years ago. It is composed of a layer of volcanic rock at least 4,000 feet thick. As the highest summit in the range, it is thought to be a central point of the White Mountain Volcanic Field. Characterized by rounded valleys and canyons, Mount Baldy wears the distinguishing marks of glacial activity as well.

History

Considered sacred by the White Mountain Apache, Mount Baldy is traditionally said to be the home of the mountain spirits. It is, therefore, of great religious significance to the Apache people, who still make pilgrimages to the summit.

ACTIVITIES
Hiking

Two trails enter Mount Baldy Wilderness and converge near the summit. To reach them, drive west from Eagar on Arizona Highway 260 to the turnoff for Arizona Highway 273. Follow this road south for 18 miles. Turn right and drive 4.5 miles to the Phelps Cabin trailhead, or continue for another 2.7 miles to where the road crosses the West Fork of the Little Colorado River. This is the Sheep Crossing trailhead. From here, the West Fork Trail follows the West Fork of the Little Colorado for nearly 7 miles to a point just below the summit of Mount Baldy. This well-maintained route is easy, even though it climbs 2,000 feet in all. Along the way, you'll cross some beautiful meadows and take in some great views. The turn-around point for hikers is usually marked by some sort of sign. Beyond this point, you'll be trespassing on Fort Apache Reservation land, which can lead to confiscation of your pack, even arrest. Near its upper end, the West Fork Trail connects with the East Fork Trail. Following the East Fork of the Little Colorado, this trail begins at the Phelps Cabin trailhead and climbs 2,000 feet in 6.7 miles. Like the West Fork Trail, this route accesses pristine forests, meadows, and streambeds. It also passes some nice outcrops of basalt.

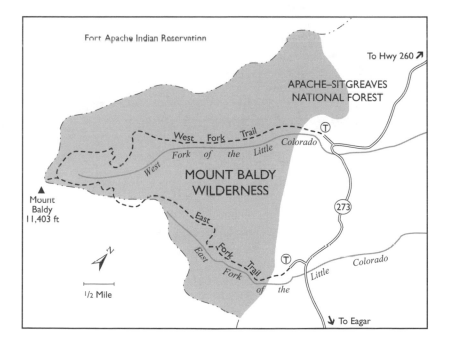

Plans are in the works for a 3- to 4-mile connecting trail between the two trailheads.

Watch for lightning and rapidly changing weather in the higher reaches of the wilderness. Water is found in creeks, but it should be treated before drinking.

Cross-Country Skiing

Although the nearest regularly plowed road is a few miles away from the wilderness, you can ski to it. The West Fork Trail offers some nice touring terrain, with mostly gentle grades and open meadows along the way. Even if you don't reach the wilderness boundary, there are still plenty of nice touring areas nearby.

37　Escudilla Wilderness

Location: 5 miles N of Alpine
Size: 5,200 acres
Status: Wilderness area (1984)
Terrain: Forested mountains
Elevation: 8,700 feet to 10,912 feet
Management: Apache–Sitgreaves NF
Topographic map: Escudilla

A significant presence on the horizon north of Alpine, Escudilla Mountain figures prominently in the lore of the area. Surpassed only by Arizona's San Francisco Peaks and Mount Baldy in elevation, Escudilla is home to the highest fire lookout in the state. The mountain was also featured in the writings of forester and naturalist Aldo Leopold.

Seasons

Because it receives heavy snowfall in winter, the wilderness is best visited from late May through October. On the other hand, cross-country skiers will enjoy the wonderful ski touring conditions.

Plants and Wildlife

Escudilla Mountain has some fine subalpine forests and meadows. Mature forests include mixed stands of Engelmann spruce, Colorado blue spruce, Douglas fir, white fir, and ponderosa pine. An extensive wildfire wiped out 23,000 acres of timberland in 1951 and has led to the proliferation of aspen trees, a pioneer species in newly cleared land. Young evergreens sprouting up among the aspen will eventually shade out the deciduous trees and return the area to a climax forest of conifers. The area also includes some beautiful meadows, which feature colorful displays of red Indian paintbrush, yellow cinquefoil, and white sego lily in July and August. Elk, mule deer, black bears, mountain lions, and coyotes live here.

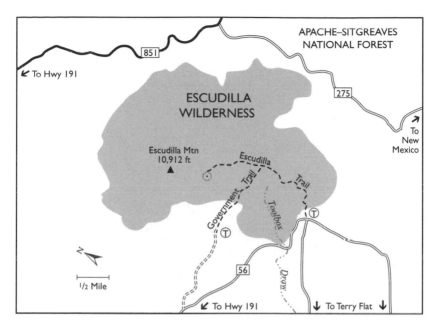

Geology

Part of the White Mountain Volcanic Field, Escudilla Mountain is an extinct volcano. Eruptions in this part of Arizona date back to the Tertiary period, a time of much volcanic activity throughout the Southwest. It appears that Escudilla's relatively level summit area resulted from a valley filling up with lava flows. Given the mountain's high elevation, it is not surprising that glaciers also have had a hand in shaping the terrain.

History

During Aldo Leopold's tenure as a forest ranger in the area earlier in the twentieth century, he often wrote of Escudilla's prominence on the eastern Arizona skyline. He also wrote about an incident that occurred on the mountain: the killing of one of the last grizzly bears in Arizona. In his book *A Sand County Almanac,* he penned, "Escudilla still hangs on the horizon, but when you see it you no longer think of the bear. It's only a mountain now."

ACTIVITIES
Hiking

The Escudilla Trail, a national recreation trail, is the primary access to the wilderness. To reach the trailhead, drive 5.5 miles north of Alpine on US Highway 191 to Forest Road 56. Follow this 2WD gravel road east for 5 miles. Climbing easily—first through a section cleared by the 1951 fire, then through a pristine meadow encircling the head of Toolbox Draw—this 3-mile route climbs 1,300 feet before reaching a fire lookout, which is situated 0.25 mile south of the actual summit. On clear days, the views from the lookout take in the San Francisco Peaks near Flagstaff, the Blue Range to the south, Gila Wilderness in New Mexico, and Mount Graham near Safford. Bead Springs is located in a meadow north of the lookout, but camping is prohibited to allow wildlife free use of this, the only water source on the mountain.

About 2 miles in, the Escudilla Trail connects with the upper end of the Government Trail. Climbing steeply from an obscure forest road just west of the wilderness, this route is not maintained and may be difficult to follow. Less than 2 miles long, it served as the original trail to the lookout on top.

Water is sometimes available at the lookout, but don't count on it. Watch for lightning in the exposed higher terrain.

Cross-Country Skiing

The gentle nature of Escudilla Wilderness makes ski touring a pleasant possibility in winter. You will need to ski 5 miles of forest road to reach the Escudilla trailhead before entering the wilderness, but the wonderful touring terrain and scenic vistas will be well worth your time.

38 Bear Wallow Wilderness

Location: 30 miles S of Alpine
Size: 11,080 acres
Status: Wilderness area (1984)
Terrain: Forested drainages
Elevation: 6,700 feet to 9,000 feet
Management: Apache–Sitgreaves NF
Topographic maps: Hoodoo Knoll, Baldy Bill

Encompassing a small drainage with the same name, Bear Wallow Wilderness offers an intimate look at a pristine forest environment. Among its attractions are virgin stands of timber, quiet stream pools, small forest glades, and a variety of wildlife.

Seasons

The primary hiking season in Bear Wallow extends from June to October. Winters typically bring heavy snows and cold temperatures.

Plants and Wildlife

Heavily forested, this wilderness is known for its stands of ponderosa pine, Engelmann spruce, Colorado blue spruce, Douglas fir, and aspen. Upland riparian communities of ash, alder, box elder, and oak are common along Bear Wallow Creek, and poison ivy grows in places. Black bears do indeed inhabit the wilderness. The name, in fact,

Old-growth forest in the Bear Wallow Wilderness

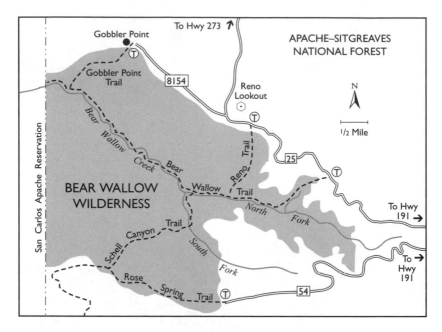

comes from the many wallows that early explorers found here. Deer, elk, coyotes, mountain lions, and bobcats also frequent the wilderness. And, as with other areas within the White Mountains, Mexican gray wolves also reside within Bear Wallow Wilderness.

A small population of native Apache trout, a threatened species, live in Bear Wallow Creek. They have been the focus of habitat enhancement efforts over the years. In 1979, a fish barrier was built to keep rainbow trout from polluting the gene pool, but flooding in 1983 wiped out the barrier. It was replaced in 1992.

Geology

Stream erosion has affected this wilderness greatly. Water has cut a pathway through the massive volcanic field that makes up the White Mountains. The Mogollon Rim borders the wilderness to the south.

ACTIVITIES
Hiking

The obvious route for exploring this wilderness is the Bear Wallow Trail, which follows the drainage all the way to the San Carlos Apache Reservation boundary. To reach the trailhead, drive 28 miles south of Alpine on US Highway 191 to Forest Road (FR) 25. Turn right and drive 3 miles on this 2WD gravel road. From beginning to end, this trail drops 2,000 feet in 7.6 miles. It starts out with a descent into a side drainage of the North Fork of Bear Wallow Creek, then, a little more than a mile later, it reaches the North Fork of the creek. About 2.5 miles from the trailhead, the trail connects with the lower end of the 1.9-mile Reno Trail, which begins along FR 25, west of the Bear Wallow trailhead. About 3.5 miles in, the Bear Wallow Trail also connects with the Schell Canyon Trail. Dropping into the drainage from the south, this route connects with the Rose Spring Trail, which begins at a trailhead along FR 54. From this access point to the Bear Wallow Trail, it is 5.8 miles.

Beyond the Schell Canyon Trail, the Bear Wallow Trail crosses the creek many times and, nearly 7 miles from its start, reaches a stream barrier built to prevent rainbow trout from migrating upstream. A little farther on, you reach the lower end of the Gobbler Point Trail. Dropping some 2,000 feet in 2.7 miles, this side route begins at scenic Gobbler Point, which is reached by driving FR 25 and FR 8154. The hike ends at the reservation boundary, 0.5 mile beyond the Gobbler Point Trail/Bear Wallow Trail junction. The boundary is marked by a fence.

Water is plentiful in Bear Wallow Creek, but it should be treated before drinking.

39 Blue Range Primitive Area

Location: 14 miles S of Alpine
Size: 173,726 acres
Status: Primitive area (1933)
Terrain: Forested mountains and canyons
Elevation: 4,500 feet to 9,346 feet
Management: Apache–Sitgreaves NF
Topographic maps: Hannagan Meadow, Beaverhead, Bear Mountain, Strayhorse, Dutch Blue Creek, Alma Mesa, Blue, Maness Peak, Rose Peak, Fritz Canyon, Maple Creek

At nearly 175,000 acres, the Blue Range Primitive Area is one of Arizona's larger tracts of wild land. Included in its boundaries is a variety of terrain: from semidesert hills and canyon bottoms to subalpine forests and meadows. Major features include the Blue River, which bisects the region from north to south, and the Mogollon Rim, which traverses the southern half of the primitive area. Because the Blue Range Primitive Area, or more simply the "Blue," is situated in an isolated portion of eastern Arizona, it is overlooked by all but a handful of hikers. It is an area, however, that deserves investigation.

Seasons
Hiking in the higher elevations is possible only from May to October. Lower elevations are typically open all year; however, access may prove difficult and temperatures may be uncomfortably cold from December to February.

Plants and Wildlife

Beginning in the area's lowest elevations, plant life includes alligator juniper, Mexican pinyon pine, and various desert oaks. Riparian communities at these elevations support bigtooth maple, ash, Arizona walnut, and box elder, and other deciduous trees. Large Douglas firs also grow along many perennial streams at higher elevations. Wildlife in these lower areas includes Coues white-tailed deer and javelinas. At the middle elevations of the primitive area, ponderosa pine and Gambel oak become prevalent. And in the higher, western section of the wilderness, Engelmann spruce, white fir, Douglas fir, and aspen are common. Among the birds living here are bald eagles, peregrine falcons, Mexican spotted owls, turkeys, and blue grouse. Big game in these areas includes elk and mule deer. Coyotes, black bears, and mountain lions range throughout the primitive area. And, given the Blue's vast expanse of undeveloped land, this wilderness is also front and center in a reintroduction project for the Mexican gray wolf. Begun in 1998, a small number of wolves were released into the White Mountains. Some setbacks have been experienced, but successive releases have added to the canine's numbers and wildlife biologists believe that the project has so far been a success.

Geology

Blue Range Primitive Area was affected by major volcanic activity during the Quaternary and Tertiary periods, when large deposits of volcanic material covered the highlands of the Blue, as evidenced by dark basaltic rock. The Blue River has cut deeply and exposed red conglomerates in the depths of its canyon system. The Mogollon Rim defines the southern half of the wilderness, running for 200 miles across Arizona and into New Mexico.

History

Blue Range Primitive Area was established in the 1930s, along with seventy-five other areas. After the passage of the 1964 Wilderness Act, all but the Blue were set aside as wilderness areas. Despite the wild character of the Blue, wilderness designation for it has met with strong opposition from area ranchers who fear grazing rights in the new wilderness would be cut off. Mineral resources in the Blue are coveted by mining interests, as well. The Blue is the only designated primitive area left on national forest lands.

ACTIVITIES
Hiking

Thanks to US Highway 191, access to the higher reaches of Blue Range Primitive Area is easy. An obvious starting point is at Hannagan Meadow, which is situated at 9,200 feet in elevation. Located 23 miles south of Alpine, and a short distance east of the highway on Forest Road (FR) 29A, the Hannagan Meadow trailhead accesses two interesting routes. The 16-mile Foote Creek Trail heads east, traversing a gentle ridge before dropping into the Foote Creek drainage. From beginning to end, the route drops nearly 4,000 feet before reaching the Blue River at Blue Camp. The second route is the 13.2-mile Steeple

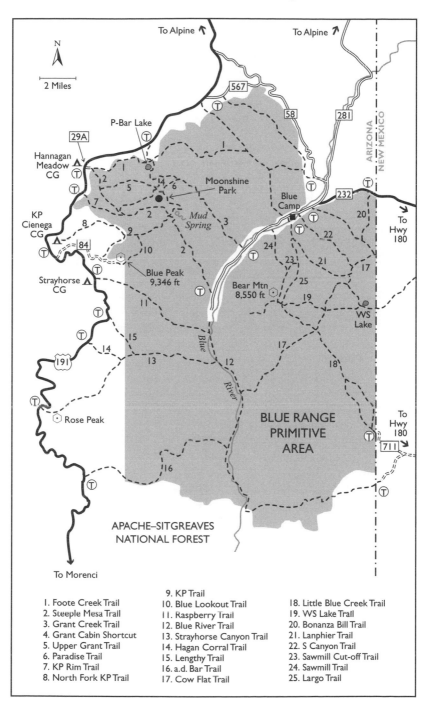

N

2 Miles

To Alpine ↗

To Alpine ↗

567

58

281

ARIZONA
NEW MEXICO

P-Bar Lake

29A

Hannagan
Meadow
CG

1

2

5

14

6

Moonshine
Park

7

2

Mud
Spring

3

Blue
Camp

232

KP
Cienega
CG

8

9

10

84

2

24

22

20

To
Hwy
180

Strayhorse
CG

Blue Peak
9,346 ft

23

21

17

11

Bear Mtn
8,550 ft

25

19

WS
Lake

15

Blue

17

18

191

14

13

12

Rose Peak

River

BLUE RANGE
PRIMITIVE
AREA

To
Hwy
180

711

16

APACHE–SITGREAVES
NATIONAL FOREST

To Morenci

1. Foote Creek Trail
2. Steeple Mesa Trail
3. Grant Creek Trail
4. Grant Cabin Shortcut
5. Upper Grant Trail
6. Paradise Trail
7. KP Rim Trail
8. North Fork KP Trail

9. KP Trail
10. Blue Lookout Trail
11. Raspberry Trail
12. Blue River Trail
13. Strayhorse Canyon Trail
14. Hagan Corral Trail
15. Lengthy Trail
16. a.d. Bar Trail
17. Cow Flat Trail

18. Little Blue Creek Trail
19. WS Lake Trail
20. Bonanza Bill Trail
21. Lanphier Trail
22. S Canyon Trail
23. Sawmill Cut-off Trail
24. Sawmill Trail
25. Largo Trail

Mesa Trail, which also drops 4,000 feet to the Blue River. Because these trails explore a wide array of ecosystems, hiking their entire lengths would make for nice trips, but such an undertaking requires a shuttle.

If you would rather follow a circular route through higher elevations, several nice itineraries may be planned that use portions of both trails, along with other trails in the area. By following the Foote Creek Trail for 3.5 miles, you will reach P-Bar Lake and, just beyond, the intersection with the Grant Creek Trail. This 10-mile trail drops along its namesake to the Blue River below. In 1.5 miles, though, it reaches the Grant Cabin Shortcut, a steep but short route that connects with the Upper Grant Trail. The Upper Grant Trail, in turn, follows Grant Creek upstream, to connect with the Steeple Mesa Trail about 1.5 miles from Hannagan Meadow. The round-trip hike is 11 miles long. To add a few miles to the trip, continue past the Grant Cabin Shortcut another mile and turn right on the Paradise Trail. Passing near Moonshine Park (a natural clearing among ponderosa pines), this trail eventually connects with the Steeple Mesa Trail near Mud Spring. This makes for a trip of 17 miles in length.

Farther south along US Highway 191, additional trailheads access other trails that add to the network of trails described above. Less than 2 miles south of Hannagan Meadow is the start of the KP Rim Trail. This 3-mile route ends along the Steeple Mesa Trail, but not before passing through a scenic area. A mile south is the start of the North Fork KP Trail. It follows the primitive area boundary for 2.3 miles before reaching the KP Trail. Nearly 9 miles long, the North Fork KP Trail begins at KP Cienega Campground and drops 2,400 feet, before reaching the Mud Spring area along the Steeple Mesa Trail. Although partially outside the primitive area, the Blue Lookout Trail climbs 3.5 miles to a fire lookout that offers some spectacular views of the surrounding mountains. The lookout is situated at 9,346 feet.

Farther south along US Highway 191, the surrounding country begins to drop. Trails in this southern section of the primitive area drop as well. Raspberry Trail begins 0.25 mile east of the Strayhorse Campground—a 31-mile drive south from Alpine. For virtually its entire length, this 10.5-mile trail follows Raspberry Creek to the Blue River, where it connects with the Blue River Trail. At one time connecting with FR 281, access to the Blue River Trail from the road is now blocked by private land. A second trail, which drops from US Highway 191 to the Blue River, is the Strayhorse Canyon Trail. From a trailhead just north of the Rose Peak fire lookout on US Highway 191, this trail descends 3,200 feet in 12.7 miles. Upon reaching the Blue River, it connects with the Blue River Trail south of the Raspberry Trail intersection. Two shorter trails—the 3.1-mile Hagan Corral and 3.3-mile Lengthy Trails—feed into the Strayhorse Canyon Trail from the north. A third route to drop to the Blue from US Highway 191 is the 11.9-mile a.d. Bar Trail, which descends 2,300 feet in all. In the first few miles it follows Squaw Creek, after which it traverses several drainages to the north. It then connects with the Blue River Trail at the H.U. Bar Ranch.

Because the Blue River Trail follows the Blue River for several miles, it offers good access to the southernmost portion of the primitive area. It can be reached by way of the Raspberry, Strayhorse Canyon, and a.d. Bar trails, but no longer from FR 281. From Alpine, pick up FR 281, about 3 miles east of town, or follow US Highway 191 south for 14 miles to FR 567. Steep and winding, this 2WD road becomes FR 58 and reaches the Blue River (and FR 281) in 12 miles. From this intersection, the Upper Blue River trailhead (now closed due to private property) is 15.5 miles south. This road may be impassable during high water. Do not attempt to ford the river in flood conditions.

The hike along the Blue River as it flows downstream offers an intimate look at riparian areas, but hikers may also access the 12.5-mile Cow Flat Trail from here. Cow Flat Trail runs northeast to the New Mexico border and crosses Government Mesa nearly 5 miles from the Blue River, and then enters scenic Bear Valley. Up to this point, the trail may be difficult to follow in places. In Bear Valley, the roughly 10-mile Little Blue Creek Trail follows Little Blue Creek. North of Bear Valley, the Cow Flat Trail climbs about 1,000 feet in 1.5 miles to the top of the Mogollon Rim. Along this scenic escarpment, the trail intersects the 11.3-mile WS Lake Trail, which follows the Mogollon Rim from WS Lake, near the New Mexico–Arizona border, west to Bear Mountain and Bear Spring. Beyond the WS Lake Trail, the Cow Flat Trail continues 3.6 miles to reach the Bonanza Bill Trail at Bonanza Flat. While you'll need a shuttle to hike the entire length of the Cow Flat Trail, loop trips are possible in the vicinity of Bear Mountain. Beginning at Blue Camp—a U.S. Forest Service Administration Site—the Lanphier Trail follows the Lanphier Creek drainage for 5.6 miles to a junction with the Cow Flat Trail. From here, turn left and follow the Cow Flat Trail to the 5.5-mile S Canyon Trail, which heads northward and drops back to the Blue River. Ending about a mile upstream from Blue Camp, the entire loop is 13 miles long. Another interesting loop hike follows the Lanphier Trail to the Cow Flat Trail and then turns right, or southwest. After 2.2 miles, the Cow Flat Trail intersects the previously mentioned WS Lake Trail, which then leads west for 3.7 miles to the turnoff for the Bear Mountain Lookout. Because the WS Lake Trail follows the Mogollon Rim, it opens up to some spectacular views along the way. Beyond Bear Mountain summit, the WS Lake Trail descends 2.4 miles to Bear Spring. To return to Blue Camp, you may follow either the 5.4-mile Sawmill Trail to a point along the Blue River 1.5 miles downstream from Blue Camp, or the 5.6-mile Largo Trail to its junction with the Lanphier Trail 0.5 mile from Blue Camp. It is also possible to follow the Sawmill Trail for about 2 miles to the Sawmill Cut-off Trail which, in turn, continues for 0.9 mile to the Largo Trail. Springs along Largo Creek provide reliable sources of water. The loop that follows the Lanphier, Cow Flat, WS Lake, and Largo Trails is 18.5 miles long and ranges in elevation from 5,600 to 8,550 feet.

Water is available in the primitive area, but it should be treated before drinking. Watch for lightning in higher terrain. It is advisable to check with the Forest Service about trail conditions before heading out.

Cross-Country Skiing

The rolling forest lands and small meadows in the western section of the primitive area are accessible year-round and, therefore, ideal for cross-country skiing. Two good starting points for a tour are the Hannagan Meadow and KP trailheads. From Hannagan Meadow, the Foote Creek Trail keeps to higher country for at least 4 miles before dropping off to the Blue River. The Steeple Mesa Trail traverses the upper end of Grant Creek before dropping into Steeple Creek—also a distance of about 4 miles. This section of the Steeple Mesa route can be connected with the KP Rim Trail for a tour of about 6 miles.

Opposite: *This riparian area in the Pusch Ridge Wilderness is complete with cattails.*

chapter 3

Southeastern Basin and Range

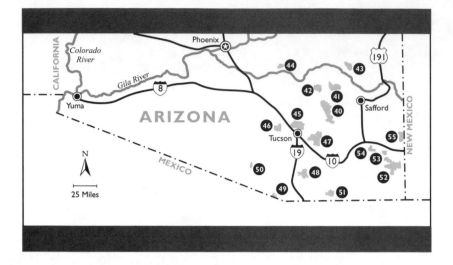

Rising suddenly and impressively in the southeastern corner of Arizona are mountain ranges that geographers call "sky islands." So definitive are these changes in elevation that they actually form ecological islands of timberland among a sea of arid desert basins. Perhaps most impressive is that of the Santa Catalina Mountains just north of Tucson. Portions of the range are embraced by Pusch Ridge Wilderness. Of course, other ranges offer similarly rugged and scenic terrain. Rincon Mountain to the east of Tucson and Mount Wrightson to the south of the city are two familiar examples. The Huachuca and Chiricahua Mountain Ranges farther to the southeast offer fine examples. They include Miller Peak and Chiricahua Wildernesses, respectively, as well as Chiricahua Monument Wilderness. East of Tucson, closer to the New Mexico border, rise the Dos Cabezas and Peloncillo Mountains, each with a wilderness by the same name. A small BLM wilderness is tucked in along the eastern slope of Baboquivari Peak south of Tucson, while the Galiuro, Santa Teresa, and Fishhook Mountains each include wilderness lands to the northeast.

Interspersed among the desert basins that yawn between each of these "sky islands" are typically small but interesting wilderness areas. Two of these (Aravaipa Canyon and Pajarita) embrace some secretive riparian areas, while two others (White Canyon and Saguaro, as in Saguaro National Park west) take in some stunning desert ecosystems. Two BLM wildernesses not included in this book are Needles Eye and Coyote Mountains. Although both are scenic and would be worth visiting, access is problematic due to neighboring private lands.

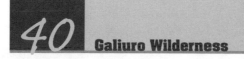

40 Galiuro Wilderness

Location: 35 miles SW of Safford
Size: 76,317 acres, plus 6,600 acres in Redfield Canyon WA
Status: Wilderness area (1964)
Terrain: Mountains and desert
Elevation: 4,000 feet to 7,671 feet
Management: Coronado NF and BLM (Tucson Field Office)
Topographic maps: Bassett Peak, Kennedy Peak, Cherry Spring Peak, Rhodes Peak, Winchester Mountains, Harrison Canyon, Kielberg Canyon, The Mesas

Because it is reached only after driving many miles of gravel road, Galiuro Wilderness is bypassed by most hikers and, therefore, offers plenty of solitude. Other attractions include diverse plant and animal life, some rugged and beautiful terrain, and one of the most colorful histories to be found anywhere in the West. In addition to the 76,317-acre Galiuro Wilderness, which is administered by the Coronado National Forest, this section also discusses the adjoining 6,600-acre Redfield Canyon Wilderness, which is administered by the BLM.

Seasons

Summers in the Galiuro Mountains can be hot, especially below 5,000 feet. Similarly, winters typically bring subfreezing temperatures at night and occasional snow. Approach roads may be muddy after rains. The best times of the year for hiking Galiuro Wilderness are mid- to late spring and fall.

Plants and Wildlife

Much of Galiuro Wilderness supports evergreen oak, pinyon pine, juniper, mountain mahogany, and manzanita. The lowest reaches feature desert grasslands and scattered pricklypear cactus, cholla, yucca, and century plant. In the highest elevations are ponderosa pine, Chihuahua pine, Mexican white pine, Arizona cypress, occasional Douglas fir, and, across the northern slope of the wilderness area's high point—7,671-foot Bassett Peak—quaking aspen. Riparian areas are good places to find cottonwood, Arizona sycamore, Arizona walnut, and bigtooth maple. Wildlife includes deer, desert bighorn sheep, pronghorn antelope, javelinas, coyotes, bobcats, mountain lions, black bears, and coatimundis. Until the mid-1950s, Mexican gray wolves also inhabited these isolated mountains.

Geology

A classic example of the fault-block mountains that make up Arizona's Basin and Range province, the Galiuros feature some breathtaking cliff faces and steep slopes in places. Much of the rock exposed is volcanic. Some sedimentary rocks are also found, as are

Along the Tortilla Trail in the Galiuro Wilderness

Precambrian granites and quartzites. Two major canyon systems dissect the wilderness lengthwise: Rattlesnake and Redfield. In Redfield Canyon, walls of deep red rock today close in on the stream bottom below.

History

Prehistoric Indians lived within this rugged range many centuries ago, the Apache roamed through its canyons a few hundred years ago, and Anglo prospectors worked its canyons a little more than 100 years ago. The most colorful chapter of history in the Galiuro Mountains, however, began in 1909. That was when Jeff Power and his family took up residence in Rattlesnake Canyon. They eventually started a gold mine, complete with a stamping mill, and farmed a spot along Rattlesnake Creek. All was well for the Power family until February 1918. That was when local sheriff deputies and U.S. marshals came to arrest Tom and John Power—the two sons—for draft evasion. Just before daybreak, a shoot-out erupted that left Jeff Power and three lawmen dead. The Power brothers, along with a friend, Tom Sisson, slipped away and eventually

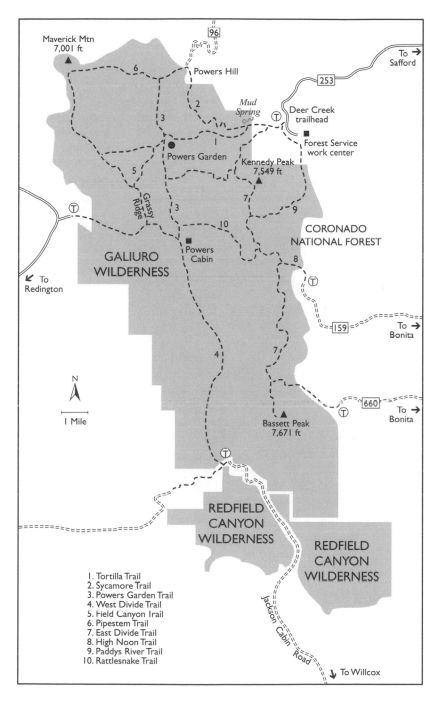

Maverick Mtn
7,001 ft

96

Powers Hill

To
Safford

253

2

Mud
Spring

Deer Creek
trailhead

3

Forest Service
work center

1

Powers Garden

Kennedy Peak
7,549 ft

5

Grassy
Ridge

3

7

9

10

CORONADO
NATIONAL FOREST

Powers
Cabin

8

GALIURO
WILDERNESS

159

To
Bonita

To
Redington

7

N

4

1 Mile

660

To
Bonita

Bassett Peak
7,671 ft

REDFIELD
CANYON
WILDERNESS

REDFIELD
CANYON
WILDERNESS

1. Tortilla Trail
2. Sycamore Trail
3. Powers Garden Trail
4. West Divide Trail
5. Field Canyon Trail
6. Pipestem Trail
7. East Divide Trail
8. High Noon Trail
9. Paddys River Trail
10. Rattlesnake Trail

Jackson Cabin Road

To Willcox

reached Mexico. Counted as one of Arizona's biggest manhunts ever, their flight ended when the three were arrested by a U.S. Army patrol that had pursued them south of the border. The Power brothers were paroled in 1961.

ACTIVITIES
Hiking

Numerous trails lace Galiuro Wilderness, creating some very nice overnight loop trips. Many of these trails follow historic routes, such as the old road to Powers Garden. For the most part, these routes either follow canyon bottoms or high ridge tops.

The easiest trailhead to access is Deer Creek trailhead, near the Deer Creek Forest Service Work Center. It is reached by driving 17 miles south from Safford on US Highway 191 to Arizona Highway 266. Turn right and drive 19 miles to Bonita. Turn north onto Aravaipa Road and drive another 19 miles to Forest Road (FR) 253. Turn left and drive 8.4 miles to the signed trailhead. From this point, the Tortilla Trail climbs west, into the foothills of the range. Crossing several drainages, the 8.2-mile trail eventually feeds into Rattlesnake Canyon at Powers Garden. Elevations do not vary more than 1,500 feet on the trail but there is, nevertheless, a lot of climbing involved. This trail also intersects the Sycamore Trail at Mud Spring. Following the riparian bottom of Sycamore Canyon for much of the way, this occasionally rugged route continues north to reach Powers Hill in 5.5 miles.

From Powers Hill, the Powers Garden Trail follows the original road constructed by the Powers family to access their home. Because most of this route stays in the bottom of Rattlesnake Canyon, elevations range from 4,660 feet to 5,280 feet. After 4 miles, the route reaches Powers Garden, where comparatively little remains of the Powers' farming and ranching activities. About 5 miles farther upcanyon, however, you will find the old Powers Cabin, which is now listed on the National Register of Historic Places. The Powers Cabin and mine site is actually located 0.5 mile beyond the southern end of the Powers Garden Trail, on the West Divide Trail.

A major route that mostly stays close to the high ridges and summits along the western portion of the wilderness, the West Divide Trail runs for nearly 24 miles in all. Covering elevations between 4,200 feet and 6,800 feet, this difficult trail boasts some incredible views. Despite the trail's name, the West Divide Trail also explores some canyons in the first 6 miles. The route follows Redfield Canyon north from the vicinity of Jackson Cabin, then climbs to reach the Powers Cabin near its halfway point. The route then climbs Grassy Ridge, beyond which the 2-mile long Field Canyon Trail turns northeast to reach Powers Garden. The West Divide Trail eventually approaches Maverick Mountain, where it ends and the Pipestem Trail begins. The Pipestem Trail, in turn, heads east for 4.4 miles to eventually connect with the Powers Garden Trail about a mile west of Powers Hill. To access the Redfield Canyon end of the West Divide Trail, drive 15 miles west from Willcox on Cascabel Road to the signed turnoff for Muleshoe Ranch, a Nature Conservancy property. Turn right and drive north through the ranch to continue up the 4WD Jackson Cabin Road. The last few miles pass through BLM's Redfield Canyon Wilderness.

The East Divide Trail follows ridges on the east side of Galiuro Wilderness. Starting out at the above-mentioned Deer Creek trailhead, this route heads south to skirt the highest summits in the range by only a short distance. Along the way, side trails access the summits of 7,549-foot Kennedy Peak and 7,671-foot Bassett Peak. Some 22 miles south of the Deer Creek trailhead, the East Divide Trail ends at the 4WD FR 660, which is reached by driving south from Bonita on Fort Grant Road, then west on FR 651. Of the side trails that feed into the East Divide Trail, the 2-mile-long High Noon Trail connects FR 159 with the middle portion of the East Divide route; the Paddys River Trail heads south from the Deer Creek trailhead and connects back up with the East Divide Trail a few miles south of Kennedy Peak; and the Rattlesnake Trail heads west from the East Divide Trail for 5 miles to connect with the Powers Garden Trail about 4 miles south of Powers Garden.

While no actual hiking trails exist in adjoining Redfield Canyon Wilderness, the above-mentioned 4WD Jackson Cabin Road, which runs along the bottom of Redfield Canyon to the national forest boundary, has been cherry-stemmed out of the wilderness. This provides vehicle access to the mouths of various side canyons, which, in turn, may be followed into wilderness lands to the east and west.

Caution should be used when hiking along trails in the rugged Galiuro Wilderness, and when bushwhacking in the Redfield Canyon area. Water is available at springs and in some streams, but it should be treated before drinking. Watch for lightning in exposed places, and be aware that flash flooding may occur along canyon bottoms. Keep in mind that historical structures, such as Powers Cabin, and all artifacts are strictly protected by federal law.

41 Santa Teresa Wilderness

Location: 30 miles NW of Safford
Size: 26,780 acres, plus 5,800 acres in the North Santa Teresa Wilderness
Status: Wilderness areas (1984)
Terrain: Mountains and canyons
Elevation: 4,000 feet to 7,550 feet
Management: Coronado NF and BLM (Safford Field Office)
Topographic maps: Buford Hill, Cobre Grande Mountain, Klondyke, Jackson Mountain

Creating a contiguous parcel of wilderness 32,580 acres in size, the Coronado National Forest's Santa Teresa Wilderness and the BLM's North Santa Teresa Wilderness encompass much of the small, yet beautiful, Santa Teresa Mountains. Reaching an elevation of 7,550 feet along Pinnacle Ridge, the Santa Teresa Range can be quite rugged. Because of their remote location and the difficulties involved in accessing trails into the area, the two wildernesses in the Santa Teresa Mountains offer real solitude.

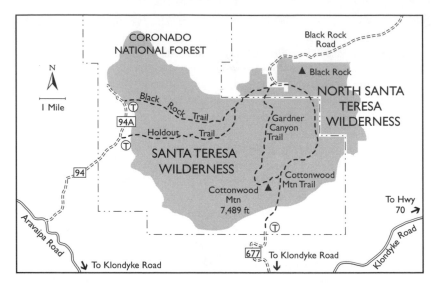

Seasons

Although Santa Teresa Wilderness can be visited any time of the year, spring and fall are the best seasons for hiking into the area. Winters often bring cold nighttime temperatures and occasional snow to the higher reaches of the wilderness. Summer days are typically hot.

Plants and Wildlife

Much of Santa Teresa Wilderness features thickets of evergreen oak, manzanita, pinyon pine, and juniper. Ponderosa pine is common in the higher terrain, and Douglas fir grows across some north-facing slopes. Streambeds support riparian growth, including Arizona sycamore, ash, and cottonwood. Wildlife includes mule deer, javelinas, coatimundis, coyotes, mountain lions, and black bears.

Geology

The primary geological features of the Santa Teresa Mountains are its eroded granite boulders, outcrops, and cliff faces. This Precambrian rock constitutes much of the core of the mountains. Located in adjoining North Santa Teresa Wilderness is Black Rock, a rhyolitic plug that towers nearly 1,000 feet above the surrounding terrain. This striking volcanic structure has religious significance for the Apache who live nearby.

ACTIVITIES
Hiking

Three trails cross Santa Teresa Wilderness. Unfortunately, these routes have not been maintained in several years and sections are close to nonexistent. Adding to the woes of poorly maintained trails is the fact that access to these routes is limited due to the closure of Forest Road (FR) 94 (Black Rock Road) by a private landowner. Black Rock Road heads southwest from US Highway 70, across a portion of the San Carlos Apache Reservation and across several parcels of private land, to reach the eastern end of the Black Rock Trail and the northern terminuses for the Cottonwood Mountain and Holdout Trails. These routes may be accessed west and south of the wilderness, however.

To reach the Cottonwood Mountain Trail, drive 13.5 miles north from Safford on US Highway 70 to Klondyke Road. Turn left and drive 18 miles to FR 677. Continue north on this high-clearance, 2WD road for nearly 4 miles, to road's end. Heading north up Cottonwood Canyon, this trail eventually gains the northeastern flank of Cottonwood Mountain, where it intersects the Gardner Canyon Trail. The Gardner Canyon Trail continues west and north for 5.5 miles before reaching Black Rock Road. The Cottonwood Mountain Trail continues northeast from this trail intersection, to eventually reach Black Rock Road as well. In its 7.9-mile length, the Cottonwood Mountain Trail gains a couple thousand feet as it travels north over the range. Because of the Black Rock Road closure, you will have to return to your car by way of either the Cottonwood Mountain or Gardner Canyon Trails.

Entering the wilderness area from the west is the 7.8-mile Black Rock Trail. It begins along FR 94A, which turns off FR 94 and follows a high ridge south for a few miles. Both roads require a 4WD vehicle, as they are steep in places. FR 94 is reached by driving north from Safford to Klondyke Road. Turn left and drive 32 miles to Aravaipa Road. Turn right and drive about 10 miles northwest to a right-hand turn. Since the western end of the Black Rock Trail is located along a high ridge that forms the western boundary of the wilderness, it is all downhill from this point to the route's eastern end along Black Rock Road. Of course, you then have to climb back up because of the road closure. About two-thirds of the way in, the Black Rock Trail intersects the eastern end of the 6.9-mile Holdout Trail, which may also be accessed via FR 94A, about 1.5 miles south of the start of the Black Rock Trail. Just as the Black Rock Trail follows a canyon by the same name, the Holdout Trail pretty much follows the bottom of Holdout Canyon.

Currently, access to BLM-administered North Santa Teresa Wilderness is not practical, due to the closure of Black Rock Road. It is possible, however, to enter North Santa Teresa Wilderness via the above-mentioned Cottonwood Mountain and Black Rock Trails. The last mile of each of these routes, in fact, falls within BLM-administered land. Beyond these trails, no other trails access North Santa Teresa Wilderness. Nevertheless, cross-country routes may be found by following canyon bottoms and some ridges.

Water is found in springs and streams, but it should be treated before drinking. Because portions of the trails mentioned above may be faded and difficult to find, due to low use and negligible maintenance, inexperienced hikers should not attempt to enter Santa Teresa Wilderness alone. Watch for lightning, especially during summer thunderstorms.

42 Aravaipa Canyon Wilderness

Location: 23 miles SE of Winkelman
Size: 19,410 acres
Status: Wilderness area (1984)
Terrain: Desert canyons
Elevation: 2,600 feet to 4,900 feet
Management: BLM (Safford Field Office)
Topographic maps: Booger Canyon, Brandenburg Mountain, Holy Joe Peak, Oak Grove Canyon

Aravaipa Canyon is one of Arizona's finest riparian areas. It features not only the perennial waters of Aravaipa Creek but also a prodigious riparian community of verdant cottonwood, thick underbrush, and a great variety of wildlife. Packaged between high walls, this desert canyon is one of Arizona's scenic treasures and is easy to explore. To help protect the canyon's pristine beauty, the BLM has instituted a permit system that restricts use of the wilderness.

Seasons

Conceivably, Aravaipa Canyon can be visited at any time of the year, but the best times are in spring and fall. From November through February, cool temperatures make for some chilly stream crossings and frosty nights. And the summer months—from May to September—are typically quite hot. Shade is plentiful, however, and the many stream crossings that must be made offer a way to cool off.

Plants and Wildlife

Cottonwood, ash, Arizona sycamore, and willow are just four of the many deciduous species growing along the riparian corridor of Aravaipa Creek. Beyond this verdant strip of life, typical desert plants, such as saguaro cactus, barrel cactus, cholla, ocotillo, and yucca, are abundant. Aravaipa Canyon is also home to many different species of wildlife: desert bighorn sheep, mule deer and Coues white-tailed deer, mountain lions, coyotes, bobcats, and coatimundis, among others. The creek supports minnows and suckers. Aravaipa Canyon is famous in birding circles for its many feathered residents, which range in size from hummingbirds and desert wrens to peregrine falcons and bald eagles.

Geology

Aravaipa Canyon cuts through the northern end of the Galiuro Mountains, which are composed of volcanic tuff and lava, sedimentary rocks, and Precambrian granites and

Opposite: Cottonwoods grow tall along Aravaipa Canyon.

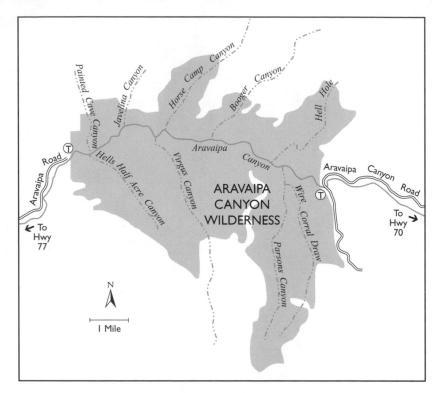

quartzites. Within the canyon itself, precipitous faces of volcanic rock make up canyon walls, although other rock types are found here as well.

History

Used by the Salado people during prehistoric times, the Aravaipa Canyon area was also inhabited by the Apache more recently. In 1860, Fort Breckenridge was established west of what is now Aravaipa Canyon Wilderness. In 1871, suspecting that the Apache were perpetrating murders in the area, the U.S. Army carried out what came to be known as the Aravaipa Massacre. During the melee, an Apache camp was raided along Aravaipa Creek and 144 Apache men, women, and children were killed or captured. To this day, it is still not known whether these victims were actually responsible for the crimes.

ACTIVITIES
Hiking

There are no maintained trails in Aravaipa Canyon Wilderness, but then none are needed, as it is easy to follow the canyon bottom. Running for 11 miles, this hike includes many stream crossings (most are knee-deep or less at normal water level). Side canyons may also be explored, but it is difficult to venture beyond the stream bottoms because the surrounding terrain is especially rugged. To reach the canyon's western trailhead, drive 11 miles south from Winkelman, on Arizona Highway 77. Turn left on Aravaipa Road, and drive 12 miles to road's end. Paved for the first few miles, then graveled for the rest of the way, this road is passable to most vehicles. The eastern trailhead is accessed by driving 15 miles northwest from Safford on US Highway 70 to Klondyke Road. Turn west and continue for another 45 miles to the trailhead. Upon reaching the Aravaipa Valley (24 miles from US Highway 70), bear right on the Aravaipa Canyon Road. Although graveled the entire way, the last few miles of Klondyke Road may require a high-clearance vehicle. Contact the BLM well in advance of your trip to make sure you can get a permit. The popularity of the canyon has led the BLM to institute a permit system that allows for a total of fifty people per day. Further, the length of stay is limited to 3 days and 2 nights. Obtain your permit by contacting the BLM's Safford Office. Permits cost $5.00 per person per day, payable at the trailhead. Pets are prohibited in the wilderness. For more information, contact the BLM, Safford Field Office, 711 14th Avenue, Safford, AZ 85546; (520) 348-4400.

Treat all water before drinking. Watch for flash floods, especially in the summer months.

43 Fishhooks Wilderness

Location: 30 miles NW of Safford
Size: 10,500 acres
Status: Wilderness area (1990)
Terrain: Desert mountains and canyons
Elevation: 4,000 feet to 6,629 feet
Management: BLM (Tucson Field Office)
Topographic maps: Gila Peak, Bylas, Ash Creek Ranch

Encompassing the southwestern flank of the Gila Mountains, Fishhooks Wilderness comprises a wonderful mixture of desert, canyons, and rugged peaks. A variety of desert species live here, and there are a few riparian areas. Although there are no established hiking trails, several natural hiking corridors provide nice opportunities for getting away from the crowds.

Seasons

Because of its low elevation, a visit to this wilderness is best made in October and November, or between March and May. The summer months frequently see temperatures above 100 degrees. Winters are a nice time to visit, as well, as long as rains do not make reaching the wilderness difficult, if not impossible.

Pricklypear cactus in the Fishhooks Wilderness

Plants and Wildlife

Growing in the lower western end of the wilderness are a few saguaro, plenty of prickly-pear, cholla, barrel cactus, yucca, sotol, and beargrass. Pinyon pine and juniper become more prevalent at higher elevations. Along some of the canyons—especially Upper and Lower Fishhook Canyons—there are some nice riparian communities, where stands

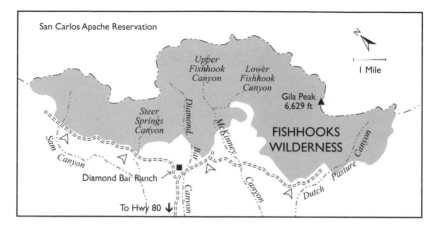

of Lowell ash may be found. Wildlife includes deer, javelinas, mountain lions, coyotes, and bobcats. Bald eagles have also been sighted in the area.

Geology

The rugged western cliffs of the Gila Mountains consist of vermilion- and ochre-colored volcanic rocks. These include tuff compositions and more recent lava flows. In contrast, the eastern slopes of this range (all of which falls within the San Carlos Apache Reservation) are characteristically gentle.

ACTIVITIES
Hiking

There are no trails accessing this wilderness, but some canyon bottoms may be explored. To reach them, drive north from Safford on US Highway 70 to Fort Thomas. Turn on Fort Thomas River Road and follow it north across the Gila River. Turn left just beyond the bridge and continue northwest for 5 miles or so. Turn right and drive roughly another 3 miles to a third intersection. Turn right and continue north toward the wilderness boundary. About 16 miles from Highway 70 is the Diamond Bar Ranch, where a right turn takes you past ranch headquarters to Upper Fishhook, Lower Fishhook, and Dutch Pasture Canyons. By continuing straight at the ranch, you will climb up and over a bench that separates Diamond Bar Canyon from Steer Springs Canyon. Continuing for several miles, this road provides access to Diamond Bar, Steer Springs, and Sam Canyons in the northern portion of the wilderness. On either route, a 4WD vehicle is required beyond the ranch. Be sure to leave gates open or closed, exactly as you find them. All of these canyons offer possible hiking routes into Fishhooks Wilderness.

Although some stock tanks may be found within or just outside the wilderness, don't count on finding water here. Bring all that you will need instead. Watch for rattlesnakes. Keep in mind that hiking cross-country can be a hazardous endeavor.

44 White Canyon Wilderness

Location: 14 miles S of Superior
Size: 5,800 acres
Status: Wilderness area (1990)
Terrain: Desert canyons and mountains
Elevation: 2,200 feet to 4,053 feet
Management: BLM (Tucson Field Office)
Topographic maps: Teapot Mountain, Mineral Mountain

Although small, White Canyon Wilderness offers hikers a real treat. At the heart of this wilderness is White Canyon itself, a deep drainage ringed by soaring cliffs. Beyond the reaches of the canyon's occasionally flowing stream is found a pristine land with good examples of desert flora. Unfortunately, a large open-pit copper mine is planned for Cooper Butte, just south of the wilderness.

Seasons
Somewhat hot for a summer hike, this wilderness is best visited between the months of November and April. Nighttime temperatures in the winter may dip below freezing, but daytime temperatures are mostly pleasant.

Plants and Wildlife
The bottom of White Canyon supports a variety of riparian trees, including willow, cottonwood, and Arizona walnut. Growing across the lower nonriparian reaches of the wilderness are saguaro cactus, cholla, pricklypear cactus, paloverde, ocotillo, and other desert plants. Communities of shrub live oak, juniper, and other low-growing trees grow in the area's higher reaches. Animal residents in this watery environment include the Sonoran mud turtle, which may be seen in pools along the creek bed. Other wildlife includes mule deer, javelinas, coyotes, mountain lions, and a variety of birds—from colorful songbirds to hawks and falcons.

Geology
The primary geographical features of this wilderness are its sheer cliffs of Apache Leap tuff, formed from volcanic ash deposits, which tower up to 1,000 feet above the canyon floor. Rhyolite, sedimentary rocks, and Pinal schist dating back some 1.7 billion years are also found here.

ACTIVITIES
Hiking
The main access point for White Canyon Wilderness is about a mile up White Canyon, from where it intersects Walnut Canyon. To reach this trailhead (there is a trail

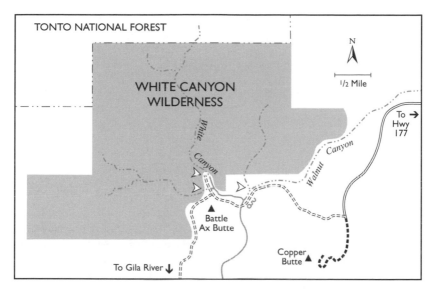

register a short distance beyond the end of the road), drive 9.5 miles south from Superior on Arizona Highway 177 to a dirt road that turns right. Continue down this good 2WD road 1.9 miles to a maintained dirt road that turns right. Follow this road north into Walnut Canyon. Nearly 4 miles from the pavement, the road appears to end in the Walnut Canyon wash near a developed spring. The route continues, however, into White Canyon. Up to this point, the road is fairly good and is usually passable to high-clearance, 2WD vehicles, but the last mile to the trailhead requires a 4WD vehicle. To reach the trailhead, keep right at a fork in the road slightly less than a mile up from Walnut Canyon. The road that turns left at this last intersection circles around Battle Ax Butte, which rises to the south before reaching the Gila River several miles to the south. If you don't have a 4WD vehicle, you can do an interesting little hike along the lower end of White Canyon, following the stream bottom. Pools of water, boulder chokes, and verdant riparian plant life make for some interesting explorations. From the trailhead, White Canyon can be explored for another 3 miles before it exits the wilderness and enters the Tonto National Forest. Travel along the wash bottom of White Canyon alternates between sandy stretches and slickrock shelves.

Besides White Canyon, it is possible to explore other drainages as well. Branching north from Walnut Canyon, less than a mile upstream from White Canyon, is an unnamed side canyon that extends for more than a mile into the eastern section of the wilderness. By bearing left at the above-mentioned road intersection, just south of the White Canyon trailhead, you will soon reach a side drainage of White Canyon. This drainage also offers some interesting desert scenery.

Hikers should use extreme caution when traveling cross-country. Watch for rattlesnakes during warmer months. Treat all water drawn from creeks before drinking. Better yet, pack in all the water you need for your hike.

45 Pusch Ridge Wilderness

Location: 5 miles N of Tucson
Size: 56,933 acres
Status: Wilderness area (1978)
Terrain: Desert foothills, canyons, and mountains
Elevation: 2,800 feet to 9,000 feet
Management: Coronado NF
Topographic maps: Mount Lemmon, Oro Valley, Tucson North, Sabino Canyon

Pusch Ridge Wilderness encompasses the southern slopes of the Santa Catalina Mountains, just outside Tucson. In so doing, it highlights the fact that these quickly rising mountains span an incredible change in elevation—6,000 feet in only a few miles. Because of this, the wilderness includes life zones comparable to those found in both Mexico and Canada: from impressive saguaro cactus stands to cool forests of pine and fir. For hikers, this unique area offers good access and terrific scenery, thanks to a network of trails. The wilderness is named for a prominent rocky ridge in the southwestern corner of the range.

Seasons

Hiking at the lower elevations—along the canyon bottoms and in the foothills—is best done between the months of October and April, since summer months are typically quite hot. At the middle elevations, hiking is possible year-round, although summers may be somewhat hot and winters a bit cool. Because winters typically bring snow (there is actually a ski area nearby) and cold, hiking is largely a late spring, summer, and early fall activity here.

Plants and Wildlife

In the Lower Sonoran Zone, which climbs to about 3,500 feet, are beautiful stands of saguaro cactus, along with cholla, ocotillo, pricklypear cactus, paloverde, and other desert species. In the Upper Sonoran Zone, thick patches of shrub live oak, mountain mahogany, pinyon pine, and juniper may be found. Above the 7,000-foot mark, picturesque stands of ponderosa pine and an occasional Gambel oak characterize the Transition Zone. Growing above the 8,000-foot level, in the Canadian Zone, are fir and aspen forests. Animal residents include javelinas, coatimundis, mule deer and white-tailed deer, desert bighorn sheep, coyotes, bobcats, mountain lions, black bears, a variety of songbirds, and numerous birds of prey.

Geology

At the heart of the Santa Catalina Mountains is a dome-shaped core of Catalina granite, exposed in the higher elevations as interesting boulders and strangely eroded

A climber tops a pinnacle in the Windy Point area.

hoodoos. The southern face of the range consists of Catalina gneiss with characteristic bands of white quartzite. Forming a steep anticline (an arch of stratified rock in which the layers bend downward in opposite directions from the crest) this southern face is separated from the main core of the range by valleys that run parallel to the faces of the mountains.

History

Named in 1697 by a Jesuit priest, Father Eusebio Kino, the Santa Catalina Mountains were exploited for their minerals from the earliest days of European American rule. First gold and then silver drew Spaniards into these mountains. Their mining exploits eventually led to tales of lost mines that have circulated ever since. In the 1870s, Anglo-American miners began combing the range in earnest. In 1881, the botanist, Sarah Lemmon, and her husband led a scientific expedition to the summit of the range where they discovered many new species of plants. The famed Mount Lemmon Highway was completed in 1949, thanks mostly to prison labor.

ACTIVITIES
Hiking

A number of trails interlace the wilderness, offering numerous hiking possibilities. Many routes begin at the foot of the mountains and climb steadily to the upper reaches of the wilderness. Because these trails begin very close to Tucson, they receive a lot of use. Other routes make higher-elevation wilderness walks possible. Many of the higher trails are also quite popular, especially in the summer when the desert basin below is sweltering.

Beginning at popular Sabino Canyon, hikers may enter the wilderness via three established trails. Following Sabino Canyon for about 4 miles is a paved road that is closed to vehicles but may be accessed by way of a shuttle bus from Sabino Canyon Visitor Center. At road's end, the Sabino Canyon Trail begins its trek upcanyon. Climbing for a short distance, the trail soon levels off and continues 2.5 miles along the east side of rugged and beautiful Sabino Canyon, before reaching Sabino Basin. Turning west from the basin to follow the west fork of Sabino Creek is the West Fork Sabino Trail. It continues for 5 miles before intersecting the Cathedral Rock Trail. Along the way, the West Fork Sabino route encounters Hutchs Pool, a lengthy stillwater section of the creek encased by rock walls. Heading north up Box Camp Canyon is the 7-mile-long Box Camp Trail. It climbs some 4,300 feet to reach the Mount Lemmon Highway in the vicinity of Soldier Camp. Paralleling the Box Camp Trail is the Palisade Trail. It eventually ends at the Girl Scout Camp, which is off Mount Lemmon Highway. Heading east from the upper end of the Sabino Canyon Trail is the 2.6-mile East Fork Trail. In approximately 2 miles, the East Fork Trail climbs out of Sabino Basin and into Sycamore Canyon, where it intersects the top of the 8.3-mile Bear Canyon Trail. A popular route in its own right, the Bear Canyon Trail begins at the Lower Bear Picnic Area, 1.7 miles east of Sabino Canyon Visitor Center. You can take a foot trail or hop a shuttle bus along the few miles of road. The main attraction in Bear Canyon is a series of falls and deep pools known as Seven Falls. While most hikers turn around at this point (2.2 miles from the end of Bear Canyon Road), a nice loop hike of 11 miles is possible, using two shuttle buses to get you there and back. A side trip along this loop could follow the Sycamore Reservoir Trail, which heads east from the Bear Canyon Trail to meet a secondary road that branches off Mount Lemmon Highway. All of these drainages support lush riparian growth, thriving bird life, and rugged scenery. Expect crowds, though.

Also heading into Pusch Ridge Wilderness from Sabino Canyon Visitor Center is the 10-mile Esperero Canyon Trail, which climbs more than 4,000 feet up the Esperero Canyon drainage. The first few miles cross desert country, then the route starts to wander through juniper forests toward the head of Ventana Canyon, the next canyon to the west. Along the way, the Esperero Trail intersects the southern end of the above-mentioned Cathedral Rock Trail, thereby closing a loop route of about 17 miles, using the shuttle bus up Sabino Canyon to get you to your starting point. North of its intersection with the above-mentioned West Fork Sabino Trail, the Cathedral Rock Trail climbs along a ridge that separates the wilderness area's south-draining canyons from those

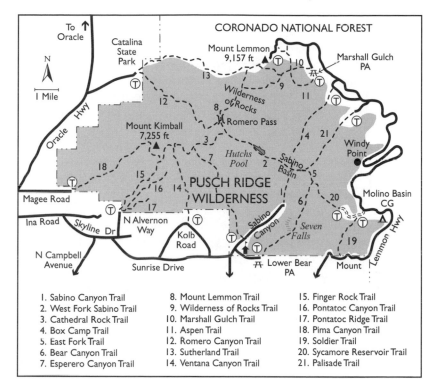

CORONADO NATIONAL FOREST

To ↑ Oracle

Catalina State Park

N

I Mile

Oracle Hwy

Mount Lemmon 9,157 ft

Marshall Gulch PA

Wilderness of Rocks

Romero Pass

Mount Kimball 7,255 ft

Windy Point

Hutchs Pool

Sabino Basin

Molino Basin CG

Magee Road

PUSCH RIDGE WILDERNESS

Ina Road

Skyline Dr

N Alvernon Way

Kolb Road

Sabino Canyon

Seven Falls

N Campbell Avenue

Sunrise Drive

Lower Bear PA

Mount

Lemmon Hwy

1. Sabino Canyon Trail
2. West Fork Sabino Trail
3. Cathedral Rock Trail
4. Box Camp Trail
5. East Fork Trail
6. Bear Canyon Trail
7. Espero Canyon Trail
8. Mount Lemmon Trail
9. Wilderness of Rocks Trail
10. Marshall Gulch Trail
11. Aspen Trail
12. Romero Canyon Trail
13. Sutherland Trail
14. Ventana Canyon Trail
15. Finger Rock Trail
16. Pontatoc Canyon Trail
17. Pontatoc Ridge Trail
18. Pima Canyon Trail
19. Soldier Trail
20. Sycamore Reservoir Trail
21. Palisade Trail

that drain west. At Romero Pass, 1.8 miles north of the upper terminus of the West Fork Sabino Trail, the Cathedral Rock Trail ends and the Mount Lemmon Trail begins. Continuing to climb northeast toward the crest of the range, the 5.8-mile Mount Lemmon Trail gains an additional 1,600 feet before reaching a trailhead located near the summit of Mount Lemmon.

As it climbs, the Mount Lemmon Trail traverses a portion of the Wilderness of Rocks—an area of interesting granite formations. A route that more thoroughly explores this geological wonderland is the aptly named Wilderness of Rocks Trail. It branches off the Mount Lemmon Trail, about 2 miles north of Romero Pass, and continues 4 miles to Marshall Pass. A little more than 2 miles from its start, the Lemmon Rock Lookout Trail branches off and heads 2 miles north to its namesake. The fire lookout is about 0.5 mile south of the Mount Lemmon summit. Upon reaching Marshall Pass, the Wilderness of Rocks Trail intersects the western portions of the Marshall Gulch and Aspen Trails. A popular and relatively easy 3.7-mile loop hike—often called the Aspen Loop—follows the Marshall Gulch and Aspen Trails west from the Marshall Gulch Picnic Area.

Climbing into Pusch Ridge Wilderness from the west and intersecting the Mount Lemmon and Cathedral Rock Trails at Romero Pass is the 5.6-mile Romero Canyon Trail. Gaining 3,200 feet as it ascends its namesake drainage, this popular route begins inside Catalina State Park, which is located along the foot of the mountains on their west side. The route accesses some nice riparian areas in Romero Canyon and passes some beautiful stands of mature saguaro cactus. The Romero Canyon Trail is easy to follow as it is well maintained. A second trail, which climbs from the Catalina State Park into the Santa Catalina Mountains but mostly stays outside the wilderness, is the 8.7-mile Sutherland Trail. It eventually connects with the Mount Lemmon Trail.

Upon reaching the head of Ventana Canyon, the above-mentioned Esperero Trail joins the upper end of the 4.7-mile Ventana Canyon Trail. This trail begins at the Flying V Guest Ranch, which is located at the end of a private road that branches off Kolb Road, off Sunrise Drive. You must obtain permission from the Flying V Guest Ranch before using this trail. Along the way is the Maiden Pools, a section of canyon bottom that features several water pockets.

Farther west are three additional canyons that may be accessed by trails. From the end of North Alvernon Way, two routes—the Finger Rock and Pontatoc Canyon Trails—head northeast into two separate canyons. The 4-mile Pontatoc Canyon Trail follows Pontatoc Canyon before ending on a ridge that overlooks Ventana Canyon to the east. It also accesses the 1.8-mile Pontatoc Ridge Trail, which climbs along Pontatoc Ridge. The Finger Rock Trail climbs along Finger Rock Canyon to reach the summit of 7,255-foot Mount Kimball. This route offers stunning panoramic views of Tucson below, as well as views of Finger Rock, a formation that rises along the canyon's north rim. The trail is 6.3 miles long and climbs 3,100 feet. Because it passes through a big-horn sheep management area, dogs are not permitted beyond Finger Rock Spring, which is 1.1 miles in.

Once it reaches the area around the summit of Mount Kimball, the Finger Rock Trail connects with the upper end of the 8.6-mile Pima Canyon Trail. Popular with locals, this route begins at the end of Magee Road, which turns east from Oracle Highway. Continuing along its namesake for much of the way, the trail eventually climbs up the northwestern slope of Mount Kimball. Gaining 4,350 feet in all, the last 3 miles are steep and the trail may be difficult to find in places.

An additional trail entering Pusch Ridge Wilderness from a trailhead along the Mount Lemmon Highway is the 2.6-mile Soldier Trail. From the highway, it heads north and eventually picks up the upper portion of Soldier Canyon. It ends on a secondary road, which turns off the highway less than 2 miles past Molino Basin Campground. The Soldier Trail gains 1,700 feet in all.

Although wilderness trails are maintained and well represented on maps, hikers should consider the elevation changes on many of these routes. Think carefully about your fitness level before heading out into rugged desert country. Watch for lightning in exposed locations. Water is available at scattered springs and in streams, but it should be treated before drinking. Because many of these routes see a lot of hiking activity, you may want to plan your trip for a weekday, especially if you are looking for solitude. In addition, because desert bighorn sheep are greatly disturbed by dogs, it is best to leave your pet at home when hiking anywhere in the wilderness.

Rock Climbing

The Santa Catalina Mountains are highly favored by technical rock climbers for their beautiful granite boulders and faces. Two especially well known places are Sabino Canyon, where sheer rock walls ring the canyon, and the Windy Point area, which is located partway up Mount Lemmon Highway. Spreading out below the Windy Point vista is a vast garden of granite boulders and cliff faces. The Wilderness of Rocks also features some interesting climbs.

46 Saguaro Wilderness

Location: 10 miles W of Tucson
Size: 13,470 acres
Status: Wilderness area (1976)
Terrain: Desert mountains
Elevation: 2,600 feet to 4,687 feet
Management: Saguaro NP
Topographic maps: Avra Valley, Brown Mountain, Jaynes, Cat Mountain

Split into two districts—one on the east side and one on the west side of Tucson—Saguaro National Park (upgraded from national monument to national park status in 1994) protects some exceptional areas of the Sonoran Desert. Of the two sections of the national park, the smaller western unit (officially known as the Tucson Mountain District) includes some of the most impressive stands of saguaro cactus to be found anywhere. Growing close together, these monarchs of the Sonoran Desert create what are often referred to as cactus "forests." Of course, other desert plants grow here as well. For wilderness enthusiasts, a number of hiking trails explore the backcountry of this interesting area. Set aside by an act of Congress in 1976, the 71,400-acre Saguaro Wilderness is divided between the two units of the park. The Tucson Mountain District (which this section covers) includes 13,470 acres of designated wilderness.

Seasons

Summers are too hot for safe and comfortable hiking. Winters, on the other hand, are quite pleasant. Late autumn and spring are the best times of the year for hiking in the park. Early spring brings a glorious display of wildflowers, especially after wet winters.

Plants and Wildlife

As the name suggests, the dominant plant species here is the saguaro cactus, a giant weighing several tons that can reach heights of up to 50 feet and live as long as 150 years. Other plants typical of the Sonoran Desert include pricklypear cactus, cholla, barrel cactus, ocotillo, mesquite, and paloverde. Javelinas are commonly sighted, as

Sunset in the Saguaro Wilderness

are jackrabbits, kangaroo rats, and other desert-adapted rodents. Bird life includes roadrunners, Gambel's quail, cactus wrens, Gila woodpeckers, red-tailed hawks, Harris' hawks, and screech owls. Look for gilded flickers and Gila woodpeckers in nests they have excavated in saguaros; screech owls, elf owls, and cactus wrens often use abandoned nests. Red-tailed and Harris' hawks like to nest in the upturned arms of saguaro. The park is also home to endangered desert tortoises and Gila monsters.

Geology

Encompassing a portion of the Tucson Mountains, Saguaro National Park's western unit includes faulted formations of sedimentary rocks that date back to the Paleozoic and Mesozoic eras. Evidence of volcanic activity during the Tertiary period is also found in the form of lava flows and light-colored tuff. Additionally, outcrops of coarse-grained granite are found on Wasson and Amole Peaks. Sizable alluvial fans of sand and gravel extend in all directions from the range.

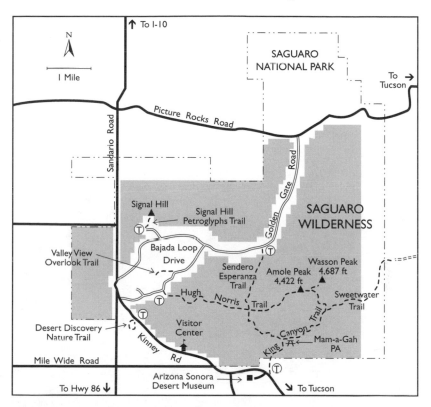

History

Long before the first Europeans first set foot in what is now southern Arizona, the Hohokom people inhabited the desert lands that today include Saguaro National Park. Evidence of their stay here is found in the petroglyphs at Signal Hill. Vanishing from the scene by A.D. 1450, the Hohokom were followed by the Tohono O'odham, or "People of the Desert." The Tohono O'odham still live in the area and continue to harvest the desert bounty. The most important of these sources is the saguaro cactus itself. Setting up special camps in early summer, they harvest the ripened fruit of the saguaro cactus to make ceremonial wine, jams, and syrups.

ACTIVITIES
Hiking

The high point of the western unit of Saguaro National Park, 4,687-foot Wasson Peak is accessed by two popular trails. The shortest of these two routes, the 3.5-mile King Canyon Trail, begins along Kinney Road, just south of the park boundary and near the entrance to the Arizona Sonora Desert Museum (a living museum with animal and plant exhibits in desert settings). From Kinney Road, the King Canyon Trail heads northeast along its namesake drainage. Nearly a mile in, the route encounters the Mam-a-Gah

Picnic Area, then begins to climb along the north side of the canyon. About 2.3 miles from the trailhead, the route grows quite steep as it switchbacks up the southern slope of Wasson Peak. In the last 0.3 mile, it levels off as it follows a ridge to the summit. Just below the switchbacks, the King Canyon Trail intersects the western section of the Sweetwater Trail, which enters the park from a residential section to the east. The second route to climb Wasson Peak is the 4.9-mile Hugh Norris Trail, which begins along

Impressive saguaro cacti are plentiful in this namesake park and wilderness.

the Bajada Loop Drive, 2.5 miles north of the Saguaro National Park Visitor Center. Climbing steeply for the first mile, this route then follows a ridgeline east for 3 miles, before reaching Amole Peak. From there, it is another 0.8 mile to Wasson Peak. Both the King Canyon Trail and the Hugh Norris Trail climb about 1,700 feet in all.

One additional trail that traverses the rugged mountainous portion of the western unit of Saguaro National Park is the Sendero Esperanza Trail. Beginning at a trailhead located along Golden Gate Road, about 6 miles north of the visitor center, this 3.2-mile route heads south to the Mam-a-Gah Picnic Area and the King Canyon Trail. Climbing for the first 1.8 miles, the Sendero Esperanza Trail then intersects the Hugh Norris Trail, after which it drops 1.4 miles to the picnic area. In so doing, it adds a link between the Hugh Norris and King Canyon Trails, thereby creating a nice loop route.

Besides the above-mentioned trails, a few short routes offer quick trips into the Saguaro National Park backcountry. These include the 0.25-mile Signal Hill Petroglyphs Trail, the 0.5-mile Desert Discovery Nature Trail, and the 0.4-mile Valley View Overlook Trail. Although short, these routes access some pristine desert lands.

Hikers in the western unit of Saguaro National Park should bring plenty of water, avoid the hot times of the day, and watch their footing. Additionally, watch for lightning, especially during the frequent summertime thunderstorms.

47 Rincon Mountain Wilderness

Location: 10 miles E of Tucson
Size: 98,520 acres
Status: Wilderness area (1976)
Terrain: Forested mountains and deserts
Elevation: 3,000 feet to 8,666 feet
Management: Saguaro NP and Coronado NF
Topographic maps: Tanque Verde Peak, Mica Mountain, Rincon Peak, Soza Canyon, Piety Hill, Happy Valley, Galleta Flat West

Rising some 6,000 feet above the desert floor, the Rincon Mountains are home to a variety of life zones—from Lower Sonoran to Canadian. In all, more than 900 plant species have been identified here. Add to this an extensive trail system that seems to receive comparatively little use, and you have a real treasure of a wilderness area. In 1976, 59,930 acres of what was then Saguaro National Monument's eastern unit were set aside as part of the larger Saguaro Wilderness (which takes in both units of what is now Saguaro National Park). In 1984, an additional 38,590 acres of adjoining Coronado National Forest land was designated as Rincon Mountain Wilderness. Combined, these two areas encompass much of the pristine Rincon Mountains. To avoid confusion, this text refers to the combined wilderness areas simply as Rincon Mountain Wilderness.

Blooming pricklypear cactus

Seasons

At the lowest elevations, summertime temperatures are hot, often in excess of 100 degrees; October and April are the most pleasant times to visit. In the higher reaches, snow and cold temperatures are common during the months of December, January, February, and March. Late fall and spring may provide the best times of the year to hike, although access to the high country may be blocked by snow even into April.

Plants and Wildlife

Although the change from one life zone to the next is gradual, it is quite noticeable. In the lower western portion of Rincon Mountain Wilderness are desert scrub communities consisting of beautiful saguaro cactus, cholla, pricklypear cactus, ocotillo, mesquite, and paloverde. Moving higher in elevation, various desert grasses, such as beargrass and sotol, become common. Around the 5,000-foot level, juniper and shrub live oak begin to make an appearance, first as scattered loners and then in increasingly thicker stands. In short order, Mexican pinyon pine, Arizona white oak, and manzanita are added to the mixture. Around 7,000 feet, ponderosa pine becomes common. At the highest reaches of the Rincon Mountains, tall ponderosa pine is joined by

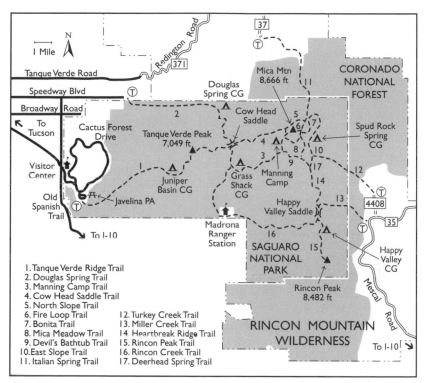

1. Tanque Verde Ridge Trail
2. Douglas Spring Trail
3. Manning Camp Trail
4. Cow Head Saddle Trail
5. North Slope Trail
6. Fire Loop Trail
7. Bonita Trail
8. Mica Meadow Trail
9. Devil's Bathtub Trail
10. East Slope Trail
11. Italian Spring Trail
12. Turkey Creek Trail
13. Miller Creek Trail
14. Heartbreak Ridge Trail
15. Rincon Peak Trail
16. Rincon Creek Trail
17. Deerhead Spring Trail

Douglas fir to create a cool, moist forest environment. Scattered stands of aspen are also found in the high country. Wildlife includes deer, javelinas, coyotes, mountain lions, black bears, and a host of smaller creatures. Birds are plentiful as well.

Geology

Although very little of it is exposed, a large dome of Precambrian granite forms the foundation of the Rincon Mountains, giving them their distinctive rounded shape. This dome is overlain by Precambrian metamorphic rocks. The two most common of these are Catalina gneiss and phyllite. A major component of phyllite is mica, which can readily be seen in the rock. A part of the Santa Catalina–Rincon Mountain complex, this chain of mountains constitutes the largest range within Arizona's Basin and Range province.

ACTIVITIES
Hiking

Although day hikes are possible in this wilderness, it takes a backpacking trip of 3 or more days to really experience the area. A good place to begin is in the western section of Saguaro National Park's Rincon Mountain District. Here, two trailheads—Tanque Verde and Douglas Spring—access a pair of interesting trails that climb steadily eastward toward the higher reaches of the wilderness. Beginning at the Javelina Picnic Area, the Tanque Verde Ridge Trail heads south for less than a mile, before picking up the southwestern end of Tanque Verde Ridge. Staying close to the crest of the ridge for the next several miles, this route climbs mostly along moderate grades, to gain some 3,000 feet in 6 miles. About 7 miles in, the trail reaches Juniper Basin, the first of six designated backcountry campgrounds found within the Saguaro National Park portion of the wilderness. All camping in the park is restricted to these small, primitive campgrounds. A free permit is required to reserve a space at each campground you plan to visit. This permit may be obtained in person, by mail (write: Saguaro National Park, 3693 South Old Spanish Trail, Tucson, AZ 85730), or by phone, (520) 733-5153.

About 2 miles beyond Juniper Basin, the Tanque Verde Ridge Trail reaches 7,049-foot Tanque Verde Peak, after which it drops nearly 1,000 feet in 2.5 miles to reach Cow Head Saddle. At this point, the Tanque Verde Ridge Trail intersects two other routes—the Douglas Spring and Manning Camp Trails. Approaching Cow Head Saddle from the north, the 8.3-mile Douglas Spring Trail begins in the northwestern corner of the park, at the end of Speedway Boulevard. Climbing easily for the first 6 miles, this route reaches its namesake, the site of another backcountry campground. It then turns south, climbing more moderately to reach Cow Head Saddle itself. Heading south from Cow Head Saddle is an unnamed trail that connects with the Manning Camp Trail in 1.4 miles. From this trail intersection, the Manning Camp Trail heads south for 4.2 miles to reach the Madrona Ranger Station, just south of the wilderness boundary. Unfortunately, public access is not available at this trailhead. From the above-mentioned

Young hiker along the Tanque Verde Ridge Trail

trail intersection, 1.4 miles south of Cow Head Saddle, the Manning Camp Trail also heads east for 5.1 miles, eventually reaching Manning Camp in the higher reaches of the wilderness. Manning Camp has a backcountry campground and an old log structure built in 1905. The structure now houses park personnel. Gaining some 2,700 feet in all, this section of the Manning Camp Trail climbs easy to moderate grades. The Grass Shack Campground, which is located along the western section of the Manning Camp route, adds to the choices of backcountry camp sites.

Although the Tanque Verde Ridge Trail ends at Cow Head Saddle, hikers can continue climbing eastward from this point along the Cow Head Saddle Trail. Gaining 2,000 feet in the next 3.3 miles, the Cow Head Saddle Trail intersects the North Slope Trail, the first of several short trails that make up a network of trails stretching across the Mica Mountain area. The Cow Head Saddle Trail intersects the Fire Loop Trail less than 0.25 mile beyond the North Slope Trail. In another 0.5 mile, it reaches its terminus at Manning Camp. The 4.5-mile Fire Loop Trail heads northeast from its intersection with the Cow Head Saddle Trail to the top of 8,666-foot Mica Mountain—the high point of the Rincon Mountains. It then circles back around to again intersect the Cow Head Saddle Trail at Manning Camp. Still other short trails—the Bonita, Mica Meadow, Mica Mountain, Devil's Bathtub, and East Slope Trails, plus the above-mentioned North Slope Trail—crisscross the broad, forested summit of the range. These routes offer hikers who are camped at Manning Camp an interesting array of day hikes. For hikers who must return to the Tanque Verde trailhead, it is possible to add some variety (not to mention a few miles) to the return trip by way of the above-mentioned Manning Camp Trail. If you arrange a shuttle beforehand, you could also try turning north from the Cow Head Saddle and following the Douglas Spring Trail out.

Approaching the Mica Mountain area of the wilderness from the Coronado National Forest to the north is the Italian Spring Trail. In 4.8 miles, this route climbs 3,200 feet to reach the North Slope Trail, in the vicinity of Italian Spring. While this route offers the shortest access to the highest portion of the wilderness, access to the route's trailhead is by way of the 4WD Forest Road (FR) 37. This rough road turns south from FR 371 (also known as Redington Road) nearly 10 miles from where the paved Tanque Verde Road ends.

Accessing the higher reaches of the wilderness from national forest lands to the east are the Turkey Creek and Miller Creek Trails. With their trailheads located either along or a short distance off Mescal Road, both routes climb about 2,000 feet before intersecting other trails within Saguaro National Park. From a trailhead located just north of Miller Ranch along FR 35 (Mescal Road) the 4.4-mile Miller Creek Trail climbs to Happy Valley Saddle, where it connects with the Heartbreak Ridge Trail. The Heartbreak Ridge Trail, in turn, heads south and north along the crest of the Rincon Range. To the south, this route terminates in 0.5 mile, at the Rincon Peak Trail. The Rincon Peak Trail then continues south for another 3.2 miles to the summit of 8,482-foot Rincon Peak. The Rincon Creek Trail heads west from the Rincon Peak Trail for 8 miles to the above-mentioned Madrona Ranger Station. Heading north from the Happy Valley

Saddle, the Heartbreak Ridge Trail eventually connects with the above-mentioned East Slope and Devil's Bathtub trails in 4 miles. In so doing, it reaches the network of trails that cover the Mica Mountain area.

Beginning at the end of FR 4408—a 4WD route that turns off Mescal Road—the Turkey Creek Trail reaches this network of higher trails in 6.2 miles. The top end of the Turkey Creek Trail connects with the Deerhead Spring Trail, which, in turn, runs between the above-mentioned Heartbreak Ridge and East Slope Trails.

When considering a trip in Rincon Mountain Wilderness, hikers should keep in mind that camping is restricted to six backcountry campgrounds. In addition to the above-mentioned Juniper Basin, Douglas Spring, Grass Shack, and Manning Camp sites, these include Happy Valley Campground near Happy Valley Saddle and Spud Rock Spring Campground located along the East Slope Trail. Because reservations at all of these sites are limited, you should obtain a permit up to 2 months ahead of time, especially if you plan to visit in the spring. Water is available at several springs and in some small creeks, but it should be treated before drinking. Piped water is also available at Manning Camp in the summer. Watch for lightning in the higher exposed terrain and be prepared for long hiking distances, major elevation gains, and very remote terrain.

Mount Wrightson Wilderness

Location: 40 miles S of Tucson
Size: 25,260 acres
Status: Wilderness area (1984)
Terrain: Forested mountains
Elevation: 3,700 feet to 9,453 feet
Management: Coronado NF
Topographic maps: Mount Wrightson, Mount Hopkins, Helvetia

Rising abruptly some 7,000 feet above the surrounding deserts, the Santa Rita Mountains offer some of the most unusual country in Arizona. Topped by 9,453-foot Mount Wrightson (or Old Baldy as some locals still call it), the Santa Ritas are home to a wide variety of plants and animals. Madera Canyon, which drains northwest from Mount Wrightson, is world renowned for its numerous species of birds that either live there or visit during annual migrations. Many of these species may be well known in Mexico but are a rare sight in this country.

Seasons

The best months to visit the wilderness are between April and November. While summer days are quite hot in the nearby deserts, the higher reaches of Mount Wrightson remain decidedly comfortable. From mid-July to mid-September, however, the monsoon

A hiker approaches the summit of Mount Wrightson.

season (a time of numerous thunderstorms) can make for hazardous hiking at times. During the winter months, the lower reaches of the wilderness are usually snow-free, although cool nights may prevail.

Plants and Wildlife

Growing in the lowest portions of Mount Wrightson Wilderness are a variety of desert grasses, cholla, ocotillo, mesquite, and other desert species. A bit higher, Mexican pinyon pine, alligator juniper, a variety of evergreen oaks, sotol, and yucca start to appear. Across the mid- to upper level lands are found stands of Chihuahua pine, Apache pine, ponderosa pine, and Douglas fir. Growing in the vicinity of springs are leafy riparian communities that include magnificent old Arizona sycamore, cottonwood, Arizona walnut, and other deciduous tree species. Wildlife includes Coues white-tailed deer, javelinas, mountain lions, coyotes, bobcats, and black bears. The elegant trogon is one of the bird species for which Madera Canyon is famous. A relative of the quetzal, this unusual bird migrates north from Mexico to Madera Canyon (and other mountainous areas of southeastern Arizona) and takes up residence until late summer. Other

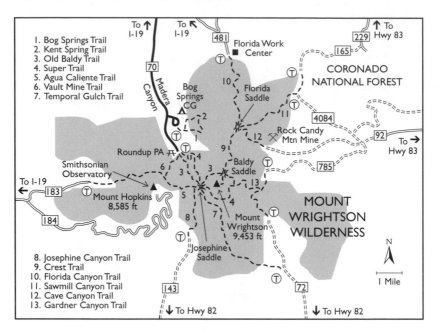

interesting species include the sulphur-bellied flycatcher, the Lucifer hummingbird, and the flammulated owl. The prime birding season in Madera Canyon is from early March through September.

Geology

Part of Arizona's Basin and Range province, these mountains are typically steep. While the range includes a Precambrian core of granite, layers of sedimentary rocks that date back to the Paleozoic era are also revealed here. This is probably due to thrust faulting, which occurred some 75 to 80 million years ago. As with other parts of the range, Mount Wrightson itself is partially composed of volcanic rocks. As you approach Madera Canyon, you may also notice an extremely broad alluvial fan, or *bajada,* which extends west of the range.

ACTIVITIES
Hiking

Laced with interconnecting trails, Mount Wrightson Wilderness offers many possibilities for interesting hikes. Because of its easy access, Madera Canyon is a good place to begin most trips. To reach Madera Canyon, drive south from Tucson on Interstate 19. Turn east at the Continental exit and drive 13 miles to Madera Canyon. Here, two trailheads access the most popular trails in the wilderness. Creating a loop of 5 miles are the Bog Springs and Kent Spring Trails. Beginning at Bog Springs Campground, the Bog Springs Trail heads 0.7 mile south to where the two routes split. Turning left, the Bog Springs Trail first accesses Bog Springs in 0.8 mile. A riparian area of old sycamores and other deciduous trees, Bog Springs offers a wonderful respite for hikers. From the springs, the trail climbs a bit, before contouring south for 1.2 miles to Kent Spring. From this permanent spring, the Kent Spring Trail then drops steeply for 1.6 miles to return to the above-mentioned divide in the loop. It is then 0.7 mile back to the campground. In all, this loop hike has an elevation change of 1,500 feet.

The second trail access point within Madera Canyon is found at the Roundup Picnic Area, which is at the road's end. From here, two trails—the 5.4-mile Old Baldy Trail and the 8.1-mile Super Trail—climb 4,000 feet to the Mount Wrightson summit. With the Old Baldy Trail taking a more direct route up the mountain's north slope, and the Super Trail climbing more easily around the south side of the peak, these two trails intersect at Josephine Saddle (near the trails' midpoints). In so doing, they form a distorted figure eight. Depending on how strong you feel, you may want to consider using portions of both routes to complete your hike. No matter which trail you use, the scenery is superb.

Along the way, the Super and Old Baldy Trails intersect other routes that approach the higher reaches of the range from trailheads outside Madera Canyon. At Josephine Saddle, you can turn west to follow the Agua Caliente Trail 4.7 miles to a trailhead located along Forest Road (FR) 183, just west of the wilderness. This route passes to the north of the 8,585-foot summit of Mount Hopkins, home to the Smithsonian Observatory. The Agua Caliente Trail intersects the Vault Mine Trail, a little more than 2 miles west of Josephine Saddle. The Vault Mine Trail continues about 2 miles, before dropping back to the Roundup Picnic Area. In so doing, the trail closes a 7.7-mile loop.

Also connecting with the Super and Old Baldy Trails at Josephine Saddle is the 6.5-mile Temporal Gulch Trail. This trail drops into a drainage with the same name and ends up at FR 72, a high-clearance, 2WD route that begins near Patagonia, along Arizona Highway 82. Turning south from the above-mentioned Agua Caliente Trail, just west of Josephine Saddle, is the 2.8-mile Josephine Canyon Trail. It heads south to reach the end of FR 4082, a 4WD route that turns off FR 143. It also begins along Arizona Highway 82 near Patagonia.

At Baldy Saddle, located just north of the Mount Wrightson summit, the Super and Old Baldy Trails combine to complete the 0.9-mile climb to the summit. At the saddle, these two routes also connect with the southern end of the Crest Trail. The 2-mile-long Crest Trail follows the crest of the range north to the Florida Saddle, where it intersects with three other trails. The Florida Canyon Trail covers 4.7 miles to reach a trailhead located at the U.S. Forest Service's Florida Work Center. Roughly paralleling Florida Canyon, this route drops 3,500 feet in all. Heading northeast from Florida Saddle is the 4.5-mile Sawmill Canyon Trail. After following its namesake drainage for most of the way, the Sawmill Canyon Trail reaches the end of the 4WD FR 4084, which is accessed by following FR 92. FR 92 turns west from Arizona Highway 83 a few miles north of Sonoita. Lastly, the 1.9-mile Cave Canyon Trail drops southwest from the Florida Saddle to reach the Rock Candy Mountain Mine, which is located at the end of FR 92. The last few miles of FR 92 may require a 4WD vehicle.

One additional trail that branches off the Super–Old Baldy network is the Gardner

Canyon Trail. This 3-mile route drops directly east from a point on the Super Trail nearly a mile southeast of Baldy Saddle. The Gardner Canyon Trail can be accessed by way of the 4WD FR 785, which turns off the above-mentioned FR 92.

Water is available at springs located within the wilderness, but you need to treat the water before drinking. Watch for lightning during the summer months and for rapidly changing weather conditions in the spring and fall. A sudden snowstorm in November 1958 killed three Boy Scouts on Josephine Saddle.

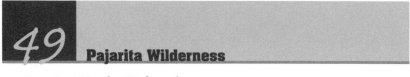

49 Pajarita Wilderness

Location: 21 miles W of Nogales
Size: 7,420 acres
Status: Wilderness area (1984)
Terrain: Desert canyons and mountains
Elevation: 3,800 feet to 4,800 feet
Management: Coronado NF
Topographic map: Ruby

Although small, Pajarita Wilderness includes the highly interesting Sycamore Canyon. Draining south to the Mexico–United States border, this perennial drainage is a delight to explore in more ways than one. Not only does it protect rugged canyon scenery but it is also home to a fascinating array of plants, many of which are found nowhere else in the United States. Highlighting the canyon's biological diversity is the Goodding Research Natural Area, which has been designated within the wilderness area.

Seasons

Because of the summer heat, spring and fall are the best seasons to visit the Pajarita, although wading through the perennial stream does offer an invigorating way to cool off in the summer. Winter is often too cold for this type of exploring. Heavy spring runoff may block passage in places in the canyon and monsoon rains typical in the summer months may produce flash-flood conditions.

Plants and Wildlife

Some 625 species of plants have been identified within Pajarita Wilderness. This is primarily because of the perennial stream that runs through Sycamore Canyon and its proximity to Mexico. Among these plants are several rare or endangered species, including the Goodding ash and a species of fern found only in the Himalayas, Mexico, and Sycamore Canyon. Beyond the well-watered confines of Sycamore Canyon grows a variety of desert plants, including ocotillo, cholla, saguaro cactus, mesquite, and several types of oak. In addition to deer, javelinas, bobcats, mountain lions, and coyotes, Sycamore

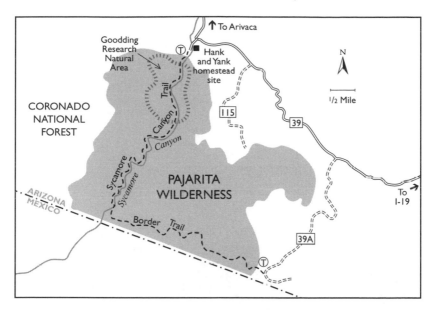

Canyon is also home to elegant trogons, green kingfishers, beardless flycatchers, and other rare bird species. Sycamore Canyon harbors the rare Tarahumara frog and Sonora chub, as well. The Goodding ash and the Goodding Research Natural Area were both named after Leslie N. Goodding, a noted botanist who called Sycamore Canyon a "hidden botanical garden."

Geology

Stream erosion has sliced deeply through the Pajarita Mountains in Sycamore Canyon, exposing cliff faces and spires of volcanic rhyolite and conglomerates of shale and sandstone.

History

Just north of the wilderness boundary, at the trailhead for Sycamore Canyon, are the Hank and Yank ruins. Although today little more than crumbling adobe walls, this was once the ranch of John (Yank) Bartlett and Henry (Hank) Hewitt. Established in the 1880s, the ranch was attacked by Indians in 1886. After Hewitt was wounded and a neighbor was killed, Bartlett escaped to summon help from nearby Oro Blanco. Despite surviving this episode, the ranch eventually failed.

ACTIVITIES
Hiking

Two trails access Pajarita Wilderness. The most popular of these begins at the Hank and Yank homestead site. To reach this trailhead, turn west on Peña Blanca Road (State

Highway 289) from Interstate 19 and drive 9 miles to Peña Blanca Lake. Bear left on Forest Road (FR) 39 and drive 8.8 miles to the signed turnoff for Sycamore Canyon. Following Sycamore Canyon downstream for 5.3 miles to the United States–Mexico border, the Sycamore Canyon Trail encounters several pools that must be waded. Stretches of large boulders must also be negotiated. Spring runoff may raise the water level in some pools to chest-height or deeper. The trail ends at the international border, which is marked by a barbed wire fence. This is a very scenic canyon with an interesting array of flora and fauna.

The second trail within the Pajarita roughly parallels the border from the 4WD FR 39A westward for 4 miles to the end of the Sycamore Canyon Trail. Established to service the border fence, this route cuts mostly across grassy foothills. To reach the trailhead, drive west from Peña Blanca Lake to the turnoff for FR 39A.

Because this area (along the border) is a high-intensity drug smuggling area, hikers should use considerable caution when hiking here.

Water should be treated before drinking. Watch for flash floods after heavy rains.

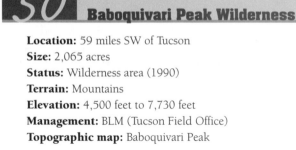

50   Baboquivari Peak Wilderness

Location: 59 miles SW of Tucson
Size: 2,065 acres
Status: Wilderness area (1990)
Terrain: Mountains
Elevation: 4,500 feet to 7,730 feet
Management: BLM (Tucson Field Office)
Topographic map: Baboquivari Peak

If you have ever traveled through southeastern Arizona, you can hardly fail to have had your imagination sparked by Baboquivari Peak. A distinctive feature of the Baboquivari Mountain Range, this dominant landmark can be spotted from dozens of miles away. It is, in fact, the only major summit in Arizona to require technical climbing skills. Not surprisingly, the distinctive peak figures prominently in the beliefs of the Tohono O'odham Indians, who have lived in the area for many centuries. Today, the 2.8-million-acre Tohono O'odham Reservation (the second-largest Indian reservation in the United States) forms the western boundary of this small but highly scenic wilderness area.

Seasons
Baboquivari Wilderness can be visited at any time of the year, although summer afternoons are usually too hot for hiking. Winter may also bring an occasional snow shower to its higher elevations. Snow cover does not last for long, however.

Plants and Wildlife

In the lowest elevations, saguaro cactus, paloverde, mesquite, and other desert species are found. Higher up, Mexican pinyon and a variety of oaks are common. Arizona walnut is a feature of riparian areas. The endangered rainbow cactus is also found on Baboquivari Peak. Trampled by livestock in most other areas, this succulent still grows in rugged portions of Baboquivari that have remained free from grazing. Animals that call the small wilderness home include Coues white-tailed deer, javelinas, coyotes, and the occasional mountain lion.

Geology

Topped by a large granite dome, Baboquivari Peak is the highest peak in the largely granitic mountain range that bears its name. Long and narrow, the Baboquivari Range was pushed upward during a major period of mountain building known as the Laramide Orogeny, which began some 65 million years ago.

History

According to Tohono O'odham legend, Baboquivari Peak is home to I'itoi, or "Elder Brother." A benevolent spirit, Elder Brother taught the Tohono O'odham how to live in this desert homeland. Some believe that he still watches over the "People of the Desert" from the mountain today. Baboquivari Peak was mentioned in the journals of Jesuit missionary Father Kino, who made many expeditions into this region of the Sonoran Desert, beginning in 1699. More recently, the peak's challenging slopes have made it a focus for climbing parties, ever since Dr. R. II. Forbes and companion Jesus Montoya made the first recorded ascent to the summit in 1898. Lacking modern climbing gear, Forbes used a grappling hook to help the two men claw their way to the top. Forbes climbed Baboquivari five more times, the last being on his eighty-second birthday.

ACTIVITIES
Hiking

Hiking in the wilderness is limited to one rough route. To reach the wilderness boundary, drive 22 miles west from Tucson on Arizona Highway 86 to Three Points Junction. Turn south on Arizona Highway 286 and continue 29.5 miles. Then turn right on an unmarked, 2WD, dirt road and continue 2.7 miles to where a second road turns right. Follow this road for 5 miles into Thomas Canyon. The last few miles require a 4WD vehicle to cross rugged washes. The road ends at a gate, beyond which is private land. Hikers must park here and walk the next mile, across the Humphrey Ranch. Currently, the Nature Conservancy holds a pedestrian right-of-way across this primitive land. After crossing the ranch, the trail dips in and out of the stream bottom as it continues up Thomas Canyon. Receiving little use, the route eventually fades as it approaches the head of the canyon. It is possible, however, to reach a saddle along the ridgeline north of the peak, provided you are up for some bushwhacking. This saddle is also accessible from the Tohono O'odham Reservation, by way of the Summit Trail.

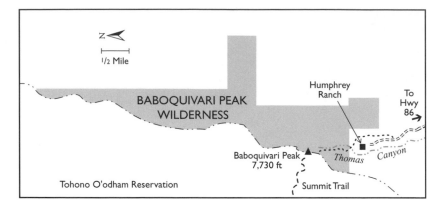

Requiring a permit from the tribe, this route climbs 2,600 feet in 4 miles along a trail constructed by the Civilian Conservation Corps (CCC) in 1934.

Rock Climbing

The fact that you need technical climbing gear to reach the top of Baboquivari makes it a particularly alluring destination for rock climbers. The standard route to the top follows the Great Ramp, a 45-degree façade on the peak's west side, to the 80-foot high Cliff-Hanger Pitch. This pitch is often impassable in wintertime due to ice. The CCC built a precarious wooden ladder along this route in the 1930s, but it has since fallen down. The Southeast Arête offers a more challenging ascent, up the southern face of the summit. A third ascent, known as the Spring Route, offers one of the only multiday climbs in Arizona. It follows the east face, which has a number of overhangs.

51 Miller Peak Wilderness

Location: 10 miles S of Sierra Vista
Size: 20,190 acres
Status: Wilderness area (1984)
Terrain: Forested mountains
Elevation: 5,200 feet to 9,466 feet
Management: Coronado NF
Topographic maps: Miller Peak, Huachuca Peak, Montezuma Pass

Towering nearly 5,000 feet above the San Pedro Valley, the Huachuca Mountains are especially vivid examples of the often sudden changes in topography that typify southeastern Arizona's Basin and Range province. For hikers, these steep mountains offer many challenges. Their efforts are rewarded, though, by the far-reaching panoramas, pristine forests, and diverse wildlife found along the way.

Seasons

Although summer afternoons are sometimes hot in the lower elevations of Miller Peak Wilderness, the best time of year to visit is between the months of May and October. Winter regularly brings snow and cold temperatures to the higher reaches of the range. Early spring, late fall, and even most winter days may be warm enough for visiting the lower canyons, however.

Plants and Wildlife

Because these mountains are characteristically steep, plant communities change from one to the next quite rapidly. In the lowest elevations of the wilderness, you will find desert grasslands, thick forests of oak (Arizona white, Emory, and silverleaf, to name but three), and stands of Mexican pinyon pine and alligator juniper. Moving up in elevation, ponderosa pine and Gambel oak are common, and Douglas fir—some of which are quite large—are found along north-facing slopes and in drainages. The occasional limber pine and aspen also grow in the higher portions of the Huachuca Mountains. Thriving riparian plant communities of Arizona sycamore, bigtooth maple, Arizona walnut, and other deciduous trees are also found here. Mule deer and white-tailed deer, javelinas, coatimundis, coyotes, mountain lions, and black bears are known residents of the mountains. Birds are numerous and quite varied, thanks to the area's proximity to Mexico. Birders come to the Huachucas in great numbers to spot elegant trogons and other exotic species. The principal birding area is the Nature Conservancy's Ramsey Canyon, a lush canyon that attracts fourteen different species of hummingbird,

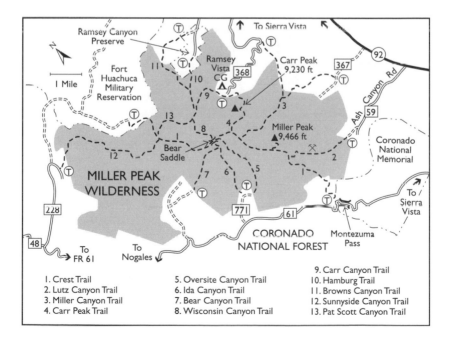

1. Crest Trail	5. Oversite Canyon Trail
2. Lutz Canyon Trail	6. Ida Canyon Trail
3. Miller Canyon Trail	7. Bear Canyon Trail
4. Carr Peak Trail	8. Wisconsin Canyon Trail

9. Carr Canyon Trail
10. Hamburg Trail
11. Browns Canyon Trail
12. Sunnyside Canyon Trail
13. Pat Scott Canyon Trail

as well as numerous other bird species. Miller Peak Wilderness is also home to the Mexican spotted owl—a relative of the endangered northern spotted owl.

Geology

Towering above broad desert valleys, the Huachuca Mountains are a faulted block range with numerous geological features. Across much of the range, you will find limestone and Precambrian granite. In other areas, however, rhyolite and other volcanic rocks attest to past volcanic activity in the area. Considerable faulting and folding have greatly added to the complexity of the range.

History

Reminders of nineteenth-century mining activity abound in many corners of Miller Peak Wilderness. Homesteads in the Huachuca Mountains sprang up around the turn of the century (one of these eventually became the Nature Conservancy's Ramsey Canyon Preserve). Adjacent to the northern boundary of the wilderness is Fort Huachuca. First established in 1877, the military outpost became headquarters during the U.S. government campaign to capture famed Apache leader Geronimo. In 1954, the fort was chosen as a site for testing electronic gear.

ACTIVITIES
Hiking

Although small, Miller Peak Wilderness offers a sensibly laid out network of trails that explore both canyon bottoms and high ridges. The central avenue of this web of backcountry routes is the Crest Trail, which begins at Montezuma Pass, south of the wilderness, in the Coronado National Memorial (a nearby NPS site). The Crest Trail continues northwest for 11.5 miles to a trailhead outside the wilderness, on Fort Huachuca property. This well-maintained route follows ridge tops and goes over various peaks. The prime attraction for most hikers along the Crest Trail is 9,466-foot Miller Peak itself. From Montezuma Pass, the Crest Trail gains 1,500 feet in 2.5 miles. It then levels off as it follows a ridge north toward Miller Peak. Approximately 4 miles in, the trail intersects the upper end of the Lutz Canyon Trail, a 3-mile trail that follows an old mining road for its first 2 miles, to reach an old mine site. It then continues climbing steeply along an overgrown foot trail until it reaches the Crest Trail. Shortly beyond this intersection, a 0.5-mile side trail turns left from the Crest Trail to access Bond Spring. About 4.5 miles from Montezuma Pass, the Crest Trail reaches the turnoff for the Miller Peak summit. Reached via a 0.5-mile side trail that switchbacks up the western slope of the mountain, Miller Peak was once the site of a fire lookout tower. It now provides incredible views in all directions. To reach Montezuma Pass, drive south from Sierra Vista on Arizona Highway 92 to Montezuma Pass Road. Turn right and drive west through Coronado National Memorial along a twisting but well-maintained gravel road. The trailhead for the Lutz Canyon Trail is reached by driving south on Arizona Highway 92 to Ash Canyon Road. Turn right and continue 2.2 miles to the Lutz Canyon trailhead.

North of Miller Peak, the Crest Trail continues for 1.6 miles before reaching the upper ends of the Miller Canyon and Carr Peak Trails. Following its namesake for about 3 miles, the Miller Canyon Trail climbs about 2,700 feet in all before connecting with the Crest Trail. It begins at the end of Miller Canyon Road, which turns off Arizona Highway 92 a few miles south of Sierra Vista. The 3.5-mile Carr Peak Trail begins at the end of Carr Canyon Road (this narrow gravel road, Forest Road [FR] 368, climbs from Arizona Highway 92 to Ramsey Vista Campground) and ascends about 1,600 feet before reaching a short side trail that takes you to the top of 9,230-foot Carr Peak. The Carr Peak Trail then continues another mile to reach the Crest Trail, also near Tubb Spring.

After passing the head of Miller Canyon, the Crest Trail intersects three additional trails in the next 1.5 miles. The first, the 3-mile Oversite Canyon Trail, climbs along its namesake drainage for 3 miles. It begins at the end of the 4WD FR 771, which branches off FR 61, west of Montezuma Pass. The second is the Ida Canyon Trail, which also begins along FR 771. In about 3 miles, this route climbs from 6,500 feet to the 8,200-foot Bear Saddle on the Crest Trail. The third trail, the seldom-used Bear Canyon Trail, climbs 1.3 miles along Bear Creek to intersect the Ida Canyon Trail near Bear Spring. It is accessed by way of an unnamed jeep trail, which branches off FR 61 a few miles west of the turnoff for FR 771.

Heading north from Bear Saddle is the Wisconsin Canyon Trail. In 1.4 miles, this route drops to Hamburg Spring in the upper end of Ramsey Canyon. Here, a left turn will take you 2.1 miles up Pat Scott Canyon to the Crest Trail in the vicinity of Pat Scott Peak; a right turn leads to the lower end of the 2.3-mile Carr Canyon Trail, which climbs 600 feet to reach the above-mentioned Ramsey Vista Campground. Continuing downcanyon from Hamburg Spring, the 2.3-mile Hamburg Trail continues all the way to Ramsey Canyon Preserve. If you begin at the preserve, you must first pick up a trail pass from the visitor center. Because the number of visitors allowed to use the trail each day is limited, you may need to make reservations ahead of time.

In addition to the Ramsey Canyon Preserve, the Hamburg Trail also accesses the Browns Canyon Trail. From an intersection 1 mile north of the Wisconsin Canyon Trail/Hamburg Trail intersection, the 5-mile Browns Canyon Trail climbs out of Ramsey Canyon to reach the head of Browns Canyon to the north. It then drops down Browns Canyon to Ramsey Canyon Road, 1.5 miles northeast of the Ramsey Canyon Preserve headquarters. Most of this route lies outside the wilderness boundary.

Back on the Crest Trail, it is 2 miles from the above-mentioned Bear Saddle to the next trail intersection to the north, where the upper end of the 4.7-mile Sunnyside Canyon Trail meets the Crest Trail. Climbing first along an old jeep road, and then along a foot trail, this route follows its namesake canyon west from FR 228. Requiring a high-clearance, 2WD vehicle in places, FR 228 turns off FR 48, which, in turn, branches north from the above-mentioned FR 61.

Shortly beyond its intersection with the Sunnyside Canyon Trail, the Crest Trail picks up the upper end of the above-mentioned Pat Scott Canyon Trail. It then continues nearly a mile before exiting the wilderness and entering the Fort Huachuca

Military Reservation. From here, the route drops into Sawmill Canyon, where it meets an old road that accesses the Garden Canyon area. To hike on the military reservation, you must first pick up a visitor's pass at the entrance gate.

Water is found at various springs and in some of the major drainages. It should be treated before drinking. Watch for lightning, especially during the summer season. Be prepared for rapidly changing weather in the higher terrain of the Huachuca Mountains.

52   Chiricahua Wilderness

Location: 40 miles N of Douglas
Size: 87,700 acres
Status: Wilderness area (1964)
Terrain: Forested mountains
Elevation: 5,200 feet to 9,796 feet
Management: Coronado NF
Topographic maps: Rustler Park, Chiricahua Peak, Portal, Portal Peak, Fife Peak, Stanford Canyon, Swede Peak

Encompassing the higher reaches of a mountain range by the same name, Chiricahua Wilderness is an incredible place for hikers to explore. One of southeastern Arizona's famed "sky islands," the verdant Chiricahua Mountains form a pleasant contrast with the surrounding desert basins. Tall pine, spruce, fir, aspen, and other montane flora are common, and because of the range's proximity to Mexico, there are plants and animals here that are usually found only south of the border. Hikers may explore most corners of the wilderness using a variety of trails. The Chiricahua Mountains were named for a band of Apache that once roamed this portion of the Southwest. In 1994, a 27,000-acre wildfire burned across much of Chiricahua Wilderness, an event that has changed the look of the land but will eventually lead to renewal, as with all wildfires.

Seasons
Because of its mostly high elevations, the wilderness is best visited during the late spring, summer, and early fall. Winters bring snow to the wilderness, though usually not enough to support a cross-country ski season.

Plants and Wildlife
Stands of Mexican pinyon pine, alligator juniper, Arizona cypress, and several varieties of evergreen oak are found at lower elevations in the wilderness. Moving up a bit in elevation, you will find Chiricahua and Apache pine—species that are more commonly found in Mexico. Ponderosa pine and Douglas fir grow in considerable numbers here, and nice stands of Engelmann spruce prosper in the very highest reaches of the wilderness. Following 1994's devastating Rattlesnake Fire, which destroyed 27,000

A recent forest fire has left much of the Chiricahua Wilderness scarred for generations to come.

acres, pioneer species such as aspen have sprouted up. The mountains are home to deer, black bears, coyotes, mountain lions, and bobcats, as well as Mexican species such as coatimundis, Apache fox squirrels, elegant trogons, Mexican chickadees, and sulphur-bellied flycatchers. Another Mexican bird that occasionally resides here is the thick-billed parrot, a former permanent resident that became extinct in this country due to hunting and deforestation. In 1986, thick-billed parrots were successfully reintroduced into these mountains. Additional releases have since followed, and it is hoped that the bright green-and-red bird will once again enliven the pine forests of southern Arizona.

Geology

Although the Chiricahua Mountains occasionally exhibit their Precambrian roots in the form of granite and schist exposures, it was a period of volcanism that led to what you see today. Volcanic explosions covered the mountain range with thick deposits of ash, which eventually cooled to form a layer of rhyolite and tuff up to 2,000 feet thick. Many summits within the Chiricahua Mountains are rounded and comparatively gentle, but some of the canyons are rocky and rugged. Cave Creek on the east side of the range, for instance, is characterized by impressive pinnacles and cliff faces. Here, pockets of gas collected as the lava cooled, forming the caves that visitors see today.

ACTIVITIES
Hiking

Interwoven with numerous trails, Chiricahua Wilderness offers hikers an exhaustive array of interesting day hikes and overnight trips. A good place to begin is Rustler Park. Situated along the crest of the range just north of the wilderness, Rustler Park serves as the northern access point for the popular Crest Trail. From Rustler Park, this easy trail heads south along a highline route toward Chiricahua Peak. It then splits to continue in two southerly directions from the peak. Along most of its length, the Crest Trail varies little in elevation (between 8,400 feet and 9,796 feet), and the trail is well maintained throughout. Rustler Park is accessed by way of Forest Road (FR) 42. From the west, this well-maintained gravel road turns off Arizona Highway 181 just outside Chiricahua National Monument; from the east, it can be reached by driving up the popular Cave Creek drainage, west of Rodeo, New Mexico.

Within the 5 miles between Rustler Park and Chiricahua Peak, the Crest Trail intersects the upper ends of several other routes that drop off the range. The first route to head west is the Rattlesnake Trail, which runs from Bootlegger Saddle down Rattlesnake Canyon, then on to FR 357 (Pine Canyon Road). The Rattlesnake Trail first connects with the Rock Creek Trail, a primitive route that continues for nearly 4 miles to where it connects with the 3.3-mile Turkey Pen Canyon Trail. The Turkey Pen Canyon Trail then continues south to FR 41 in Turkey Creek Canyon. The Rattlesnake Trail also connects with the primitive Witch Canyon Trail, which follows its namesake west for a few miles before reaching two additional primitive routes: the 3.8-mile Hoovey Canyon Trail and the 3.2-mile Green Canyon Trail. These routes both descend to FR

357 in Pine Canyon. About 2 miles south of Bootlegger Saddle, the Crest Trail intersects the upper end of the Saulsbury Trail. Dropping more than 2,000 feet in 4.4 miles, this well-maintained route crosses 8,715-foot Little Bull Mountain before descending into Saulsbury Canyon. The lower trailhead for the Saulsbury Trail is found along FR 41. Branching east from the Crest Trail about a mile north of Chiricahua Peak is the

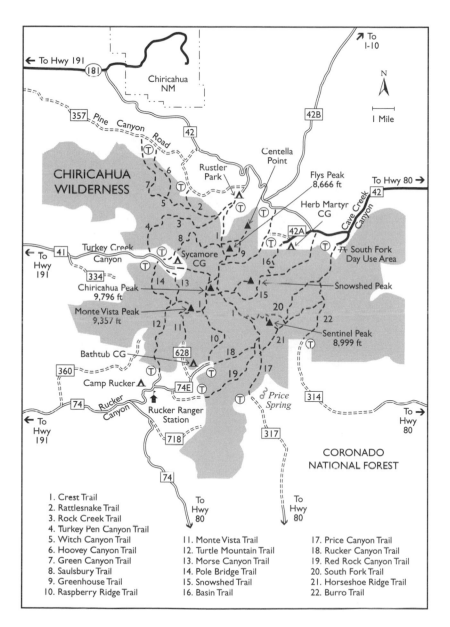

1. Crest Trail
2. Rattlesnake Trail
3. Rock Creek Trail
4. Turkey Pen Canyon Trail
5. Witch Canyon Trail
6. Hoovey Canyon Trail
7. Green Canyon Trail
8. Saulsbury Trail
9. Greenhouse Trail
10. Raspberry Ridge Trail

11. Monte Vista Trail
12. Turtle Mountain Trail
13. Morse Canyon Trail
14. Pole Bridge Trail
15. Snowshed Trail
16. Basin Trail

17. Price Canyon Trail
18. Rucker Canyon Trail
19. Red Rock Canyon Trail
20. South Fork Trail
21. Horseshoe Ridge Trail
22. Burro Trail

Greenhouse Trail. Heading east from Cima Park, the Greenhouse Trail descends some 2,800 feet in a little more than 4 miles, to reach the end of a spur road in Cave Creek Canyon. Another trail that heads east from the Crest Trail is a 2-mile side route that goes to scenic Centella Point. This trail can be accessed in two ways: either by a segment of trail that turns north from Flys Peak or a trail that turns south from the 8,666-foot summit.

Once it reaches Junction Saddle, just north of Chiricahua Peak, the Crest Trail splits in two: one segment heads southeast and the other southwest. In so doing, the Crest Trail forms an inverted Y at the heart of the wilderness. Approximately 2 miles south of Chiricahua Peak, the western leg of the Crest Trail intersects the Raspberry Ridge Trail. This 4.6-mile primitive route follows the top of Raspberry Ridge before dropping into Bear Canyon. It terminates near the end of FR 74E, a short way beyond Rucker Lake. A little more than 0.5 mile beyond the Raspberry Ridge Trail, the Crest Trail reaches the 9,357-foot summit of Monte Vista Peak. The site of a fire lookout, Monte Vista Peak affords some memorable views as it rises between Turkey Creek to the north and Rucker Canyon to the south. Shortly beyond the Monte Vista summit, the Monte Vista Trail heads directly south for 2.7 miles before reaching the end of FR 628, a high-clearance, 2WD road that turns off FR 74 near Bathtub Campground. Continuing west for another 1.4 miles to the summit of Johnson Peak, the Crest Trail intersects the primitive Turtle Mountain Trail, which, in turn, heads south 4.5 miles to reach a trailhead in the Rucker Canyon drainage. This trail terminates near the Rucker Ranger Station. The site of several campgrounds and trailheads, Rucker Canyon is reached by turning off US Highway 191 onto Arizona Highway 181, then following it eastward to FR 74. Most of the Rucker Canyon trailheads are found along FR 74E, which turns left from FR 74 about 3 miles past the Coronado National Forest boundary.

In the vicinity of Johnson Peak, the Crest Trail also connects with the upper ends of the Morse Canyon and Pole Bridge Trails. The Morse Canyon Trail descends 2.4 miles into its namesake drainage before reaching the end of the above-mentioned FR 41. The Pole Bridge Trail drops down Pole Bridge Canyon for 2.4 miles to reach a trailhead that is about a mile northwest of the Morse Canyon trailhead. A portion of Pole Bridge Canyon is included in the Pole Bridge Research Natural Area and supports some nice stands of Apache and Chiricahua pine and impressive old alligator juniper.

From Chiricahua Peak, the southeastern leg of the Crest Trail continues for 5.5 miles before reaching the summit of 8,999-foot Sentinel Peak. Spectacular views occasionally open up along this segment of the Crest Trail, taking in the upper reaches of Rucker Canyon to the west and portions of Mexico in the far distance. At Sentinel Peak itself, though, the view is obscured by trees, just as it is from Chiricahua Peak. The Chiricahua Peak–Sentinel Peak segment of the Crest Trail also accesses a number of side routes. The first to be reached while traveling south is the 8.5-mile Snowshed Trail. After skirting around the south side of Snowshed Peak (the summit of which can be reached by way of a 0.6-mile side trail), the Snowshed Trail descends along a ridge top to FR 42 (Cave Creek Road), a short distance east of the Southwestern Research Station. The Basin Trail turns north from the Snowshed Trail near its halfway mark and continues 2.8 miles to the end of FR 42A, near Herb Martyr Campground. Cave Creek Canyon itself is a spectacular drainage ringed by stunning rock outcrops. It has also been identified as an important natural area, especially for its prodigious bird and plant life.

About 1.5 miles south of the Snowshed Trail, the Price Canyon Trail turns off the Crest Trail to head south into Price Canyon. Along its 5.7-mile length, this route drops about 3,000 feet. Its lower terminus is reached by driving north from US Highway 80 on FR 317 to Price Spring. Along the way, the Price Canyon Trail picks up the western end of the 3.8-mile Rucker Canyon Trail, which begins at the end of the above-mentioned FR 74E, just east of Rucker Lake. The Rucker Canyon Trail perhaps offers the best access to the southern end of Chiricahua Wilderness. Also intersecting the Rucker Canyon Trail—nearly a mile from the Price Canyon Trail—is the 7.4-mile Red Rock Canyon Trail. After topping Sage Peak, this route drops into its namesake canyon and ends up at FR 354, which turns off FR 74E.

Just before it reaches Sentinel Peak, the Crest Trail intersects the uphill end of the South Fork Trail. This route descends 3,500 feet in 6.8 miles, following the South Fork of Cave Creek to reach the South Fork Day Use Area, about 1.5 miles south of the above-mentioned FR 42. The Crest Trail ends in the vicinity of Sentinel Peak, but three other trails continue from here. Roughly paralleling the South Fork Trail, the 3.6-mile Horseshoe Ridge Trail heads northeast to where it intersects the Burro Trail. The Burro Trail, in turn, runs for 6.6 miles, between a trailhead located at the end of the 4WD FR 314 (this road turns west from US Highway 80) and the South Fork Trail. From the intersection of the Burro and South Fork Trails, it is about 1.5 miles to the South Fork Day Use Area. Heading south from the end of the Crest Trail is a 1.5-mile side route, which dead-ends on top of 8,411-foot Jones Peak.

Water is readily available at many springs and in major drainages, but it should be treated before drinking. Watch for lightning in the higher portions of the wilderness.

53 Chiricahua Monument Wilderness

Location: 38 miles S of Willcox
Size: 10,290 acres
Status: Wilderness area (1984)
Terrain: Forested canyons and rock formations
Elevation: 5,300 feet to 7,310 feet
Management: NPS
Topographic maps: Cochise Head, Rustler Park

Encompassing one of the more unusual collections of rock formations in the Southwest, Chiricahua National Monument offers some memorable opportunities for wilderness exploration. Countless grottos, cliff faces, and spires, or hoodoos, await those

who venture along one of several trails that lace the monument's backcountry. Of the monument's 11,985 acres, 10,290 acres have been designated as wilderness.

Seasons

It is possible to hike in Chiricahua National Monument throughout the year. Summer temperatures rarely top 100 degrees and winters occasionally bring snow to the monument, but it is usually not enough to close trails. While fresh snow may make some trails slippery, it can also greatly enhance the beauty of the monument's geologic wonders.

Plants and Wildlife

Situated at the northern end of the Chiricahua Mountains, Chiricahua National Monument offers a natural corridor for plants and animals from both north and south of the border with Mexico. Cool in summer, the monument is a protected retreat for a variety of flora and fauna. Douglas fir and Apache and Chiricahua pine (both of which are more common south of the border than north) grow here, as does aspen. Arizona cypress is plentiful in the bottoms of washes, while alligator juniper and a variety of evergreen oaks are found in the more arid terrain. Wildlife includes Coues white-tailed deer, javelinas, coyotes, mountain lions, black bears, coatimundis, and Apache fox squirrels—a species more at home in Mexico than in the United States.

Geology

Known as the "Land of the Standing-up Rocks" by the Chiricahua Apache, the geological wonders of Chiricahua National Monument have long impressed those who come here. Geologists believe that the formation of this scenic wonderland began with volcanic eruptions at a nearby caldera some 27 million years ago. After layer upon layer of ash was deposited, a 2,000-foot-thick layer of rhyolitic tuff resulted. Water, ice, and wind erosion then went to work along fractures in the stone. Differential erosion led to the strange gray hoodoos at the center of the monument.

History

For many years, the rugged Chiricahua Mountains served as a hideout for Chiricahua Apaches who were evading capture by the army. From deep within the mountains, Cochise and his Apache followers launched surprise attacks on the U.S. cavalry. Years later, a medicine man named Geronimo broke away from the San Carlos Apache Reservation with renegade bands of Apache warriors and hid out in the Chiricahua area. After Geronimo surrendered in 1886, settlers began to pour into the southeastern corner of the state. Two of these were Neil and Emma Erickson, who homesteaded Faraway Ranch in the western portion of what is now the monument. The area gained early recognition for its wonders in 1924, when President Calvin Coolidge set aside 11,000 acres as a national monument.

Opposite: *Inside the Heart of Rocks*

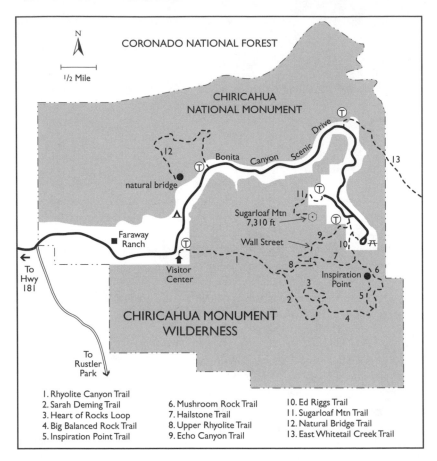

N
CORONADO NATIONAL FOREST

1/2 Mile

CHIRICAHUA
NATIONAL MONUMENT

12

Bonita Canyon Scenic Drive

natural bridge

13

Sugarloaf Mtn
7,310 ft

11

9

Wall Street

Faraway
Ranch

Visitor
Center

To
Hwy
181

8

7

10

3

Inspiration
Point

6

2

5

4

CHIRICAHUA MONUMENT
WILDERNESS

To
Rustler
Park

1. Rhyolite Canyon Trail
2. Sarah Deming Trail
3. Heart of Rocks Loop
4. Big Balanced Rock Trail
5. Inspiration Point Trail

6. Mushroom Rock Trail
7. Hailstone Trail
8. Upper Rhyolite Trail
9. Echo Canyon Trail

10. Ed Riggs Trail
11. Sugarloaf Mtn Trail
12. Natural Bridge Trail
13. East Whitetail Creek Trail

ACTIVITIES
Hiking

A number of hiking routes make up the monument's 20-mile network of backcountry trails. Although overnight backpacking is prohibited, all of these routes may be explored by day hikers. A good place to start is at the visitor center, which is located a mile beyond the monument entrance. Beginning at the eastern end of the parking lot is the 1.5-mile Rhyolite Canyon Trail. Climbing steadily along its namesake canyon, this route divides at the mouth of Sarah Deming Canyon. A right turn heads up Sarah Deming Canyon and the Sarah Deming Trail. After 1.6 miles, this trail accesses the 0.9-mile Heart of Rocks Loop, which circles through a wondrous collection of rock formations. Along the loop are such aptly named formations as Pinnacle Balanced Rock, Camel's Head, Punch and Judy, Duck on a Rock, and Kissing Rocks. Vistas along this trail take in the high peak of Cochise Head to the northeast and Sulphur Springs Valley to the west.

Beyond the turnoff for the Heart of Rocks, the 1-mile Big Balanced Rock Trail continues to climb toward the turnoff for the 0.5-mile Inspiration Point Trail. The hike from the visitor center to Inspiration Point climbs some 1,600 feet in 4.6 miles. Beyond the turnoff for Inspiration Point, the 1.2-mile Mushroom Rock Trail drops into the upper end of Rhyolite Canyon, where it eventually connects with the Hailstone Trail. The Hailstone Trail, in turn, continues down Rhyolite Canyon for 0.8 mile, to connect with the Upper Rhyolite Trail. In 1.1 miles, this trail connects back up with the Rhyolite Canyon Trail, to complete a loop through some of the most scenic portions of the monument. This entire hike covers 8.7 miles in all.

By taking the Hailstone Trail, you can make a pleasurable 3.3-mile circle hike known as the Echo Canyon Loop. Beginning at the Echo Canyon trailhead, 5.5 miles past the visitor center, the 1.6-mile Echo Canyon Trail heads southwest to connect

Rock formations along Rhyolite Canyon in the Chiricahua National Monument

with the Hailstone Trail. Along this first leg of the hike, the Echo Canyon Trail passes through Wall Street—an interesting corridor between closed-in rock walls—before dropping into Echo Canyon. The Echo Canyon Loop turns left on the Hailstone Trail, which it then follows to the 0.9-mile Ed Riggs Trail. The loop is finally completed by following the Ed Riggs Trail back to the trailhead.

In addition to the Heart of Rocks–Echo Canyon network of trails, a few other routes explore other areas of the monument. Gaining 500 feet in 0.9 mile, the Sugarloaf Mountain Trail takes you to the high point of the monument, 7,310-foot Sugarloaf Mountain, the site of a fire lookout. Starting from a trailhead on the Bonita Canyon Scenic Drive, 1.25 miles beyond the visitor center, the Natural Bridge Trail climbs 500 feet in 2.4 miles to reach a natural bridge. And heading eastward from the Bonita Canyon Scenic Drive, the unmaintained East Whitetail Creek Trail exits the monument to pick up the Indian Creek Trail on adjacent Coronado National Forest land, to access Cochise Head beyond.

Hikers should watch their footing at all times, particularly when it is wet. Water is not available in the backcountry of the monument, so be sure to pack plenty beforehand. Watch for lightning in higher, exposed areas, especially during the frequent thunderstorms in the summer months.

54 Dos Cabezas Mountains Wilderness

Location: 40 miles S of Safford
Size: 11,998 acres
Status: Wilderness area (1990)
Terrain: Desert mountains
Elevation: 4,080 feet to 7,950 feet
Management: BLM (Safford Field Office)
Topographic maps: Dos Cabezas, Bowie Mountain North, Luzena

Named after Dos Cabezas (Two Heads) Peaks, Dos Cabezas Mountains Wilderness offers a collection of rugged summits and canyons. Thick desert shrubbery makes hiking difficult along many slopes and in most drainages, but hiking access is possible along a few closed-off vehicle routes and in the lower, eastern portions of the wilderness. In the southeastern corner, eroded granite boulders and outcrops make for some rather interesting hiking.

Seasons
The low elevations of the wilderness can be quite hot in summer, while the higher elevations are noticeably cooler. The spring and fall are most pleasant. Winters are not uncomfortable, but the higher elevations may occasionally experience subfreezing temperatures and periodic snow.

Plants and Wildlife

Mesquite, turpentine bush, and snakeweed typically grow here, along with prickly-pear cactus, sotol, yucca, agave, and ocotillo. At higher elevations, mountain mahogany begins to appear, as well as juniper and oak. Drainages and areas near springs support riparian vegetation, including Arizona sycamore, cottonwood, and velvet ash. White-tailed

Yucca growing within the Dos Cabezas Mountains Wilderness

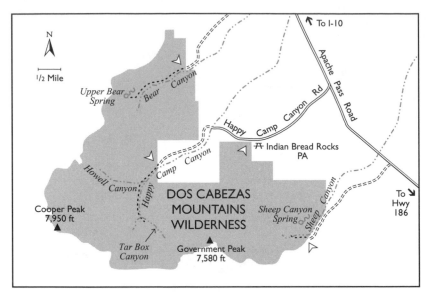

deer, mule deer, javelinas, mountain lions, coyotes, and other creatures of the desert mountains are found here. A variety of game birds inhabit the area, and both golden and bald eagles have been spotted here.

Geology

Typical of Basin and Range topography, the Dos Cabezas Mountains are a fault block range, composed primarily of Pinal schist and Precambrian granite. Where there are granite exposures, interesting rock gardens have been formed as a result of erosion. A handful of old mines (all of them shut down) offer evidence of the mineral wealth of the Dos Cabezas.

ACTIVITIES
Hiking

Hiking access to Dos Cabezas Mountains Wilderness is possible only from the east side of the range, since the western access is blocked by private land. To reach the wilderness, drive to the small town of Bowie, on Interstate 10, then head 4.5 miles south on Apache Pass Road. Turn right on Happy Camp Canyon Road and follow this good dirt road 3 miles to the Indian Bread Rocks Picnic Area on the left. Although no trails begin at the picnic site, it is easy to hike cross-country from here, heading south and southwest among the granite boulders and faces that characterize this section of the wilderness. Directly behind the picnic site is a small ridge that, when crossed, leads to a wide open area at the foot of the mountains.

Beyond the Indian Bread Rocks Picnic Area, Happy Camp Canyon Road becomes noticeably rougher (4WD may be required), as it continues west into Happy Camp Canyon. Because the road traverses private land, you will need to continue all the way to its end (about 6 miles from Apache Pass Road) to reach the wilderness boundary. From road's end, you can then hike up Happy Camp Canyon. Within the first mile, Howell Canyon branches off to the right. This is followed by Tar Box Canyon, which branches off to the left. Tar Box provides the best route for reaching Government Peak, along the wilderness's southern boundary. Happy Camp Canyon eventually leads to the foot of Cooper Peak, the highest point in the wilderness.

Forming the southeastern border of the wilderness is a 4WD route that follows Sheep Canyon for a couple of miles. Extending into the wilderness a short distance (vehicles are prohibited beyond the wilderness boundary), this road accesses Sheep Canyon Spring, beyond which cross-country explorations are possible.

Approaching the wilderness from the north, a 4WD road heads south from Bowie for about 4.5 miles, before reaching the wilderness boundary at the mouth of Bear Canyon. Beyond the boundary, the old vehicle way continues for another 2 miles to reach Upper Bear Spring. Now closed to vehicles, this route makes for some good canyon hiking.

Because there are no established trails within this wilderness, hikers should proceed with caution. There are several springs in the wilderness, but it is safest to bring your own water. Watch for rattlesnakes in the warmer months and lightning when hiking on exposed ridges and peaks.

55 Peloncillo Mountains Wilderness

Location: 9 miles NE of San Simon
Size: 19,440 acres
Status: Wilderness area (1990)
Terrain: Desert mountains and canyons
Elevation: 4,100 feet to 6,400 feet
Management: BLM (Safford Field Office)
Topographic maps: Doubtful Canyon, San Simon, Engine Mountain, Orange Butte

Straddling the Arizona–New Mexico border, the Peloncillo Mountain Range is a rugged collection of desert peaks that break up the skyline in spectacular fashion. Encompassing nearly 20,000 acres of the central portion of the range, the Peloncillo Mountains Wilderness includes some of the range's more scenic sections. Slicing through these mountains are deep canyons that offer some excellent backcountry hiking routes.

Seasons

Hot in the summer and somewhat cool in the winter, the Peloncillo Mountains are best visited in the spring and fall: from March to May and October to early December.

Ward Canyon in the Peloncillo Mountains

Of course, if you don't mind a little discomfort and the roads are dry, it is possible to visit during other months, as well.

Plants and Wildlife

Plants in the Peloncillo Mountains are characterized by both desert shrub and mountain shrub communities. At lower elevations, you'll find pricklypear and cholla cactus, ocotillo, yucca, sotol, mesquite, creosote bush, catclaw, and various desert grasses. In the higher elevations, oak and juniper are common. In addition to the Coues white-tailed deer, mule deer, javelinas, mountain lions, and coyotes that inhabit this range, desert bighorns were reintroduced to the area in 1986 (there was a second release in 1990). Among the species of birds known to frequent this wilderness is the endangered peregrine falcon, which likes to nest on precipitous cliff faces.

Geology

Mostly volcanic in nature, the wilderness portion of the Peloncillo Mountains consists of both light-colored rhyolite and much darker basalts. Some breccia is also found. Breccia is formed from larger pieces of volcanic rock that were spewed from volcanoes and then cemented together with lava or volcanic ash. It is believed that the Peloncillo Range resulted from volcanic activity that occurred during the Tertiary period.

ACTIVITIES
Hiking

Given the fact that this wilderness includes a number of cherry-stemmed roads, access to some sections of the area is possible. A good place to begin is along the western side. From San Simon, which lies along Interstate 10, turn north on Kennedy Road

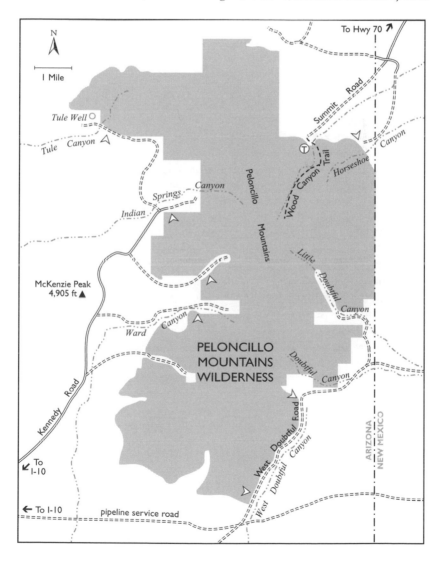

and drive 2.5 miles to where the main road bends to the left. Continue straight, then turn right a little farther on. Approximately 4 miles from town, a natural gas line and accompanying service road head east, while the main road continues north. This pipeline road provides access to the southern and southeastern portions of the wilderness discussed below. About 9 miles from town, a right turn accesses a cherry-stemmed road that heads up Ward Canyon. Ending a little more than 2 miles beyond, at a stock well, this route soon turns to 4WD. Shortly before road's end, the main drainage of Ward Canyon heads to the left. This canyon bottom could be followed for a way if you do not mind bushwhacking. It is also possible to hike north from various points along the road to access the ridgeline above.

North of the turnoff for Ward Canyon, the main road continues past McKenzie Peak before dropping into a broad valley beyond. Here, the road encounters a seldom-used 4WD route that heads up an unnamed canyon just north of Ward Canyon (this route is better walked than driven). The main road then reaches Indian Springs Canyon, where a locked gate blocks access to the canyon bottom. It is possible, however, to access Indian Springs Canyon by walking cross-country on BLM land that runs south of the private holding. Beyond the turnoff for Indian Springs Canyon, the main road forms the wilderness boundary for a way, in the vicinity of Tule Well. From the road, open terrain and Tule Canyon offer possible access routes to the wilderness.

By following the above-mentioned natural-gas pipeline road east for nearly 5 miles, it is possible to access the 4WD West Doubtful Road, which reaches the wilderness boundary approximately 0.5 mile north of the pipeline road. Upon reaching the head of West Doubtful Canyon (3 miles beyond the intersection), the road drops into the Doubtful Canyon drainage, where a locked gate prevents further travel. While this gate prevents access to Little Doubtful Canyon to the north, it is possible to hike cross-country into the southeastern corner of the wilderness.

Access to the northern portion of the wilderness is possible by driving 17 miles east from Duncan on Arizona Highway 70. Near mile 12, turn south on Summit Road and continue 5 miles to where it crosses Wood Canyon. Just beyond the canyon, a locked gate prevents direct access to the wilderness. It is possible, however, to reach the boundary by following the canyon upstream for 2 miles. A second interesting drainage system—Horseshoe Canyon in the east side of the wilderness—can also be accessed by way of Summit Road.

Be careful when hiking cross-country. Water is available at springs and stock wells, but don't count on these sources. Pack in all you will need. Watch for rattlesnakes in warmer weather. Electrical storms are common; stay away from high, exposed areas during thunderstorms.

Opposite: *Organ pipe cactus often grows side by side with saguaro cactus in Organ Pipe Wilderness.*

chapter 4

Western Basin and Range

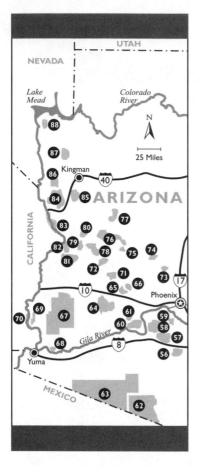

The western portion of Arizona's Basin and Range province takes in the most arid and remote areas of the state. Repeating the same pattern of broad desert basins spiked by sudden rises of mountain as found in the southeastern corner of Arizona, this western third of the state features some dramatic scenery. But here the mountains are typically not high enough to provide a suitable climate for timber and other montane plant life. Instead, these mountains are mostly covered with desert ecosystems and they are, for the most part, very dry. Despite its bone-dry environs, however, this region is home to thirty-three different wilderness areas.

Located south and southwest of Phoenix, three wilderness areas—Table Top, South Maricopa Mountains, and North Maricopa Mountains—are now included in the newly established Sonoran Desert National Monument. Nearby is Sierra Estrella Wilderness and a bit west are the adjacent Woolsey Peak and Signal Mountain Wildernesses. Along the Mexican border Organ Pipe Cactus National Monument and Cabeza Prieta National Wildlife Refuge encompass two expansive wilderness areas. As Interstate 10 tracks west from Phoenix, a number of wilderness areas form the broad skyline. They include Eagletail Mountains, Big Horn Mountains, Hummingbird Springs, Harquahala Mountains, and Harcuvar Mountains. The Hells Canyon and Hassayampa River Canyon are located not far from Phoenix to the northwest. And farther west, several wilderness areas— Tres Alamos, Arrastra Mountain, Rawhide Mountains, Upper Burro Creek, Aubrey Peak, Swansea, East Cactus Plain, and Gibraltar Mountain—form an impressive collection of pristine desert landscapes. Crowning the southwest corner of Arizona is the expansive Kofa National Wildlife Refuge. Smaller wilderness parcels nearby include the Muggins Mountains, Trigo Mountains, and the Imperial National Wildlife Refuge. North along Colorado River the Havasu National Wildlife Refuge straddles both shores of the river. And ringing Kingman to the south, west, and north are the Wabayuma Peak, Warm Springs, Mount Nutt, Mount Tipton, and Mount Wilson Wildernesses.

56 Table Top Wilderness

Location: 20 miles W of Casa Grande
Size: 34,400 acres
Status: Wilderness area (1990)
Terrain: Desert mountains and *bajadas*
Elevation: 1,800 feet to 4,373 feet
Management: Sonoran Desert NM, BLM (Phoenix Field Office)
Topographic maps: Antelope Peak, Little Table Top, Indian Butte, Vekol Mountains NE

A prominent landmark from many miles around, Table Top Mountain dominates the desert plains west of Casa Grande. As the name suggests, the mountain's blocked-off summit appears level from most angles, and its slopes are of a seemingly uniform grade. Hikers reach the summit by following a 3.5-mile-long trail that ascends the southwestern slope of the mountain. There are a few other interesting hiking routes within the 34,400-acre wilderness, as well. Thanks to a directive approved by then President Clinton in January 2001, the Table Top Wilderness falls within the expansive Sonoran Desert National Monument.

Seasons
Because it is somewhat higher than other wilderness areas in the vicinity, Table Top Wilderness offers a slightly extended hiking season. Comfortable hiking here may be

A trailhead sign

Along the trail to Table Top Mountain

had from October through May. Summers are still very hot, even in the highest reaches of Table Top Mountain. March and April bring showy displays of wildflowers after wet winters.

Plants and Wildlife

The lower reaches of the wilderness are characterized by stands of saguaro cactus, cholla, pricklypear cactus, ocotillo, paloverde, and creosote bush. On top of the mountain is an isolated 40-acre patch of desert grassland, which, because of its pristine condition, may offer scientists important research opportunities. Desert bighorn sheep, mule deer, javelinas, coyotes, numerous species of birds, desert tortoises, and a variety of snakes and lizards call this wilderness home.

Geology

The Table Top Mountain Range is composed of Precambrian granite and gneiss, which, where exposed, have been greatly weathered. Volcanic activity has led to numerous

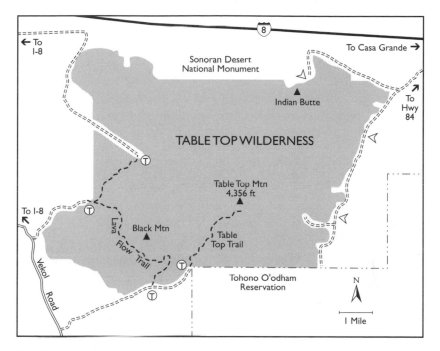

lava flows and dark basaltic rock here. The caprock of Table Top Mountain, in fact, is a remnant of an old lava flow.

ACTIVITIES
Hiking

The 3.5-mile Table Top Trail accesses the high point of Table Top Wilderness. Climbing from a trailhead elevation of 2,299 feet to the 4,356-foot summit, this trail is steep in places, as well as rocky along the switchbacks up the southwestern slope of the mountain. Reach the trailhead by turning off Interstate 8 at the Vekol Road exit, 34 miles west of Casa Grande. Drive south on Vekol Road for 2.1 miles until you reach a fork in the road. Keep right and drive another 5.7 miles to where the route bears right again. Approximately 11 miles south of the interstate, turn left at a corral and go over two cattle guards. Follow this high-clearance, 2WD road 4.5 miles to its end. Note that this route is impassable when wet.

Some closed roads now make up another hiking trail that traverses the southwestern corner of the wilderness. Known as the Lava Flow Trail, this route heads north from the approach road to the above-mentioned trailhead, then heads west along the foot of Black Mountain to reach a trailhead just outside the wilderness boundary. The Lava Flow Trail then continues northeast to reach a third trailhead, located at the end of a cherry-stemmed 4WD road. This road is reached by turning left from Vekol Road 0.7 mile south of the interstate, then continuing east and south for 8.4 miles.

Another old vehicle way in the northeastern corner of the wilderness takes you to the area around Indian Butte before continuing into an interior basin. Gaining access to this route requires a lot of driving first, though. You will need to drive a long dirt road south from Arizona Highway 84 and pass under Interstate 8 before reaching the wilderness area's northeastern corner. From this point, turn northwest and drive another 2 miles or so.

Jeep roads form the eastern boundary of the wilderness and provide access to cross-country routes into the *bajadas* in the eastern portion of the wilderness. To reach these jeep roads, use the route described above to get to the Indian Butte access point.

Be careful when hiking cross-country. Bring water, as none is available in the wilderness. Watch for rattlesnakes while hiking during the warmer months and for lightning during thunderstorms.

57 South Maricopa Mountains Wilderness

Location: 16 miles E of Gila Bend
Size: 60,100 acres
Status: Wilderness area (1990)
Terrain: Desert mountains and basins
Elevation: 1,250 feet to 3,183 feet
Management: Sonoran Desert NM, BLM (Phoenix Field Office)
Topographic maps: Big Horn, Estrella, Bosque, Lost Horse Peak, Conelly Well

South Maricopa Mountains Wilderness encompasses a 13-mile stretch of the Maricopa Mountain Range located directly north of Interstate 8. It is characterized by rugged peaks that shelter interior basins. Because access to this wilderness is restricted, any worthwhile trip into the area requires a lot of planning and trip time—a few days or more. If you go, though, you'll be rewarded by plenty of solitude and some interesting desert scenery. This wilderness now falls within the newly created, 496,337-acre Sonoran Desert National Monument.

Seasons

It is very hot from May to October in this low-elevation wilderness. November and April are usually much nicer, and the winter months of December, January, and February can be pleasant as well. March may be the best month for a visit, as wet winters produce a plethora of wildflowers in this desert area.

Plants and Wildlife

Like nearby North Maricopa Mountains Wilderness, this wilderness area includes some grand old saguaro cactus, patches of cholla, paloverde, mesquite, ocotillo, and a lot of creosote bush. Animal residents include desert bighorn sheep, mule deer, coyotes, bobcats, foxes, jackrabbits, and desert tortoises.

Fallen saguaro cactus in the South Maricopa Mountains Wilderness

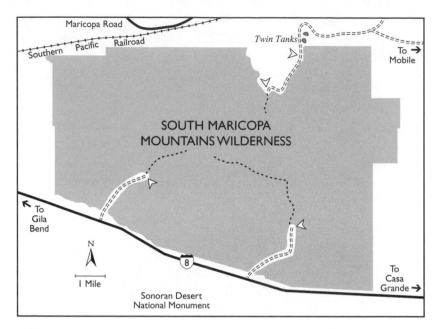

Geology

The Maricopa Mountains consist mostly of Precambrian granite and gneiss. In the south-ernmost portion of the wilderness, however, ancient lava flows have left behind expo-sures of dark basaltic rock.

ACTIVITIES
Hiking

Bordering a 13-mile stretch of the wilderness area's southern boundary is Interstate 8. Two cherry-stemmed roads turn off the highway and head north for 3 miles or more. Closed to vehicular traffic inside the wilderness, these roads then continue for a few additional miles to offer suitable hiking routes. Since no exit ramps access these roads, extreme caution should be used when leaving or entering the interstate. Gates at each road are unlocked and passable to the public. Be sure to close the gates behind you.

A few miles of the northwestern boundary of the wilderness lie within a short distance of the paved Maricopa Road. Unfortunately, access is blocked by the busy Union Pacific Railroad. The mostly flat northeastern corner of the wilderness is acces-sible by 4WD roads, but the trip is lengthy. From Maricopa, drive 11.2 miles west on Arizona Highway 238 to Mobile (a small cluster of buildings) and turn left. Follow this road 3.4 miles south to Schumacher Lane. Turn right and continue 1.9 miles to where the road turns left. Drive 2 miles south and turn right at some old ruins. Turn west here and drive 2.1 miles to Twin Tanks. From Twin Tanks, you can either turn left and reach the wilderness in 0.9 mile or continue straight for about 6 miles. You can leave this road at almost any point and hike cross-country across mostly open basins. Another entry point is at an old jeep trail, about 3 miles south of the stock pond. Now closed to vehicles, this short route reaches an old mining area 1 mile south.

Hiking cross-country should be attempted only by experienced hikers. Use great caution when exiting Interstate 8 and when crossing the railroad tracks (on foot). Bring plenty of water, as none is available in the wilderness. Watch for rattlesnakes during the warmer times of the year.

58 North Maricopa Mountains Wilderness

Location: 12 miles NE of Gila Bend
Size: 63,200 acres
Status: Wilderness area (1990)
Terrain: Desert mountains and basins
Elevation: 840 feet to 2,813 feet
Management: Sonoran Desert NM, BLM (Phoenix Field Office)
Topographic maps: Butterfield Pass, Cotton Center SE, Margies Peak, Mobile NW

Encompassing the northern third of the Maricopa Mountain Range, North Maricopa Mountains Wilderness offers an interesting selection of rugged summits separated by open interior basins. Because of its overall low elevation, the wilderness is home to a variety of Lower Sonoran life zone plants and animals. Its size is such that some nice overnight excursions are possible. This wilderness is now included in the sizeable Sonoran Desert National Monument.

Seasons
You can forget about visiting this wilderness at any time during the summer—it's just too hot. Late spring and early fall are marginal as well. The best months are from November to April.

Plants and Wildlife
Along with some nice stands of mature saguaro cactus, North Maricopa Mountains Wilderness supports cholla, paloverde, ocotillo, brittlebush, mesquite, and creosote bush. Mule deer live here, along with coyotes, bobcats, and foxes. The wilderness is considered to be crucial habitat for desert bighorn sheep and protected desert tortoises. A number of raptors have been known to frequent the area as well.

Geology
The Maricopa Mountains trend northwest–southeast and consist mostly of Precambrian granite and gneiss. Rising as a faulted block during a period of considerable tectonic plate movement, the Maricopa Mountains have since been greatly eroded, hence the almost flat desert basins and *bajadas* within and around the peaks.

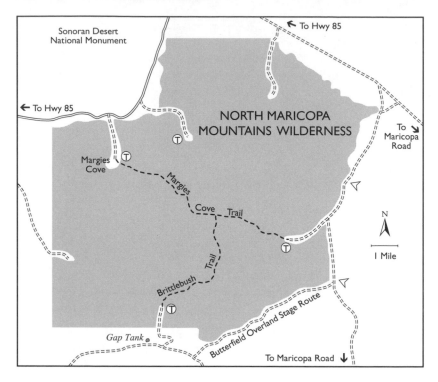

History

The historic Butterfield Stage Overland Route borders a portion of the wilderness area's southern boundary. Established in the 1850s, this well-known trail ran from St. Louis to San Francisco, carrying mail across a West that was still wild and untamed. Today, the portion of the stage route that borders North Maricopa Mountains Wilderness is a 4WD route.

ACTIVITIES
Hiking

Although the Maricopa Mountains are quite rugged, a network of interconnected interior basins make foot travel throughout the wilderness relatively easy. Even more conducive to hiking are a number of old roads that have since been turned into hiking trails. Perhaps the easiest way to reach these access points is a cherry-stemmed road that heads south into Margies Cove. To get there, drive 20 miles south from Interstate 10 on Arizona Highway 85, then turn east on a good dirt road (be sure to close the gate behind you). Drive 3.8 miles to where the 1.8-mile-long road into Margies Cove turns south. From the road closure at the wilderness boundary, follow the 8-mile Margies Cove Trail southeast to a trailhead east of the wilderness. Near its midway point, the Margies Cove Trail intersects the northern end of the 6-mile Brittlebush Trail. It heads south to reach a cherry-stemmed road in the southern end of the wilderness. The southern end of the Brittlebush Trail is reached by driving the 4WD Butterfield Overland Stage Route to the turnoff for Gap Tank; the eastern trailhead for the Margies Cove Trail is approached from a 4WD road that forms the eastern boundary of the wilderness.

Cross-country hikers enjoy even greater options. Cross-country hiking is greatly enhanced by the fact that the wilderness's northern, eastern, and southern boundaries are largely defined by existing roads. From the west, a couple of roads reach the wilderness boundary, as well. Check topographic maps to find the best routes.

Cross-country hiking here, and elsewhere, should be attempted only by experienced outdoors enthusiasts. Bring plenty of water, as none is available in this wilderness. Watch for rattlesnakes during the warmer months.

59 Sierra Estrella Wilderness

Location: 15 miles SW of Phoenix
Size: 14,400 acres
Status: Wilderness area (1990)
Terrain: Desert mountains
Elevation: 1,400 feet to 4,119 feet
Management: BLM (Phoenix Field Office)
Topographic maps: Montezuma Peak, Mobile

Of all the mountain ranges that tower over Phoenix and the Valley of the Sun, one of the most impressive is the Sierra Estrella, a range that rises nearly 3,000 feet above the surrounding desert floor. Although much of this range falls within the Gila River Indian Reservation, a portion is administered by the BLM as the 14,400-acre Sierra Estrella Wilderness. Although quite close to Phoenix, this area is seldom visited, thanks to the maze of sandy 4WD roads that access its boundaries.

Seasons
It is far too hot in the Sierra Estrellas for comfortable hiking during the summer and early autumn months. Late fall to mid- or late spring offers the best weather, as nights are cool and daytime temperatures are typically warm.

Plants and Wildlife
Most of the wilderness is characterized by saguaro cactus, cholla, ocotillo, paloverde, and creosote bush. The elephant tree reaches its northeasternmost extension in the Sierra Estrellas. There are a few isolated patches of shrub live oak and juniper in the higher reaches of the wilderness. The Sierra Estrella is home to mule deer, javelinas, coyotes, mountain lions, and a small band of desert bighorn sheep. Both desert tortoises and Gila monsters live within the wilderness boundaries. A number of raptors—prairie falcons, Cooper's hawks, and golden eagles, among others—have been sighted here as well.

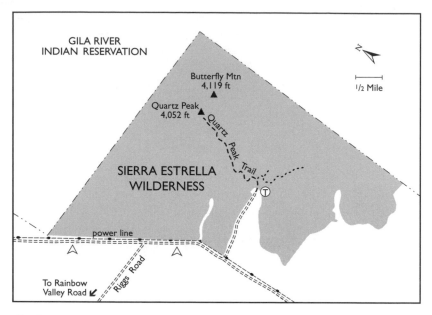

Geology

Characteristically rugged, the Sierra Estrella is a northwest–southeast-trending block of Precambrian gneiss, schist, and granite. Although the mineral wealth of the Sierra Estrellas is minimal, some deposits of mica have been exploited in the range.

ACTIVITIES
Hiking

This wilderness is accessed via the sparsely populated Rainbow Valley, which sprawls west of the wilderness. The approach drive requires a 4WD vehicle to negotiate rough desert country and good topographic maps to help you find your way. From Phoenix, drive west on Interstate 10 to exit 126. Drive 8.3 miles south on Jackrabbit Road to Elliot Road. Turn right and drive 2.6 miles to Rainbow Valley Road. Turn right and follow this road 9.3 miles south until the pavement ends. Turn left on graveled Riggs Road and continue another 4 miles to an intersection. Continue straight for 5.3 miles to where this road intersects a powerline road. Turn right and drive 1.2 miles to where another road turns left, or east. Drive 1.9 miles east to the trailhead, which is at road's end. From here, the 3-mile Quartz Peak Trail climbs northeast to a ridge 0.5 mile below 4,052-foot Quartz Peak. It is a very rugged and difficult scramble to the summit itself. Quartz Peak lies a short distance west of 4,119-foot Butterfly Mountain. Within the first 0.5 mile, the trail passes some old mica mines. The scenery to the west is tremendous.

Also accessible from the Quartz Peak trailhead is a mostly open *bajada* to the south and some short but inviting canyons that penetrate the mountain range just to the east. Mostly open, the *bajadas* are suitable for cross-country travel, and some of the canyons can be accessed by following some old mining roads. Check the topographic maps for possible routes.

From the Quartz Peak trailhead, the wilderness boundary continues northwest along the powerline right-of-way for a few additional miles. Thanks to the powerline service road, it is possible to access additional portions of the wilderness. Because this northwest side of the wilderness is characterized by sandy washes and open *bajada* terrain, the hiking possibilities are many.

Whether you follow the established Quartz Peak Trail or hike cross-country, use extreme caution because the terrain is rugged and quite isolated. Watch for rattlesnakes and don't count on finding any water in this area; bring plenty of your own. Be wary of lightning as well.

60 Woolsey Peak Wilderness

Location: 32 miles SW of Phoenix
Size: 64,000 acres
Status: Wilderness area (1990)
Terrain: Desert mountains and plains
Elevation: 700 feet to 3,270 feet
Management: BLM (Phoenix Field Office)
Topographic maps: Woolsey Peak, Spring Mountain, Quail Springs Wash, Dendora Valley, Citrus Valley East, Citrus Valley West

Encompassing a portion of the Gila Bend Mountains, the Woolsey Peak Wilderness offers an interesting collection of volcanic peaks, broad basins, and *bajadas*. The wilderness is dominated by its namesake, 3,270-foot Woolsey Peak. This steep and distinctive mountain towers above scenic desert plains that are open to hiking.

Seasons
Summers are very hot in this low-elevation wilderness, as is early autumn and late spring. The best months for a visit are November through April. Springtime displays of wildflowers can be impressive, especially after a wet winter.

Plants and Wildlife
In addition to fine stands of saguaro cactus, Woolsey Peak Wilderness supports cholla, paloverde, and creosote bush. Mesquite and ironwood typically line the desert washes of the area. A small herd of desert bighorn sheep roams the northern half of the wilderness. Mule deer are found here, along with coyotes, bobcats, mountain lions, and a variety of birds of prey.

A windmill at Woolsey Spring with Woolsey Peak rising in the background

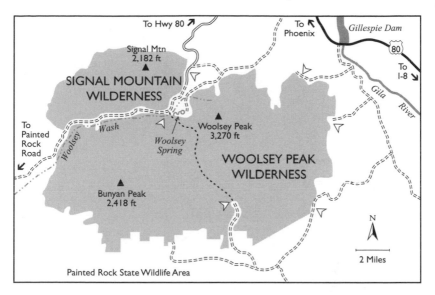

Geology

The Gila Bend Mountains, which trend northwest–southeast across the wilderness, exhibit plenty of past volcanic activity. Woolsey Peak itself is a large volcanic plug that rises more than 2,000 feet above plains of dark basaltic rock. Extensive lava flows cover portions of the area, and volcanic ridges and peaks rise in the western portion of the wilderness. On the east side of the wilderness are found some formations of Precambrian granite.

ACTIVITIES
Hiking

Woolsey Peak Wilderness is open and ideal for cross-country hiking. The best access points for the wilderness are found along a road that forms a portion of the wilderness area's northwestern boundary. From Phoenix, drive west on Interstate 10 to the exit for Arizona Highway 85. Continue 5.5 miles south to Old US Highway 80. Turn west and continue nearly 6 miles to the small town of Hassayampa. Continue south on Old Highway 80 for another 8 miles, at which point Agua Caliente Road turns west. Follow Agua Caliente Road west for about 5 miles to where an unnamed road bears left, then follow that road for another 5 miles or so to the wilderness boundary. A high-clearance, 2WD vehicle is needed to complete this approach. While it is possible to hike a number of cross-country routes south into the wilderness from this road, an established route is provided by an old road now closed to vehicles. It begins at Woolsey Spring, along Woolsey Wash, and heads southeast for 8 miles before exiting the wilderness to enter the adjoining Painted Rock State Wildlife Area. This old road offers a variety of jumping-off points for cross-country hikes in all directions.

A network of 4WD routes that head west from the Gila River offers access to the eastern section of Woolsey Peak Wilderness. Here, some closed-off roadways and a number of interesting drainages may be followed. To access these approach roads, head south from Gillespie Dam on Enterprise Road. Check the topographic maps to determine which route is right for you.

Keep in mind that cross-country hiking is an inherently risky endeavor. Water is not available in Woolsey Peak Wilderness. Watch for rattlesnakes while hiking in the warmer months.

61 Signal Mountain Wilderness

Location: 35 miles SW of Phoenix
Size: 13,350 acres
Status: Wilderness area (1990)
Terrain: Desert mountains and washes
Elevation: 800 feet to 2,182 feet
Management: BLM (Phoenix Field Office)
Topographic maps: Woolsey Peak, Quail Springs Wash

Separated from the larger Woolsey Peak Wilderness by a primitive road, Signal Mountain Wilderness is a natural extension of protected land within the ruggedly beautiful Gila Bend Mountains. The area's namesake, 2,182-foot Signal Mountain, dominates the landscape, and several small summits add to this cluster of inviting peaks.

Seasons
Don't count on visiting the Signal Mountain Wilderness between May and October because it will be too hot. Late fall and winter are ideal seasons, as is early spring.

Plants and Wildlife
Signal Mountain Wilderness features a variety of flora typical of the Lower Sonoran deserts. These include saguaro cactus, cholla, barrel cactus, paloverde, ocotillo, mesquite, ironwood, creosote bush, and bursage bush. A small band of desert bighorn sheep roams across this wilderness and the northern half of Woolsey Peak Wilderness. Mule deer, coyotes, jackrabbits, and a variety of raptors live here, as do rare desert tortoises.

Geology
Encompassing a portion of the Gila Bend Mountains, Signal Mountain Wilderness exhibits a variety of volcanic features: lava flows, basaltic rocks, and the like. Signal Mountain itself is composed of andesite, a colorful rock deposited as volcanic flows.

The sparse Signal Mountain Wilderness

The Signal Mountain Wilderness is a land of stark beauty.

ACTIVITIES
Hiking

Access to Signal Mountain Wilderness is available along a primitive road that follows Woolsey Wash. From Phoenix, drive west on Interstate 10 to the exit for Arizona Highway 85. Drive 5.5 miles south to Old US Highway 80. Turn right and drive about 6 miles to Hassayampa. Continue for another 8 miles to Agua Caliente Road. Turn right and continue 5 miles to where an unnamed road bears left. Follow this route for another few miles to where the signed wilderness boundary begins. To this point, the drive is along a high-clearance, 2WD route, but farther on it may require a 4WD vehicle. Forming the eastern and southern boundaries of the wilderness, a 6-mile stretch of this road provides a variety of access points for numerous cross-country hikes. The terrain is mostly open, and several washes offer natural hiking corridors. While Signal Mountain makes for an obvious destination, the surrounding summits provide some up-close views of this striking centerpiece of the wilderness. A portion of the wilderness area's northwestern boundary runs close to an active railroad, but public access along this front is both limited and impractical.

Hiking cross-country within this wilderness can be hazardous. Bring water, as none is available. Watch for snakes in the warmer months.

62 Organ Pipe Wilderness

Location: 15 miles S of Ajo
Size: 312,600 acres
Status: Wilderness area (1978)
Terrain: Low deserts
Elevation: 500 feet to 4,808 feet
Management: NPS
Topographic maps: Lukeville, West of Lukeville, Mount Ajo, Blankenship Well, Menagers Lake, Sentinel NE, Pozo Nuevo Well, Palo Verde Camp, Tillotson Peak, Kino Peak, Gunsight, Armenta Well, Bates Well, Diaz Peak

Spanning some of the hottest desert lands in Arizona, Organ Pipe Cactus National Monument lies at the heart of the Sonoran Desert. The monument's namesake, the organ pipe cactus, grows mostly in Mexico, but it has established itself here and in nearby portions of the Tohono O'odham Reservation to the east. Saguaro cactus and many other species of cactus also grow within the monument boundaries. Established in 1937, Organ Pipe Cactus National Monument encompasses one of the most pristine areas of Sonoran Desert in the Southwest. In 1978, 312,600 acres of the monument became a wilderness area.

Seasons

With summertime temperatures that soar well above 100 degrees (110 degrees is not uncommon), Organ Pipe Cactus National Monument is best visited between the months of October and May. Temperatures during these months range between 60 and 80 degrees and rains are typically light.

Plants and Wildlife

The organ pipe cactus blooms—but only at night. Other species of cactus that grow here include the giant saguaro, senita, cholla, pricklypear, and barrel, along with ocotillo, brittlebush, creosote bush, paloverde, and mesquite. After wet winters, colorful Mexican poppies often carpet the desert floor in the monument. Juniper and oak find suitable living conditions in the highest reaches of the Ajo Mountains, which rise more than 4,000 feet along the monument's eastern boundary. Wildlife of the monument include javelinas, coyotes, mountain lions, kit foxes, ring-tailed cats, bobcats, and kangaroo rats. If you are lucky, you may glimpse some desert bighorn

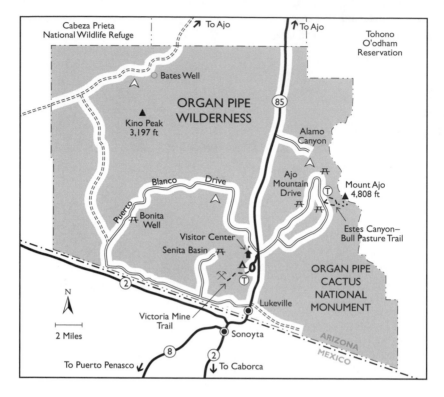

sheep or the endangered Sonoran pronghorn antelope. Of the 250-plus species of birds that have been sighted in the monument, cactus wrens, red-tailed hawks, white-winged doves, roadrunners, and Gambel's quails are most often spotted during desert walks.

Geology

The tan-and-orange-colored Ajo Mountains consist of rock formed during volcanic eruptions 14 to 22 million years ago. Other ranges, such as the Sonoyta Mountains, consist of Precambrian granite. Heavily mineralized, abandoned mines in the Sonoyta Range once produced modest amounts of gold and silver. As these desert ranges were eroded, gravels, sands, and soils were deposited in broad alluvial fans known as *bajadas*. With their loose soil and warm exposures, these *bajadas* are home to the monument's greatest mix of desert plants.

History

Archaeological evidence indicates that this desert area was inhabited by different groups during prehistoric times. In addition to archaic hunters and gatherers, the Hohokom also traveled through the area. After their disappearance in the fifteenth century, the Hohokom were followed by the Tohono O'odham, who survived partially on edible desert

An organ pipe cactus growing in its namesake monument

plants. During the nineteenth century, miners exploited various areas of the monument, as evidenced by the circa 1880s Victoria Mine. Ranchers tried their hand at making a living in the area, but grazing was phased out in the 1970s.

ACTIVITIES
Hiking

Two established trails penetrate the monument's backcountry. The 2.25-mile Victoria Mine Trail begins at the southern end of the campground loop and heads southwest across *bajadas* to the Victoria Mine. An easy hike, this route passes several old mines, some old machinery, and the dilapidated stone walls of a general store built around 1900.

The Estes Canyon–Bull Pasture Trail starts along the Ajo Mountain Drive (a 21-mile gravel road suitable for passenger cars) in the eastern portion of the monument. Climbing about 1,000 feet to reach Bull Pasture in the foothills of the Ajo Mountains, this trail is moderate in difficulty. The entire loop hike is a little more than 4 miles in length. Intrepid hikers can continue along a poorly established route to the top of Mount Ajo, which rises above Bull Pasture to the east. From the summit it is possible to see the Gulf of California, 70 miles away.

In the vicinity of the campground, three shorter trails offer good introductions to the Organ Pipe Wilderness environment. The 1.2-mile Desert View Nature Trail climbs a small rise northwest of the campground, the 1-mile Campground Perimeter Trail circumnavigates the campground, and the 1.3-mile-long Palo Verde Trail runs from the campground to the visitor center.

If you want to explore other areas of the monument's backcountry, you are on your own in terms of choosing hiking routes. In many areas, however, the terrain is open and easy to negotiate. Such cross-country explorations are greatly enhanced by two graded gravel roads—the above-mentioned Ajo Mountain Drive and the 53-mile Puerto Blanco Drive. Three additional unimproved roads also access the western and southern portions of the monument. Camping along these auto routes is prohibited, but you may obtain a permit for camping in the backcountry. You must camp at least 0.25 mile from the road.

Use extreme caution when traveling cross-country in the Organ Pipe Cactus National Monument backcountry. Be sure to bring along a topographic map and compass, and at least 1 gallon of water per person per day. Water is not available in the backcountry. Watch for rattlesnakes when hiking during warmer months and for lightning when visiting higher, exposed terrain.

63 Cabeza Prieta Refuge Wilderness

Location: 5 miles W of Ajo
Size: 803,418 acres
Status: Wilderness area (1990)
Terrain: Desert basins and mountains
Elevation: 300 feet to 3,027 feet
Management: USFWS
Topographic maps: Pozo Nuevo Well, Agua Dulce Mountains, North of Agua Dulce Mountains, O'Neill Hills, Las Playas, Monument Bluff, Palo Verde Camp, Antelope Hills, Pinta Playa, Paradise Canyon, Sierra Arida, Tule Mountains, Sierra de la Lechuguilla, Temporal Pass, Saguaro Gap Well, Granite Mountains South, Granite Mountains North, Bryan Mountains, Isla Pinta, North of Isla Pinta, Christmas Pass, Cabeza Prieta Peak, Coyote Water, Growler Peak, West of Growler Peak, Monreal Well, Point of the Pintas, Buck Peak, East of Buck Peak, Quitobaquito Springs

Larger than the state of Rhode Island, Cabeza Prieta National Wildlife Refuge is a sprawling collection of exceptionally arid desert lands. Broad valleys stretch between sudden rises of multihued mountains. Saguaro cactus and other succulents grow in some portions of the refuge, while precious little grows in others. Lava flows cast a dark hue across parts of the landscape, and dried-up mud encircles low, sunken areas known as *playas*. Cabeza Prieta National Wildlife Refuge was established in 1939, and 803,418 acres of the refuge were set aside as wilderness in 1990. Because the U.S. Air Force uses air space over the refuge at various times of the year, the desert stillness may occasionally be shattered by low-flying jets.

Saguaro cacti in the Cabeza Prieta National Wildlife Refuge

Seasons

Situated along the Arizona–Mexico border, Cabeza Prieta National Wildlife Refuge encompasses some of the hottest and driest terrain in the state. Practically speaking, the only time of year to visit the refuge is between November and April. Winters are ideal, as temperatures may climb into the 70s during the day. In the searing heat of summer, temperatures can easily top 110 degrees.

Plants and Wildlife

Cabeza Prieta National Wildlife Refuge is home to saguaro, cholla, ocotillo, creosote bush, mesquite, and paloverde trees. Wildlife of the refuge includes javelinas, mule deer, desert bighorn sheep, mountain lions, coyotes, bobcats, and the extremely rare Sonoran pronghorn antelope. Most of the 200 or so Sonoran pronghorns that live within the United States are found within the refuge.

Geology

Typical of Arizona's Basin and Range province, most of the mountain ranges rising within the refuge are fault block ranges. They differ, however, in the type and age of the base

Along El Camino del Diablo in the Cabeza Prieta National Wildlife Refuge

rock. Some special features of the refuge include extensive sand dunes and rugged lava flows. The name, Cabeza Prieta, which is Spanish for "Black Head," refers to a dark, lava-topped mountain in the western end of the refuge.

History

Before the first Spanish missionaries entered what is now southern Arizona, small bands of Tohono O'odham Indians traveled across the region in search of wild food and game. The first European to cross the area was a member of the 1540 Coronado Expedition who set out to search for a route to California. In 1699, Jesuit missionary Father Kino led a small party through the area. Other expeditions followed and, in time, an established route, stretching the length of the refuge, became known as El Camino del Diablo, or the Devil's Highway. Besides bedeviling early Spanish explorers, the extremely hot climate of the area also spelled disaster for the many parties of Anglo-American travelers headed to the California goldfields in the mid-1800s. Dozens of people died along the route for lack of water, and several gravestones still mark the way. Today, the Devil's Highway is a lengthy 4WD route that runs through the southern section of the refuge. Since World War II, the refuge has also served as an extension of the Barry Goldwater Air Force Range to the north. Although this factor occasionally leads to low-level flights that shatter the desert silence, it has probably contributed to the refuge's protection as well.

ACTIVITIES
Hiking

There are no established hiking trails within Cabeza Prieta National Wildlife Refuge, but its mostly open terrain is conducive to cross-country travel. Two 4WD roads—or "trails," as the refuge management refers to them—access different portions of the refuge. To drive either route, a permit is required. The above-mentioned El Camino del Diablo begins just south of Ajo and continues for 63 miles across the refuge. From pavement to pavement, the route's entire length is 120 miles. Depending on conditions, some or most of the drive requires a 4WD vehicle. Included among the obstacles along the way are long stretches of deep sand. The total time required to drive the entire route is 14 to 16 hours. Open desert terrain is found all along the Devil's Highway, most of which is ideal for hiking. Particular areas of interest include the Agua Dulce Mountains near Papago Well, the Pinacate Lava Flow in the south-central portion of the refuge, and the mountains near Tule Well. Additionally, about a dozen administrative 4WD trails branch off the Devil's Highway to facilitate the management of "wildlife developments," i.e., water holes. Strictly off-limits to private vehicles, these routes make for some nice hiking.

The second 4WD trail to enter the Cabeza Prieta National Wildlife Refuge is the 18-mile route to Charlie Bell Pass in the Growler Mountains. It begins in Ajo and travels west into the northeastern corner of the refuge. Along the way, open desert country offers a variety of hiking possibilities. One possible route follows the western foothills of the Growler Mountains north. Another continues directly west from Charlie Bell Pass into the expansive Growler Valley.

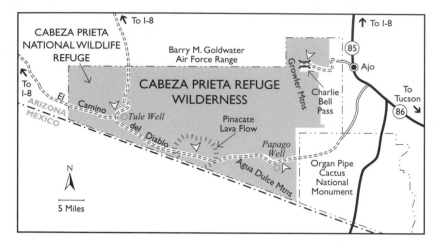

Don't be misled by the existence of Papago Well, Tule Well, and other scattered water holes; you still must pack in all the water you will need (a gallon or more per person per day), in order to be safe. Be prepared for extremely hot weather during most times of the year. Watch for rattlesnakes and other venomous creatures when visiting during the warmer months. To obtain a free permit for visiting Cabeza Prieta National Wildlife Refuge write: U.S. Fish and Wildlife Service, 1611 North 2nd Avenue, Ajo, AZ 85321; (520) 387-6483. Before setting out, stop at the refuge's center (1611 North 2nd Avenue, Ajo) to obtain updated information on road conditions, the availability of water, and other issues of concern here in the desert. And keep in mind that extensive stretches of cryptogamic soil are found here and that traversing these areas should be avoided.

64 Eagletail Mountains Wilderness

Location: 65 miles W of Phoenix
Size: 100,600 acres
Status: Wilderness area (1990)
Terrain: Desert mountains and basins
Elevation: 1,150 feet to 3,300 feet
Management: BLM (Yuma Field Office)
Topographic maps: Eagletail Mountains East, Eagletail Mountains West, Little Horn Mountains NE, Columbus Peak, Nottbusch Butte, Lone Mountain, Hope SE

The Eagletail Mountains form a line of rugged peaks, buttes, and spires that rise above the surrounding desert basins. Encompassing much of its namesake mountain range, Eagletail Mountains Wilderness has much to offer hikers: spectacular scenery, unusual geology, and interesting flora. In addition to this rugged range, the 100,000-plus-acre Eagletail Mountains Wilderness also takes in an expansive desert valley and a second, smaller uplift known as Cemetery Ridge.

Seasons

Summers are hot here, as are the early fall and late spring months. Winters often bring pleasant days, as does late fall and early to mid-spring. March often produces some nice displays of desert wildflowers, especially if there has been a wet winter.

Plants and Wildlife

Eagletail Mountains Wilderness features saguaro cactus, cholla, ocotillo, paloverde, mesquite, and acacia. A few relict junipers and oaks have also been found on the north slope of Eagletail Peak, the highest point within the wilderness. Wildlife includes mule deer, desert bighorn sheep, coyotes, bobcats, mountain lions, jackrabbits, Gila monsters, and desert tortoises. The precipitous cliffs and rock spires of the wilderness also provide suitable nesting areas for a variety of birds of prey.

Geology

The Eagletails consist almost entirely of volcanic rock. Running the length of this range is a prominent dike, which forms a row of jagged spires and peaks. A number of unusual formations, such as natural arches, are also tucked away in the range. Lava flows dating back to the Tertiary period characterize some areas of the wilderness, and *bajada* plains fan out from the range on either side.

ACTIVITIES
Hiking

Blessed with open terrain, former jeep routes, and game trails, Eagletail Mountains Wilderness is readily accessible to hikers. The most interesting routes are found within the Eagletail Mountains, which stretch across the northeastern section of the wilderness. To access the east side, drive west from Phoenix on Interstate 10 to exit 81, then turn off for Harquahala Valley. Drive 5 miles south to Courthouse Rock Road. Turn right on Centennial Road and drive west toward Courthouse Rock. Centennial Road eventually intersects a gas pipeline maintenance road, which heads northwestward beyond the wilderness boundary. Along this road, look for short side roads that head southwest to the wilderness boundary. After driving 10.8 miles west from the turn onto Centennial Road, you will reach one of these approach routes. Follow this high clearance route for 1.5 miles until you reach a trailhead; beyond this a former vehicle route now serves as a hiking route. This is the northern portion of the Ben Avery Trail. Named after a noted outdoor writer from Phoenix, this designated route covers 12 miles in all. From the trailhead near Courthouse Rock, the trail continues south across the wilderness to a trailhead near Nottbusch Butte. An extension of the Ben Avery Trail also branches off to head east to a trailhead near Double Eagle Peak.

Using Centennial Road, it is also possible to access the easternmost portion of

Small natural arch in the Eagletail Mountains

Eagletail Mountains Wilderness. Here, *bajada* terrain slopes gently up to the central portion of the Eagletail Mountains, and a former vehicle way heads west into the wilderness and circles south of Granite Mountain. After a hike of about 4 miles, it is also possible to reach the foot of 3,300-foot Eagletail Peak.

To reach the southern trailhead for the Ben Avery Trail and the western portions of the wilderness, drive west on the Arlington–Clanton Well Road. Following closely along the wilderness boundary, this high-clearance, 2WD road draws within 2 miles of Double Eagle Peak, in the southern end of the Eagletail Mountains. Beyond the range, Arlington–Clanton Well Road accesses a mostly level desert basin that spans the interior of the wilderness. This central section is not quite as spectacular as the Eagletail Mountains, but some old roads in the area offer suitable hiking routes, including the southern end of the Ben Avery Trail.

In the western section of the wilderness, Arlington–Clanton Well Road provides access to Cemetery Ridge, a low-profile ridgeline highlighted by 2,184-foot Nottbusch Butte. Cemetery Ridge is dotted with old mines and closed-off mine roads that may be used for hiking.

From Clanton Well, the 2WD Palomas–Harquahala Road heads north for nearly

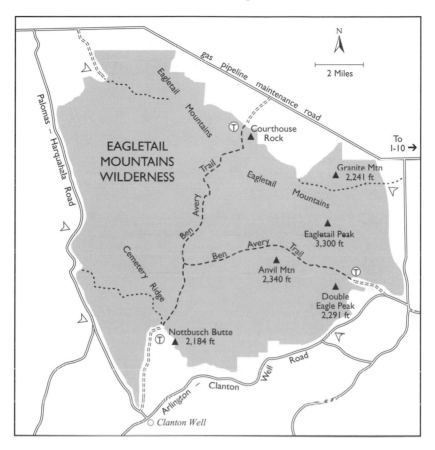

20 miles before reaching the above-mentioned gas pipeline. In so doing, it forms the wilderness area's western boundary. Here, as within the central portion of the wilderness, mostly flat terrain is the rule. But, if it's empty spaces and solitude you are looking for, then this portion of the wilderness fits the bill.

Cross-country hiking in this wilderness is an inherently risky undertaking. Water is not available, so bring all that you will need—a gallon or more per person per day. Watch for rattlesnakes in the warmer months.

Rock Climbing

Because of its relatively solid rock cliffs, walls, and spires of the Eagletail Mountains, this wilderness is a favored climbing destination for a handful of technical rock climbers. The two landmarks most visited by climbers are Courthouse Rock and Eagletail Peak. On both peaks a variety of routes are possible—from easy to difficult. From the summit of either of these prominent peaks, you will gain some wonderful views of verdant farmlands to the east and of empty desert basins to the west.

65 Big Horn Mountains Wilderness

Location: 11 miles NW of Tonopah
Size: 21,000 acres
Status: Wilderness area (1990)
Terrain: Desert mountains and basins
Elevation: 1,400 feet to 3,480 feet
Management: BLM (Phoenix Field Office)
Topographic maps: Big Horn Peak, Burnt Mountain, Little Horn Peak

Rugged Big Horn Peak rises sharply from the desert floor, and it is the most striking of a host of smaller mountains. It caps one of the more alluring mountain ranges in Arizona's western deserts. Up close, the range offers even greater rewards. Interesting flora and fauna, nice hiking terrain, and a handful of scenic summits are but three.

Seasons

Summertime temperatures are exceedingly high in this low-desert terrain, while winters often prove ideal. Late fall and early spring are also nice, with temperatures usually in the 70s and 80s. It is best to plan a visit between November and April.

Plants and Wildlife

Saguaro cactus grow in considerable numbers within Big Horn Mountains Wilderness, as do cholla and ocotillo. Washes are often thick with mesquite and ironwood, while the drier *bajadas* host scattered paloverde and creosote bush. Mule deer, coyotes, desert bighorn sheep, kit foxes, desert tortoises, and Gila monsters all reside in the wilderness. Among birds of prey that inhabit the wilderness are golden eagles and prairie falcons.

Geology

The dark complexion of Big Horn Peak reveals the volcanic origins of this range. Thought to have formed during the early Tertiary period, ranges such as this are plentiful in southwestern Arizona. Big Horn Peak itself is a central volcanic plug surrounded by layers of lighter-colored volcanic ash and breccia.

ACTIVITIES
Hiking

The best access points to the wilderness are found along a primitive road that separates the Big Horn Mountains Wilderness from Hummingbird Springs Wilderness to the northeast. To reach this unnamed road, drive 5 miles west from Tonopah on Indian School Road, a graveled route that parallels Interstate 10. Turn right onto a narrow dirt road

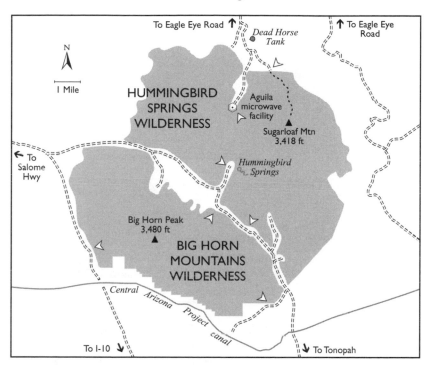

and follow it under Interstate 10 to an intersection just beyond the freeway. Turn left, then take a right soon afterward. The route crosses the Central Arizona Project canal before reaching a wire gate, about 11 miles from town. Just beyond here, wilderness boundary signs come into view on either side of the road. The terrain is mostly open and gently sloping here until it reaches the foot of the peaks, a mile or so to the west. It is possible to hike cross-country throughout much of this portion of the wilderness. If you feel more comfortable following an established route, you might try hiking an old road that heads west for a couple of miles from a windmill and corral, about 3 miles north of the wire gate.

The southern section of Big Horn Mountains Wilderness can be accessed by turning left on a 4WD road 1.2 miles north of the Central Arizona Project canal. This route follows a power transmission line that runs along the southern boundary of the wilderness. Within 2 miles, the road takes you through a wire gate, beyond which an open valley heads north into the wilderness.

Access to the western portion of the wilderness is difficult. Turning off of the Eagle Eye Road 4.5 miles north of where it crosses the Central Arizona Project canal, a high-clearance, 2WD road continues east for 3 miles to a fork in the road. Bear right and you will eventually reach the western boundary of the wilderness. By checking the topographic maps, you might find a cross-country route that goes up to the summit of Big Horn Peak.

An extremely rugged hike, the top of Big Horn is a destination reserved for expert hikers only. All cross-country hiking here can be a risky undertaking, as well. Use caution when doing so. Bring water, as none is available. Watch for rattlesnakes when hiking in the warmer times of the year.

66 Hummingbird Springs Wilderness

Location: 11 miles NW of Tonopah
Size: 31,200 acres
Status: Wilderness area (1990)
Terrain: Desert mountains
Elevation: 1,550 feet to 3,418 feet
Management: BLM (Phoenix Field Office)
Topographic maps: Hummingbird Spring, Big Horn Peak, Burnt Mountain, Little Horn Peak

Gentler and, in some respects, less dramatic than the neighboring Big Horn Mountains Wilderness, Hummingbird Springs Wilderness is often passed up by visitors to the area. Nevertheless, it does encompass a wide array of the desert terrain that surrounds 3,418-foot Sugarloaf Mountain. Add to this a variety of desert plants and wildlife, and you have a wilderness worth visiting.

Cholla cactus in the Hummingbird Springs Wilderness

Seasons

Because temperatures in this desert terrain often exceed 100 degrees, summer is a bad time to visit. November through April is ideal, though. Winter often brings periods of light rain, but temperatures are comfortable during the day.

Plants and Wildlife

As with Big Horn Mountains Wilderness, Hummingbird Springs Wilderness features many stands of saguaro cactus interspersed with cholla, ocotillo, and creosote bush. Washes provide suitable habitat for paloverde, mesquite, and ironwood trees. Mule deer, bighorn sheep, coyotes, kit foxes, and mountain lions live here, as do Gila monsters, desert tortoises, and a number of birds of prey.

Geology

Spanning the eastern portion of the Big Horn Mountains, this wilderness has features that are mostly volcanic in origin. Colorful Sugarloaf Mountain is composed of rhyolite, a rock that formed as lava and volcanic ash. Across the southern portion of the wilderness is a highly dissected *bajada,* which forms the northern end of the Tonopah Desert.

ACTIVITIES
Hiking

There are a number of possible access points to the wilderness. A good area to begin is along a high-clearance, 2WD road that separates this wilderness from Big Horn Mountains Wilderness to the west. To reach this route, drive 5 miles west from Tonopah on Indian School Road. Turn right on a small dirt track and continue beneath Interstate 10. Just beyond the highway, turn left, then right shortly afterward. Continuing north, this road crosses the Central Arizona Project canal before reaching the wilderness boundary 11 miles from town. This point is marked by a wire gate in the road. Beyond the gate, the road continues northwest for several miles before eventually reaching Eagle Eye Road. About 2 miles north of the gate, a cherry-stemmed road takes off to the right to access a spring located 2 miles beyond. From this point, it is possible to explore the relatively gentle *bajadas* of the southern part of the wilderness. About 5 miles from the gate a second cherry-stemmed road continues for a mile to the right, to reach the vicinity of the wilderness's namesake, Hummingbird Springs. The wilderness boundary precludes reaching the springs by vehicle, but you can hike the last 0.5 mile by following the closed-off portion of road. Another 4WD route that has since been closed to vehicles takes off to the north from the Hummingbird Springs area and climbs to the Aguila microwave facility, a couple miles to the north. The Aguila microwave facility can also be reached by driving a 2WD road that begins along Eagle Eye Road, south of the small town of Aguila. From the microwave facility, it is possible to access the higher ridges of the northern portion of the wilderness. Approximately 3 miles before reaching the microwave tower, a secondary 4WD road turns off to the left. It provides the best access to the top of Sugarloaf Mountain. It is a 2.5-mile walk mostly along an old road from where this road encounters Dead Horse Tank.

Cross-country hiking in this and other wilderness areas poses risks, so plan accordingly. Bring plenty of water, as springs in the area may not be suitable for drinking. Watch for rattlesnakes in the warmer times of the year.

67 Kofa Refuge Wilderness

Location: 50 miles N of Yuma
Size: 516,300 acres, plus 24,600-acre BLM New Water Mountains Wilderness
Status: Wilderness area (1990)
Terrain: Desert mountains and basins
Elevation: 700 feet to 4,877 feet
Management: USFWS and BLM (Yuma Field Office)
Topographic maps: Palm Canyon, Stone Cabin, Kofa Butte, Hoodoo Well, Arch Tank, Kofa Deep Well, Charlie Died Tank, Engesser Pass, Castle Dome Peak, Slumgullion Pass, Engesser Pass SW, Neversweat Ridge, Red Bluff Mountains NW, Salton Tanks, Livingston Hills, Livingston Hills NW, Owls Head, Cholla Tank, Crystal Hill, New Water Mountains, New Water Well, South of Quartzite

Spanning 665,400 acres of southwestern Arizona, the Kofa National Wildlife Refuge offers a stunning collection of rugged mountains and broad desert basins. The area's stark beauty and expansive terrain offer outstanding scenery at every turn. Because the refuge's two principal mountain ranges—the Castle Dome and Kofa Mountains—are characteristically rugged and relatively unspoiled, they make ideal habitat for desert bighorn sheep. A variety of other species of wildlife live here, as well. The 1990 Arizona Desert Wilderness Act set aside 516,300 acres of the refuge as wilderness. Also established was the 24,600-acre New Water Mountains Wilderness, which is adjacent to the refuge's northern boundary on BLM land. This chapter combines the two wilderness areas.

Seasons
Because Kofa National Wildlife Refuge is located in the most arid corner of the state, the best time of year to visit is between October and April. Summertime temperatures often top 110 degrees in July and August and hover around 100 degrees in June and September. During the winter, afternoon temperatures typically reach the 60s and 70s, and nighttime lows sometimes dip below freezing.

Plants and Wildlife
Among the more common desert plants that grow here are saguaro cactus, cholla, beavertail cactus, ocotillo, creosote bush, ironwood, and paloverde. In addition to these

species, there are also a few rare members of the plant kingdom to be found in this wilderness. Best known of these are California fan palm trees, which grow in a few isolated groves. These trees are either remnants from the last Ice Age or they grew from seeds that were carried to these locales in the digestive tracts of birds. In either case, these palms have found suitable habitat in a few well-shaded canyons of the Kofa

Palm Canyon is a popular destination in the Kofa Refuge Wilderness.

Mountain Range. Another unusual plant that grows in the refuge is the nolina plant, which is often mistaken for a young palm. Wildlife includes desert bighorn sheep, mule deer, coyotes, kit foxes, gray foxes, ring-tailed cats, and mountain lions. Among the 185 species of birds that have been sighted in the refuge are golden eagles, Gambel's quail, white-winged doves, mourning doves, and Gila woodpeckers.

Geology

Rising abruptly above expansive desert basins, the two principal mountain ranges within the refuge exhibit telltale signs of past volcanic activity. Much of the rock visible is dark rhyolite, but there are also examples of breccia. Breccia consists of smaller rocks and pebbles that were cemented together by lava and ash. A third mountain range—the New Water Mountains, which stretch across the northern tier of the refuge—is also volcanic in origin. Located in the northwestern corner of the refuge, Crystal Hill is a popular rockhounding area for noncommercial collectors.

History

Around the turn of the century, the King of Arizona Mine was established in the southern end of these mountains, after gold was discovered there in 1896. Taking their name from the acronym KOFA (for King of Arizona), the Kofa Mountains became the namesake for the refuge when it was established in 1939.

ACTIVITIES
Hiking

One short trail—the Palm Canyon Trail—enters Kofa Refuge Wilderness. To reach the trailhead, drive 63 miles north from Yuma (or 18 miles south from Quartzite) on US Highway 95 until you see signs for Palm Canyon. Turn east and drive 7 miles to the end of the graveled Palm Canyon Road. The trailhead lies at the foot of the Kofa Mountains. Although only 0.5-mile long, the Palm Canyon Trail is well worth the visit for its views of these impressive mountains. To reach the palms themselves, you will have to scramble up a steep and rocky side canyon. Beyond the established trail, it is possible to scramble up the main canyon for some distance to enjoy its rugged environment.

Aside from the Palm Canyon Trail, hikers are strictly on their own. Fortunately, the terrain is mostly open and easily explored, especially in the flat desert basins. The many 2WD and 4WD roads that crisscross the refuge offer access to endless hiking possibilities. One possible route follows the base of the Kofa Mountains from the Palm Canyon trailhead for as far as you like. Reached by the 22-mile King Road, the King of Arizona Mine is located on private land, but the surrounding area is of interest. King Road turns off US Highway 95 about 9 miles south of Palm Canyon Road. Heading northeast from the Palm Canyon access, a 4WD road leads into Queen Canyon to access the northwestern flank of the Kofa Mountains. A number of 4WD routes also access the Kofa Mountains from the north and east. It is best to check with the refuge manager in Yuma about the condition of these remote roads before setting out.

En route to the above-mentioned King of Arizona Mine, King Road passes through

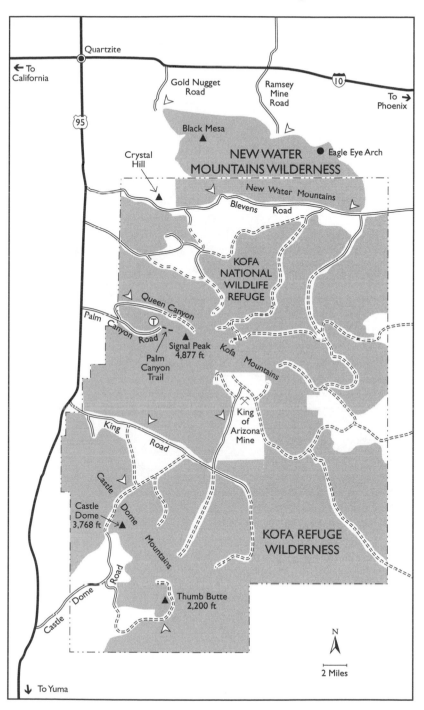

the northern end of the Castle Dome Mountains, which stretch across the southwestern portion of the refuge. From the road, it is possible to explore portions of the range to the north or south. The central and southern portions of the Castle Dome Mountains are accessed by turning east from US Highway 95 on Castle Dome Road. A 4WD spur of this road circles Thumb Butte to access a number of old mines, while the main road heads north toward the prominent Castle Dome Peak. Eventually, Castle Dome Road becomes a 4WD route as it crosses its namesake mountain range and connects with King Road to the north.

A third area of interest in Kofa National Wildlife Refuge is the New Water Mountains Range to the north. From the 2WD Blevens Road, which accesses Crystal Hill and continues eastward along the southern end of the range, it is possible to access wilderness lands to the north. Spanning an adjoining tract of BLM land, New Water Mountains Wilderness extends wilderness protection to much of the rest of the range as well. The best way to access this BLM-administered wilderness is to drive east from Quartzite on Interstate 10 to Gold Nugget Road. Two landmarks of interest in the New Water Mountains are Black Mesa, a 1,200-foot-high volcanic butte, and the Eagle Eye, an impressive natural arch. Like the Kofa and Castle Dome Mountains, the New Water Mountains are prime bighorn sheep habitat.

In addition to the above-mentioned roads and access points, several other 4WD roads extend into the refuge. Because these roads are cherry-stemmed from the wilderness, they are open to vehicles. To determine which route is right for you, study the topographic maps and check with refuge officials.

Use extreme caution when hiking cross-country in both these wildernesses. Watch for venomous creatures and be prepared for extremely hot conditions. Water is not generally available in the wilderness. Experts suggest bringing at least one gallon per person per day.

68   Muggins Mountains Wilderness

Location: 25 miles W of Yuma
Size: 7,640 acres
Status: Wilderness area (1990)
Terrain: Desert mountains and canyons
Elevation: 200 feet to 1,666 feet
Management: BLM (Yuma Field Office)
Topographic maps: Dome, Ligurta, Red Bluff Mountain West

Rising above the Dome Valley and the Gila River, the rocky and barren Muggins Mountains offer a stark backdrop to the patchwork of verdant farmlands below. Easily accessible, this wilderness offers hikers some interesting terrain for a day or overnight hike.

Rugged Muggins Peak as seen from Muggins Wash

Seasons

Because of the extreme heat that typifies this desert area, the best time to visit the Muggins Mountains is November through April. Winters here are warm and pleasant, compared with the cold, snowy conditions that may grip higher-elevation areas of the state.

Plants and Wildlife

Although it may seem that few plants could survive in the Muggins Mountains, there are, in fact, several species that have found a suitable habitat here. Saguaro cactus are scattered about, as are ocotillo, creosote bush, brittlebush, paloverde, ironwood, and smoketree. Among the creatures that call this wilderness home are mule deer, coyotes, desert bighorn sheep, and a variety of hawks.

Geology

Much of the Muggins Mountains consists of sand and gravel deposited by rivers and lakes that covered the area during the Miocene epoch. There is also evidence of volcanic

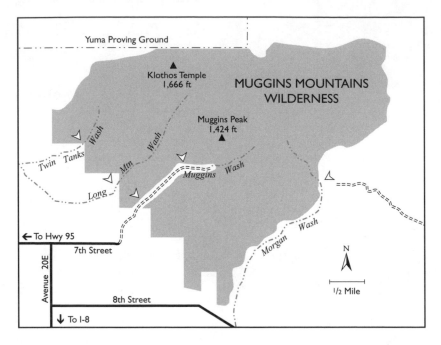

activity that occurred during the late Tertiary period. Some gold has been found here in the past, and there are still some small mining operations in the wilderness.

ACTIVITIES
Hiking

There are no hiking trails in Muggins Mountains Wilderness, but a cherry-stemmed road follows Muggins Wash for a couple of miles, providing access to the heart of the range. To reach this 4WD road, travel east from Yuma on Interstate 8 to the Dome Valley exit. Then continue east to Dome Valley Road. Turn north and continue to 7th Street. Turn east and drive past a refuse transfer station to the foot of the mountains. From here, Muggins Wash Road continues northeast across the foothills before dropping into the wash. Portions of this road cross private land. Along this road, a few washes branch off to the north toward Muggins Peak. The terrain is mostly open along these drainages and across most of the surrounding terrain.

Other washes that provide access to the range's interior include Twin Tanks, Long Mountain, and Morgan. While Morgan Wash can be reached by driving east on 9th Street for 6.5 miles, then 3.5 miles northwest along a jeep road, other access points can be reached only by driving more obscure 4WD routes. A check with the BLM office in Yuma will help you locate possible access routes to these areas.

Because hiking within Muggins Mountains Wilderness is all cross-country, be extremely careful when visiting the area. There is no water here, so bring plenty with you. Watch for rattlesnakes during most months of the year.

69 Trigo Mountains Wilderness

Location: 52 miles N of Yuma
Size: 30,300 acres
Status: Wilderness area (1990)
Terrain: Desert mountains and canyons
Elevation: 280 feet to 1,920 feet
Management: BLM (Yuma Field Office)
Topographic maps: Picacho, Picacho SW, Picacho NW, Cibola, Cibola SE, Hidden Valley

Trigo Mountains Wilderness encompasses a rugged collection of desert peaks and washes that stretch north-south, just east of the Colorado River. The wilderness area is bordered by the Yuma Proving Ground to the east and the Imperial Wildlife Refuge to the west. To say the least, it is isolated and somewhat difficult to reach. This means that hikers will find plenty of solitude among some interesting terrain.

Seasons

The Trigo Mountains are located in the hottest desert country in the state, so plan to visit this wilderness between November and March. October and April are also possibilities, if it is not unseasonably warm.

Feral burros in the Trigo Mountains Wilderness

Plants and Wildlife

Despite the apparent barrenness of the Trigo Mountains, a variety of plants grow here: widely scattered saguaro cactus, cholla, beavertail cactus, ocotillo, paloverde, creosote bush, and brittlebush. Some of the most noticeable residents are the feral burros. Every other year or so, the BLM rounds up a portion of them to control their numbers. Desert bighorn sheep inhabit the area, and predator species such as coyotes and mountain lions are also present.

Geology

Part of western Arizona's Basin and Range province, the Trigo Mountains resulted from fault blocking. Colorful rocks exposed in the ridges and summits are volcanic in origin. These include rhyolite, tuff, and basalt. Prospecting in the region has met with some success as deposits of gold, lead, zinc, chromium, and manganese have been found. Just outside the wilderness, the Red Cloud Mine—once a source of lead—has since been worked by a lone miner for its deposits of wulfenite, a lead compound that forms beautiful crystals.

ACTIVITIES
Hiking

There are no established trails in Trigo Mountains Wilderness, but the terrain is open and often dissected by easy-to-follow washes and game trails that frequently cross from one drainage to the next. The wilderness has three main points of access, all of which require a 4WD vehicle. From US Highway 95, turn west at the Martinez Lake turnoff and drive 10 miles. Make a right-hand turn just before the Martinez Lake resort. Continue 2.5 miles to a second fork in the road, keep right and drive through the Imperial National Wildlife Refuge and across its northern boundary. From this point, drive to the Red Cloud Mine, which is 13 miles north of Martinez Lake. To reach the mine, you will need a high-clearance, 2WD vehicle. Beyond the mine, however, the road becomes a 4WD route. The southern boundary of the wilderness runs along Red Cloud Wash, the

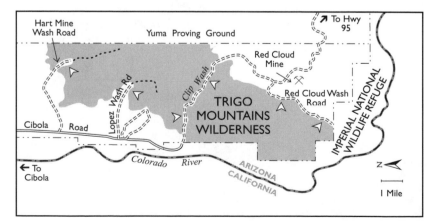

The Trigo Mountains Wilderness

length of which is driveable by way of its sandy bottom. To access Red Cloud Wash, bear left about 0.25 mile past the Red Cloud Mine, then left again in another 0.7 mile. From Red Cloud Wash Road, it is possible to hike west into Trigo Mountains Wilderness along wash bottoms and small canyon corridors.

In the middle section of the wilderness a cherry-stemmed road follows Clip Wash, effectively dividing the wilderness in half. To reach this route, continue 0.25 mile past the Red Cloud Mine, turn left and then drive 0.7 mile to where the road splits. Turn right here and follow the wash north for about 3 miles before reaching a low divide. The route then drops into the head of Clip Wash, which it follows for the next 6 miles. Most of this portion of the drive is bounded on both sides by the wilderness, which may be accessed by hiking up side drainages, or along gentler ridges. Keep in mind that the 4WD route through Clip Wash is quite rugged.

A third possibility is to drive 40 miles of the graveled Cibola Road to the small enclave of Cibola and the Cibola National Wildlife Refuge. From there, continue nearly 3 miles south on Cibola Road to where it intersects the 4WD Hart Mine Wash Road. Turn left and continue 3 miles to reach the northern boundary of the wilderness. Hart Mine Wash Road is cherry-stemmed within the wilderness for another mile. Beyond the wilderness boundary, the road continues south for 3 miles. Closed to vehicles, this portion of the road offers hikers a handy route into the heart of the wilderness area's northern portion. A second 4WD route to access this portion of the wilderness and provide hikers with several miles of a former vehicle way is Lopez Wash Road. This route turns off Cibola Road about 6 miles south of Cibola. It then continues east for 3 miles before reaching the wilderness boundary. Now closed to vehicles beyond the wilderness boundary, a portion of this route follows the rugged and scenic Lopez Wash for several miles to where it accesses some abandoned mines. Beyond Lopez Wash Road, Cibola Road eventually connects with the western end of the above-mentioned Clip Wash

Road. Cibola Road turns west from US Highway 95 about 21 miles south of Quartzite.

Use extreme caution when hiking cross-country in this and all other desert wilderness areas. There is no water available in Trigo Mountains Wilderness, so pack plenty—at least a gallon per person per day. Dress appropriately for the desert climate. Watch for rattlesnakes when hiking during the warmer months.

70 Imperial Refuge Wilderness

Location: 40 miles N of Yuma
Size: 9,220 acres
Status: Wilderness area (1990)
Terrain: River bottom and desert foothills
Elevation: 200 feet to 1,085 feet
Management: USFWS (Imperial NWR)
Topographic maps: Red Hill SW, Picacho, Picacho SW, Picacho NW

The Imperial National Wildlife Refuge encompasses two distinctly different environments. Along the banks of the Colorado River are marshes, shallow lakes, sloughs, and other wetland areas that are frequented by a variety of waterfowl species. Standing in stark contrast are extremely arid desert lands, which begin only a few meters away. Between these two ecosystems, it is possible to enjoy a great variety of flora and fauna. Of the refuge's 25,125 acres, 9,220 acres were set aside as wilderness in 1990. The end result was that it extended wilderness status to lands that fall between the BLM's Trigo Mountains Wilderness and the floodplain of the Colorado River.

Seasons

Winter is the best time to visit Imperial Refuge Wilderness, especially if you want to avoid the heat and spot migrating ducks, geese, and other waterfowl. Spring and fall are good times to find the greatest variety of songbirds, however, and March is usually the best month of the year to enjoy desert wildflowers.

Plants and Wildlife

Characteristic of the riparian plant community that grows along the Colorado River, lake shores, and in marshlands are various grasses, cattails, cottonwoods, and other water-loving plants. In the arid reaches of the refuge, you will find paloverde, ironwood, ocotillo, beavertail cactus, and a few lone saguaros. Visiting waterfowl species include Canada geese, a variety of ducks, grebes, great blue herons, egrets, white-faced ibis, and loons. Hawks, owls, quail, and doves are found within the refuge's desert environs. In all, more than 250 species of birds have been spotted here. Wildlife includes mule deer, desert bighorn sheep, feral burros, feral horses, jackrabbits, mountain lions, coyotes, and many rodents.

Geology

Sloughs, lakes, and old river channels that have been cut off from the main river have all resulted from the ever-changing course of the Colorado River. The surrounding desert landscape has been shaped by volcanic eruptions, which took place here some 23 to 30 million years ago. These fiery origins have resulted in dark basaltic rock, along with other, often colorful volcanics.

ACTIVITIES
Hiking

The easiest access point for Imperial Refuge Wilderness is found along its lower east end, near Clear Lake. No trails enter the wilderness from this point, but the desert foothill terrain is sparsely vegetated and open to cross-country hiking. To reach this section of the refuge, drive north from Yuma on US Highway 95 to Martinez Lake Road. Turn west and drive 10 miles, then make a right turn onto a gravel road. Following the signs for the refuge, continue 2.5 miles to a fork in the road. A left turn leads less than a mile to the refuge headquarters, while a right turn continues 4.5 miles through the refuge, before reaching BLM land. The wilderness area spreads west from the last 0.5 mile of the refuge road.

A second, more difficult-to-reach access point is found south of the small enclave of Cibola, which is located along the Colorado River in the Cibola National Wildlife

The Colorado River flows through the Imperial National Wildlife Refuge.

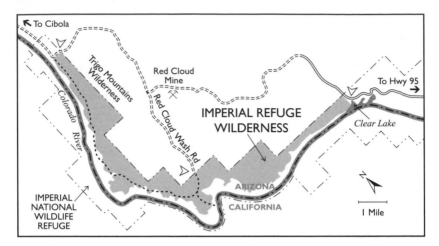

Refuge. To reach this point, turn off US Highway 95 about 21 miles south of Quartzite and drive west on Cibola Road, a good gravel road. About 40 miles from US Highway 95, Cibola Road reaches Cibola. It then continues south along the Colorado River to reach Imperial Refuge Wilderness in about 10 miles. Gated and closed to vehicles at the refuge boundary, this old road continues south for another 10 miles into the wilderness, paralleling the Colorado River to Red Cloud Wash Road (see the Trigo Mountains Wilderness section). This route might make a nice hiking route, although portions are overgrown. Red Cloud Wash Road forms the southeastern boundary of Trigo Mountains Wilderness and is open to 4WD vehicles from the Red Cloud Mine area south to the Imperial National Wildlife Refuge boundary.

Keep in mind that camping is not permitted within the refuge. Although it is possible to draw water from the Colorado River, it is best to bring all the water you will need, since river water must be treated before drinking. Watch for rattlesnakes and other venomous creatures, and be prepared for hot, dry conditions during much of the year.

River Running

Although the river itself is not included within this wilderness, canoeists are able to enjoy a nice float through the refuge if they don't mind sharing the waterway with powerboats. A 76-mile route—from Interstate 10 near Blythe, California, to Imperial Dam—offers boaters a unique look at the desert waterway. Thirty miles of this route runs through the refuge. Because camping is not permitted within the refuge, you will have to camp in Picacho State Recreation Area in California. Camping is also prohibited on both banks for a 10-mile stretch north of Picacho State Recreation Area, and for 9 river miles below the recreation area. A good description of the float is found in "A Boating Trail Guide to the Colorado River," a brochure available free from the BLM or refuge headquarters. The best time of year to float the lower Colorado is between late fall and early spring, when motorboats are not as numerous.

71 Harquahala Mountains Wilderness

Location: 34 miles W of Wickenburg
Size: 22,880 acres
Status: Wilderness area (1990)
Terrain: Desert mountains
Elevation: 2,200 feet to 5,691 feet
Management: BLM (Phoenix Field Office)
Topographic maps: Harquahala Mountain, Tiger Well, Socorro Peak

At 5,691 feet, Harquahala Mountain is the highest point in southwestern Arizona. Rising from the surrounding desert basins, the mountain's distinctive shape is clearly visible throughout the area. In the early part of this century, the Smithsonian Institution built an astrophysical observatory on the summit. Today, what remains of the facility is listed on the National Register of Historic Places and lies just outside the wilderness.

Seasons

The Harquahala Mountains are best visited between the months of October and April. Summer temperatures may top 100 degrees, making travel not only uncomfortable but possibly dangerous as well. Winters can bring pleasant daytime temperatures although snow can accumulate on the summit.

Plants and Wildlife

Nice stands of saguaro cactus, along with large patches of cholla, ocotillo, and creosote bush are common in this wilderness. Barrel cactus grow along many rocky ridges. A small stand of juniper is found in the upper reaches of Sunset Canyon and a well-established chaparral community prospers in the highest reaches of the range. The Harquahala Mountains support many species of wildlife, including mule deer, desert bighorn sheep, a number of raptors, desert tortoises, and Gila monsters. Springs and riparian areas in the range add to the diversity of wildlife.

Geology

Trending northeast–southwest, the Harquahala Mountains run against the grain of most other ranges in Arizona's Basin and Range province. The core material of the range is mostly Precambrian gneiss, schist, and granite. Rich in minerals, the Harquahala Range includes more than a thousand mining claims. Although these are nearly all abandoned, past activity has produced gold, silver, tungsten, gypsum, barium, copper, and marble.

History

Built in 1920, the Smithsonian Astrophysical Observatory was established to study the effect of sun activity on the earth's climate. Although the observatory had no telescopes,

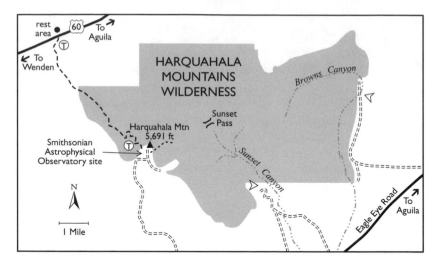

it was equipped with a variety of other scientific devices. For five years, the mountaintop was home to scientists and workers, then, in 1925, the site was abandoned in favor of a location in California. While the Harquahala Mountain site was originally reached by a rugged 4-mile mule trail, it is now accessible by a 10.5-mile 4WD road.

ACTIVITIES
Hiking

Thanks to the 4WD Harquahala Peak Backcountry Byway (do not drive when wet or icy), which climbs 10.5 miles to the summit of Harquahala Mountain, the highest reaches of the range are quite accessible. Although the 5,691-foot summit lies just outside the boundary, the wilderness itself stretches east from the summit across the crest of the range. From the observatory, it is possible to follow an old jeep road (now closed to vehicles) northeast for about a mile toward Sunset Pass.

The historic Harquahala Peak Pack Trail drops from the summit to reach the north-western corner of the wilderness. The trailhead for this route is accessed by driving 2.2 miles south from US Highway 60 on a 4WD road that turns off 13.6 miles south-west of Aguila. Having been recently maintained, this route is in good shape along its 5- to 6-mile length.

Harquahala Mountains Wilderness also includes many natural routes as well. Most of these begin along the southern section at the foot of the range. A good place to ex-plore is Browns Canyon, in the eastern portion of the wilderness. To reach this drain-age, drive 25 miles west from Wickenburg on US Highway 60 to the small town of Aguila. Turn south on Eagle Eye Road (paved for most of its length) and continue 9.8 miles, then make a right turn onto what becomes a 4WD road. Within 3 miles the route turns north, where it runs adjacent to the wilderness boundary. After 4 miles, the road crosses a wash and continues for nearly another mile to some old mines. From this road, it is possible to follow Browns Canyon north into the interior of the range.

Continuing for another 3 miles or so, this drainage accesses a scenic inner basin, complete with riparian areas lined with cottonwood and areas of large granite boulders.

Another access point is found in Sunset Canyon, which drains the south-central portion of the wilderness. To reach this canyon, drive 15.6 miles south and west from Aguila on Eagle Eye Road, then make a right turn. This high-clearance, 2WD road travels north for a little more than 3 miles before it begins to climb steeply up a mountainside. Although the last 0.5 mile of the road is too rutted and narrow for 4WD vehicles, you can walk up it to the ridgeline above. The vegetation is somewhat open here, and it is possible to pick your way to even higher terrain to the north. Another possible hiking route follows nearby Sunset Canyon, which is overgrown in places.

The rugged and isolated terrain in Harquahala Mountains Wilderness makes cross-country hiking a risky venture. Only experienced hikers should attempt it. It is best to bring water, as natural sources of drinking water are scarce. Watch for snakes in the warmer months, and be wary of lightning strikes in the higher terrain.

72 Harcuvar Mountains Wilderness

Location: 45 miles W of Wickenburg
Size: 25,050 acres
Status: Wilderness area (1990)
Terrain: Desert mountains and canyons
Elevation: 2,400 feet to 5,135 feet
Management: BLM (Phoenix Field Office)
Topographic maps: Cunningham Pass, E.C.P. Peak, Webber Canyon, Alamo Dam SE

Rising more than 3,000 feet above the surrounding desert basins, the Harcuvar Mountains are a gem of a range for desert hiking enthusiasts. Canyons dissect most portions of these mountains, and pristine plant communities grow at all elevations. A few old trails, combined with some natural corridors, make for a number of hiking route possibilities. The wilderness spans 10 miles of the Harcuvar Mountain Range.

Seasons

Because summers are too hot for comfortable and safe hiking, the best time to visit this wilderness is between October and April. Winters usually see temperatures in the upper 60s, while in autumn and spring the mercury may approach the 90-degree mark.

Plants and Wildlife

Growing among the *bajadas* that slope gently away from the range on either side are saguaro cactus, cholla, pricklypear cactus, ocotillo, and brittlebush. A 3,500-acre "island" of chaparral habitat has also been identified at the highest reaches of the wilderness. Among the species of wildlife that inhabit the Harcuvar Mountains are mule deer, desert bighorn sheep, mountain lions, and, of course, coyotes. A small population of desert tortoises live in the low desert. The isolated chaparral along the crest of the range is home to Gilbert's skinks and rosy boas.

Geology

Like the nearby Harquahala Mountains, the Harcuvars trend southwest–northeast, as opposed to the more usual northwest–southeast axis found elsewhere in the Basin and Range province of Arizona. Further, they have a metamorphic core, rather than a volcanic one. Within the wilderness, a number of mines at one time produced copper, gold, and silver, among other minerals.

Saguaro cactus in the Harcuvar Mountains

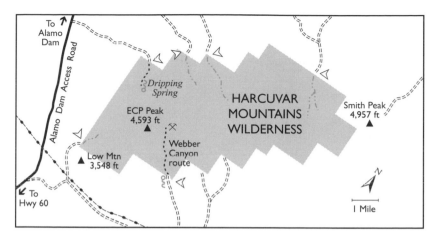

ACTIVITIES
Hiking

Thanks to an old mining road, there is a nice route into the upper reaches of Webber Canyon on the southern face of the range. To find this route, drive 24 miles from Wickenburg to the town of Aguila on US Highway 60. Continue another 13 miles, then make a right turn. After following this 2WD route for 2.9 miles, turn left and drive another mile to the power transmission line. Turn left again and drive 0.6 mile, then make another right turn. Follow this 4WD route 4.5 miles until it reaches the wilderness boundary. The trailhead is also the site of a spring, which has been developed for wildlife use. From this point, an abandoned jeep track continues up Webber Canyon for approximately 3 miles to the abandoned Webber Mine. Closed to vehicles, this old road makes for a nice hiking route. Beyond the mine, the terrain is steep, but it is possible to bushwhack about 0.5 mile to the ridge top. You can access both 4,593-foot E.C.P. Peak (to the southwest) and 4,957-foot Smith Peak (to the northeast) from here. Because it is the site of several translator towers, Smith Peak is also accessible by a 4WD route and is just east of the wilderness boundary.

Another point of entry is found in the southwestern corner of the range, near Low Mountain. From US Highway 60, turn north on Alamo Dam Access Road and drive about 7 miles to where the power transmission line crosses the road. Follow the powerline road for about 1.5 miles to where a 4WD route turns to the north. This route continues for a little more than a mile to the wilderness boundary. A small canyon may then be followed for a mile or so before the terrain becomes steeper.

Other access possibilities are found on the north side of the range. Drive about 16 miles north from US Highway 60 on Alamo Dam Access Road to a dirt road that takes off to the east. Turn here and drive about 3 miles along a high-clearance, 2WD road to the wilderness boundary. An abandoned portion of this road continues a mile farther to Dripping Spring. About 18 miles north of US Highway 60, a second high-clearance, 2WD road takes off to the east where it reaches three 4WD routes, each of which access a different canyon. With topographic maps in hand, it is possible to explore these natural hiking routes at length.

Cross-country hiking in wilderness areas can be hazardous. Use caution. Some springs are found in the area, but it is best to bring your own water. Watch for rattlesnakes when hiking during the warmer times of the year. Lightning may pose a threat in the exposed, higher reaches of the range.

73 Hells Canyon Wilderness

Location: 25 miles NW of Phoenix
Size: 9,311 acres
Status: Wilderness area (1990)
Terrain: Desert mountains and canyons
Elevation: 1,850 feet to 3,381 feet
Management: BLM (Phoenix Field Office)
Topographic maps: Garfias Mountain, Governors Peak

Although small, Hells Canyon Wilderness offers hikers highly scenic desert canyons, ridges, and peaks in which to explore. Set in the rugged and geologically interesting Hieroglyphic Mountains, this wilderness supports many fascinating desert plants and animals. Because of its close proximity to Phoenix, the wilderness receives a fair amount of use but there is still plenty of opportunity to escape the crowds.

Seasons

The low elevation of this wilderness makes for searing summers that are usually too hot for hiking. Late fall and spring are normally the best times of year to visit, while winter is also pleasant. Spring is the best time to witness the prodigious displays of wildflowers—early to late March for annuals and April to May for blooming succulents, such as saguaro cactus.

Plants and Wildlife

Featuring flora typical of the Lower Sonoran Desert ecosystem, Hells Canyon Wilderness is characterized by stands of saguaro cactus, cholla, barrel cactus, ocotillo, paloverde, creosote bush, some desert grasses, and even juniper. Wildlife of the area includes mule deer, javelinas, mountain lions, coyotes, bobcats, jackrabbits, and desert tortoises. Feral burros also frequent the area.

Geology

Most of Hells Canyon Wilderness features volcanic rock that dates back to the Cretaceous and Tertiary periods; however, outcrops of granite and schist in the Governors Peak area hint at the underlying Precambrian core of the Hieroglyphic Mountain Range.

Sunset in the Hells Canyon Wilderness

Erosion by wind and water has had a pronounced effect on the range, with water cutting deep canyons and general weathering shaping sheer cliffs and rugged summits.

ACTIVITIES
Hiking

The BLM has inventoried a number of trails and natural corridors within Hells Canyon Wilderness. Originally established by hunters, horse packers, miners, and other wilderness travelers, these trails may be faint or nonexistent in places. Nevertheless, they offer hikers a starting point for treks into the wilderness. The most easily accessible of these trails are the Spring Valley and Hermit Trails, which start along Castle Creek, a stream that borders the wilderness to the northeast. To reach this access point, drive north from Phoenix on Interstate 17 to the Carefree Highway (exit 223), then head west to Arizona Highway 74, turn right, and drive to the turnoff for Lake Pleasant. From Highway 74, drive 5.5 miles north to a stop sign. Turn left and drive another 4.9 miles along Castle Hot Springs Road. These unmarked trails begin at the

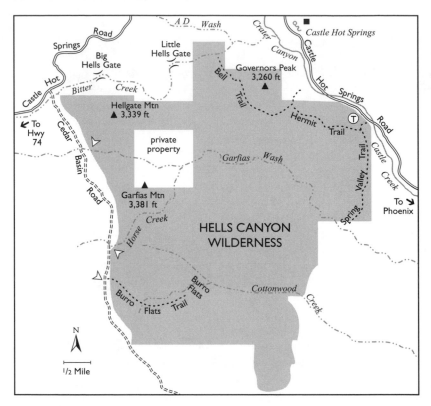

mouth of a small, narrow wash that opens up on the south side of Castle Creek. Of these two routes, the Spring Valley Trail is easiest to find. After climbing up a small hill to the left of the wash, it heads south for nearly 2 miles before reaching Garfias Wash. The second route, the Hermit Trail, is very hard to find, as it follows the small wash for a little way before continuing west toward Governors Peak. It eventually drops to private land along Castle Creek. The Bell Trail continues northwest past Governors Peak to eventually reach Bitter Creek.

Nearly 13 miles from Arizona Highway 74, Castle Hot Springs Road reaches its namesake, an old resort that is now closed to the public. Above this point, the creek continues up impressive Crater Canyon for a way. Unfortunately, this canyon is located on private land, making legal access a problem. Upstream, Crater Canyon eventually splits into the Bitter Creek and A.D. Wash drainages. Bitter Creek then crosses the northernmost portion of the wilderness, before passing through Little Hells Gate (just outside the wilderness boundary) and Big Hells Gate, about 2 miles beyond. Bitter Creek eventually crosses Castle Hot Springs Road about 7 miles beyond Castle Hot Springs. Although outside the wilderness, hikes to both Big Hells Gate and Little Hells Gate are rewarding, as both narrow passages are quite spectacular.

Just beyond the point where Castle Hot Springs Road crosses Bitter Creek, hikers can access the 4WD Cedar Basin Road. Beginning here, the road drops south along the western boundary of the wilderness and offers additional entry points for hiking routes within the wilderness. The first of these begins where the Cedar Basin Road crosses the above-mentioned Garfias Wash, about 2 miles south of Castle Hot Springs Road. Traversing the wilderness from west to east, Garfias Wash offers a wonderful natural corridor through the wilderness. The premier attraction is Hells Canyon itself, which is approximately 2.5 miles in from Cedar Basin Road. Narrow and scenic, Hells Canyon features riparian growth that has found a home beside springs along the wash. If you have access to a shuttle, lengthier hikes within the wilderness are also possible. From Cedar Basin Road, one route might take you down Garfias Wash for about 7 miles, then up the above-mentioned Spring Valley Trail to Castle Hot Springs Road. Alternatively, you could follow Garfias Wash to Hells Canyon, where Horse Creek branches off to the south. It is then possible to follow Horse Creek upstream for a few miles to where it crosses Cedar Basin Road. The Horse Creek drainage crosses Cedar Basin Road approximately 2 miles south of the Garfias Wash entry point. Keep in mind that a portion of Garfias Wash and the lower portion of Horse Creek fall within a section of private land. While this parcel is not signed or fenced, hikers may want to contact the landowner first.

An additional access point, about a mile south of Horse Creek along Cedar Basin Road, is the Burro Flats Trail. It heads into the wilderness for a few miles before reaching Burro Flats—a scenic interior basin surrounded by striking desert peaks. Much of the Burro Flats Trail follows an old road that has since been closed to vehicles.

Although water may be found in many places, you must treat it before drinking. It is best to pack in all you will need. Don't hike during the daytime heat in summer and early fall, and watch for rattlesnakes during these times. While most of the above-mentioned hikes follow washes or trails with easy grades, the surrounding summits are precipitous. Use extreme caution when attempting such excursions.

74 Hassayampa River Canyon Wilderness

Location: 20 miles N of Wickenburg
Size: 11,840 acres
Status: Wilderness area (1990)
Terrain: Desert mountains and river canyon
Elevation: 2,600 feet to 4,500 feet
Management: BLM (Phoenix Field Office)
Topographic maps: Morgan Butte, Sam Powell Peak, Wagoneer, Yarnell

As the name suggests, the primary feature of this wilderness area is a 14-mile stretch of the Hassayampa River Canyon, which cuts across the eastern, central, and southern portions of the wilderness. Although not perennial, the Hassayampa River flows

The Hassayampa River

frequently enough to support a prodigious riparian ecosystem. Like riparian areas throughout the state, the Hassayampa is a great birding spot.

Seasons
It is typically too hot for summertime visits in this low-elevation terrain, although the river (if it is flowing) allows for periodic cooling off. Late autumn is ideal, as is spring. Winters offer pleasant daytime temperatures, but stream crossings may prove a bit chilly.

Plants and Wildlife
Scattered along the river bottom are water-loving species such as cottonwood and willow. The surrounding desert hills are thick with catclaw, paloverde, saguaro cactus, cholla, and other succulents. In at least one location, a small cluster of Arizona cypress

is found. The area is home to deer, javelinas, coyotes, bobcats, mountain lions, jack-rabbits, desert tortoises, and Gila monsters. Birders will delight in spotting a variety of birds of prey here, including zone-tailed hawks, golden eagles, and peregrine falcons.

Geology

The Hassayampa River Canyon cuts deeply into the Weaver Mountains, which consist mostly of Precambrian granite, gneiss, and schist, with volcanic rock as well. A century of mining for gold and other metals, a few miles south of the wilderness, has left behind numerous old mineshafts, shacks, mining structures, and the abandoned town site of Constellation. Stream erosion along the Hassayampa River and its tributaries has resulted in a deep and meandering canyon system.

ACTIVITIES
Hiking

Access to Hassayampa River Canyon Wilderness requires a 4WD vehicle. From Wickenburg, drive north on Constellation Road. Keep driving for about 3 miles until you reach a fork in the road. Keep right and in another 5.5 miles continue straight at a second road junction. This route soon drops into a wash bottom, which the road follows upstream for 0.25 mile, before climbing out the north side. For the next 5 miles or so, the road climbs in and out of some rugged drainages, passing old mining sites along the way. Nearly 13 miles from town, a third split in the road is reached along a ridge top. Keep right and drop into Obrien Gulch. Follow it into Amazon Gulch. There is a signed trailhead, approximately 16 miles from Wickenburg. From a small parking area at the trailhead, the hiking route continues down the Amazon Gulch wash bottom for 0.25 mile before reaching the Hassayampa River. Because the portion of the route along Amazon Wash falls within a private ranch, the utmost respect for private property should be observed. It is best, in fact, to first check with the landowners, as they like to keep track of hikers in the area. They are very agreeable to allowing access to the wilderness through their land.

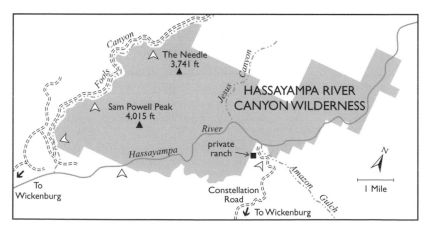

Upon reaching the river, it is possible to follow the Hassayampa River upstream or down for several miles. The going is very easy along the riverbed, but plan on making periodic stream crossings. Beyond the sinuous confines of the canyon bottom, travel is severely restricted by thick desert brush. A number of side canyons branch off the Hassayampa, offering still other hiking routes. One of these is the highly scenic Jesus Canyon, which branches north of the main river, about 2 miles downstream from the trailhead.

A second, but even more difficult, access point for Hassayampa River Canyon Wilderness is found along the western boundary. Here, a 4WD road follows the bottom of Fools Canyon for several miles. Check topographic maps for the best approach to Fools Canyon. There are rugged cross-country approaches to two high points in the western portion of the wilderness: The Needle (3,741 feet) and Sam Powell Peak (4,015 feet).

While the river bottom offers an easy and relatively safe travel corridor, a visit to other portions of the wilderness entails rigorous cross-country travel. Use caution. Watch for flash floods after heavy rains and for rattlesnakes during the warmer months. Additionally, water taken from the river should be treated before drinking.

75 Tres Alamos Wilderness

Location: 30 miles NW of Wickenburg
Size: 8,300 acres
Status: Wilderness area (1990)
Terrain: Desert mountains and plains
Elevation: 2,300 feet to 4,293 feet
Management: BLM (Kingman Field Office)
Topographic maps: Date Creek Ranch NW, Malpais Mesa SW

Although small when compared to the nearby Arrastra Wilderness, Tres Alamos Wilderness encompasses an interesting collection of mountains. At the heart of this area are Sawyer Peak and the Tres Alamos. These closely clustered summits are rugged and quite scenic. Falling away on all sides are expansive *bajadas* (alluvial fans) that are open and suitable to hiking. Separated from the eastern end of Arrastra Mountain Wilderness by a 4WD road, Tres Alamos Wilderness acts as an extension of that wilderness.

Seasons

Because of the low elevation, Tres Alamos Wilderness can be very hot in summer. Late fall is often a nice time to hike here, as is spring. Winters bring cool nights but pleasant daytime temperatures. Wildflowers are often quite spectacular in early spring, especially if there has been a wet winter.

A Joshua tree in the Tres Alamos Wilderness

Plants and Wildlife

Tres Alamos Wilderness is characterized by a variety of plant species endemic to both the Mojave and Sonoran Deserts. While creosote bush and paloverde grow throughout, you are treated here to the sight of saguaro cactus growing alongside Joshua trees. Acacia and mesquite trees line washes. Wildlife includes mule deer, coyotes, kit foxes, mountain lions, jackrabbits, Gila monsters, and desert tortoises.

Geology

The colorful peaks that form the centerpiece of Tres Alamos Wilderness display the telltale signs of past volcanic activity. This wilderness encompasses the southern section of the Black Mountains, a Basin and Range mountain chain that trends northwest–southeast. Gently sloping *bajadas,* formed from material eroding from the mountains, radiate into the desert. Date Creek, a periodically flowing stream, has carved a 200-foot-deep canyon, which now forms the wilderness area's southeastern boundary.

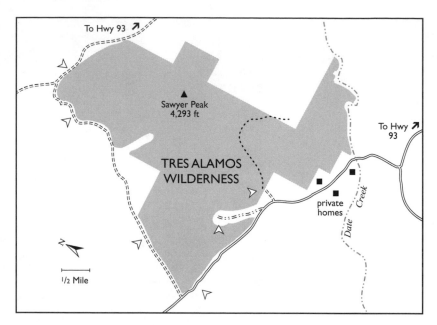

ACTIVITIES
Hiking

One old road penetrates the southern half of the wilderness, while much of the rest of the area is open to cross-country hiking. To reach the southern boundary, drive 21 miles northwest of Wickenburg on US Highway 93 to the unsigned turnoff for Alamo Lake Road. Follow this high-clearance route west for 6 miles until you reach a fork in the road. Keep right and drive 3.5 miles until the route splits a second time. Turn right again and drop into the Date Creek drainage, where a number of private homes are found. Continue across the wash bottom, then climb out the far side. A little more than 3 miles after the second right turn, the road intersects an old road that heads north. Follow this for 0.3 mile to the signed wilderness boundary. Continuing into the wilderness for another 2 miles, this former vehicle way offers a convenient hiking route to the top of a ridge that overlooks much of the southern end of the wilderness. Beyond this road, the *bajada* is open and easy to hike. The high point of the wilderness, 4,293-foot Sawyer Peak, rises north of this point.

Beyond the above-mentioned access point, the road continues along the southern boundary of the wilderness for 2.5 miles to where a 4WD road turns north. This route forms most of the western boundary of the wilderness. All along these two roads, it is possible to hike cross-country into the western side of Tres Alamos Wilderness, an area of mostly open terrain.

The northern boundary of the wilderness is also bordered by a 4WD road that turns off US Highway 93 a mile north of a highway rest stop. Drive about 6 miles west to reach the wilderness boundary. From here, it is possible to hike south into the wilderness, along washes that drop off the north slope of the Tres Alamos peaks, the highest of which is Sawyer Peak.

Cross-country hiking in this wilderness requires caution. Bring plenty of water, as none is available within the wilderness. Watch for snakes during the warmer months.

76 Arrastra Mountain Wilderness

Location: 45 miles NW of Wickenburg
Size: 129,800 acres
Status: Wilderness area (1990)
Terrain: Desert mountains and river canyons
Elevation: 1,200 feet to 4,807 feet
Management: BLM (Kingman Field Office)
Topographic maps: Arrastra Mountain, Arrastra Mountain NE, Arrastra Mountain SE, Malpais Mesa SW, Palmerita Ranch, Signal Mountain

The largest of the wilderness areas in Arizona managed by the BLM, Arrastra Mountain features a variety of desert terrain—from imposing peaks to rugged canyons and broad riverbeds. Encompassing portions of the Poachie Mountain Range along its northern boundary and the Artillery Mountains in its southwestern corner, it also contains beautiful riparian areas, which form a ribbon of green within the canyons. Several miles of the free-flowing Big Sandy and Santa Maria Rivers offer convenient hiking avenues. Volcanic plugs jut skyward at intervals, adding considerable interest to the topography.

Seasons
Summers are quite hot in Arrastra Mountain Wilderness. Spring is a nice time for visiting, although seasonal rains upstream may present brief periods of high runoff in the Big Sandy and Santa Maria Rivers. Late autumn is pleasant, and winter, while bringing cold nighttime temperatures, usually provides comfortable daytime highs.

Plants and Wildlife
In lower areas, you will find saguaro cactus, cholla, barrel cactus, ocotillo, yucca, paloverde, and other Sonoran Desert plants. Also growing here are several species commonly found in the Mojave Desert, including the Joshua tree. Higher up, chaparral and juniper forests become more common. Particularly eye-catching are the verdant riparian corridors, which support communities of willow, cottonwood, Arizona walnut, and Arizona sycamore. Wildlife includes mule deer, coyotes, bobcats, mountain lions, a variety of rodents, jackrabbits, and desert cottontails. The wilderness is also

home to the endangered desert tortoise, which lives at lower elevations. A variety of birds have been spotted here, as well. These include bald eagles, peregrine falcons, osprey, prairie falcons, snowy egrets, and great blue herons.

Geology

While the core of the Poachie Mountain Range includes Precambrian gneiss and granite, there is abundant evidence of past volcanic activity throughout the wilderness. These include old lava flows that manifest in dark mesa tops and some striking volcanic plugs. The best known of these is 3,213-foot-high Artillery Peak, which rises in the southwestern corner of the wilderness. Along the Big Sandy River rise bluffs of siltstone and other sedimentary rocks.

ACTIVITIES
Hiking

No trails enter Arrastra Mountain Wilderness, but a variety of natural hiking corridors may be found in the numerous washes and canyon bottoms. What makes visiting this wilderness difficult is that its access points are remote, with most requiring a 4WD vehicle.

Although roughly paralleling US Highway 93, sections of the northern boundary of the wilderness are hard to reach because few roads are suitable for even 4WD vehicles. One possible approach follows an old road for 4 miles, starting at US Highway 93, across from the turnoff to Bagdad. While this road is sometimes impassable, even to 4WD vehicles, you could walk it to reach the scenic Peoples Canyon area. Once inside the drainage, it is then possible to follow the stream for a few miles up- or downstream. Portions of this route cross private lands. Be sure to get permission before crossing.

A second approach to the wilderness area's northern boundary is found along 17 Mile Road, which turns off US Highway 93. This narrow but well-maintained road begins about 3.5 miles southeast from where the highway crosses Burro Creek. In approximately 6 miles, 17 Mile Road reaches the wilderness boundary, which it then follows for the next 3 miles or so. In this area, you could hike cross-country in and out of washes and along ridges until you get to flat-topped Signal Mountain or the deeply incised Hackberry Canyon.

Where 17 Mile Road first encounters the wilderness boundary (nearly 6 miles in), it intersects a 4WD route that heads south for about 3 miles before reaching Arroweed Spring. Cherry-stemmed within the wilderness, this road puts you within the northern half of the wilderness. An old jeep route that is now closed to vehicles continues south into the heart of wilderness for several miles, accessing some ridges along the head of Government Wash. This drainage flows southwest into the Big Sandy River.

The mouths of the above-mentioned Hackberry Canyon and Government Wash can be reached from the old town site of Signal, which is situated along the west bank of the Big Sandy River. From Wickenburg, drive 66 miles northwest on US Highway 93 to Signal Road. Turn left and follow this good graveled road for 12.5 miles to a short road that branches left. Drive less than 0.5 mile down this road to the town site.

From Signal, follow the Big Sandy River downstream for approximately 3 miles to where Hackberry Canyon branches to the left. At its mouth, Hackberry Canyon seems like an unassuming wash. It becomes more of a canyon farther up, however. You can follow the canyon for 4 miles or more. Although not always flowing, the Big Sandy River is a broad and sandy-bottomed waterway, which you can follow for many miles. About 2 miles beyond the mouth of Hackberry Canyon is the mouth of Government Wash. It, too, runs east into the heart of the wilderness for several miles.

After flowing for 12 miles through the western section of Arrastra Mountain Wilderness, the Big Sandy River intersects the Santa Maria River, which flows along the southern boundary of the wilderness and through its eastern section. Like the Big Sandy, the Santa Maria River provides a handy hiking route. It is accessible in a number of places. From where it crosses US Highway 93, it is possible to follow the river downstream a few miles to the point at which it enters the wilderness. A number of side canyons and washes also head north into the wilderness from the Santa Maria River.

The Big Sandy River flows through the Arrastra Mountain Wilderness.

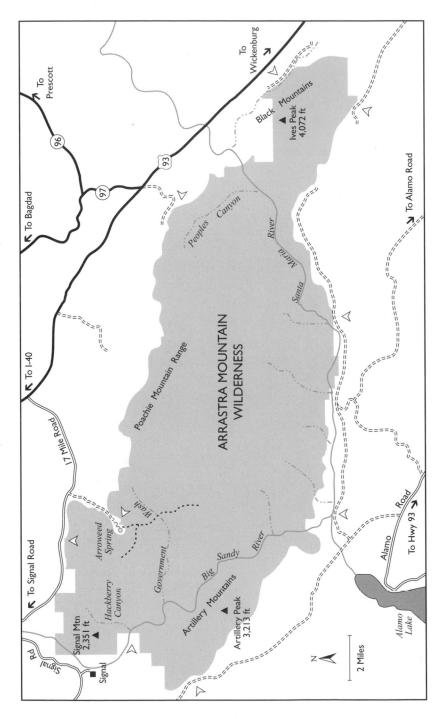

To Wickenburg

To Prescott

96

97

93

To Bagdad

To I-40

17 Mile Road

To Signal Road

Signal Rd

Signal

Signal Mtn
2,351 ft

Hackberry
Canyon

Arroweed
Spring

Wash

Government

Poachie Mountain Range

Peoples Canyon

Santa Maria River

ARRASTRA MOUNTAIN
WILDERNESS

Black Mountains

Ives Peak
4,072 ft

To Alamo Road

Big Sandy River

Artillery Mountains

Artillery Peak
3,213 ft

Alamo Road

To Hwy 93

Alamo
Lake

N

2 Miles

To determine which of these possible routes is best, check the topographic maps that cover the area. Some 4WD roads that access the river from the south can be reached by driving west on the unsigned Alamo Road. This 2WD gravel road turns off US Highway 93, approximately 21 miles northwest of Wickenburg. Here again, check the topographic maps for the best approach. Patches of private land in the area may prevent access in places.

East of the Santa Maria River, the wilderness comes to within a mile of US Highway 93. This section of the wilderness is accessed by a few 4WD roads that turn off the highway. One of these routes follows Black Canyon Wash, which forms part of the wilderness boundary line. This portion of the wilderness is dominated by Ives Peak and the Black Mountains. While the terrain is rugged in much of this area, some washes and ridges offer possible hiking routes.

Keep in mind that cross-country hiking is risky. Rough terrain, venomous snakes, and other dangers are common. Water is available in many places within the wilderness, but it should be treated before drinking. Watch for lightning in the higher reaches of the wilderness, and for flash floods along the river and canyon bottoms.

77 Upper Burro Creek Wilderness

Location: 60 miles NW of Wickenburg
Size: 27,440 acres
Status: Wilderness area (1990)
Terrain: Desert canyons and mesas
Elevation: 2,375 feet to 4,975 feet
Management: BLM (Kingman Field Office)
Topographic maps: Negro Ed, Grayback Mountains, Pilot Knob, Elephant Mountain

Difficult to reach and extremely rugged, Upper Burro Creek Wilderness is a rarely visited collection of canyons and isolated mesa tops. At the heart of the wilderness is a 13-mile stretch of Burro Creek, which flows unimpeded through a precipitous canyon. Lofty mesas and buttes tower nearby, adding vertical relief to the topography. The highest of these landforms is Negro Ed, a striking butte that reaches to within a few feet of the 5,000-foot level. Adding to the allure of this wilderness area is a variety of pristine ecosystems: from arid desert lands to verdant riparian plant communities.

Seasons
Spring and fall are the best seasons for hiking the wilderness. Summers can be hot in the lower reaches. Wintertime generally provides pleasant daytime temperatures, but stream crossings may be chilly at this time of year. There may be a few weeks in the spring when runoff may impede travel along Burro Creek entirely.

Plants and Wildlife

Thanks to the prodigious flow of Burro Creek, willow, cottonwood, and Arizona sycamore grow here. Beyond the creek, the flora includes a mixture of saguaro cactus, ocotillo, cholla, and paloverde and chaparral communities of shrub live oak. Pinyon pine and juniper are found along the higher mesas. Mule deer, javelinas, coyotes, bobcats, and mountain lions all thrive here, as do a number of species of birds. Pronghorn also frequent the mesa tops. Of primary interest to birders who occasionally visit Upper Burro Creek Wilderness are the bald eagles, ospreys, zone-tailed hawks, and black hawks that soar above canyon rims.

Geology

This wilderness area has been affected by volcanic activity, which built the land, and by erosion, which has shaped it and carried some of it away. Layers of lava and volcanic tuff are found throughout the area, exposed by the cutting action of Upper Burro Creek and its tributaries. Basalt forms the caprock for the surrounding mesas.

ACTIVITIES
Hiking

Access to the wilderness is restricted to just a few places, all of which involve difficult and lengthy drives. To get to the mouth of Upper Burro Creek Canyon, drive 50 miles northwest from Wickenburg on US Highway 93 as far as the Nothing Store. Turn north on a dirt road just east of the store and drive 3.1 miles north to a Y in the road. Keep left and drive another 6.3 miles to a second fork. Bear right here and follow a natural-gas pipeline service road east. In 2.5 miles, turn left and drive a short distance to a washed-out crossing along the perennial Boulder Creek. Although much of this drive is on roads that are passable to 2WD vehicles, the last 2.5 miles require a 4WD vehicle. After crossing Boulder Creek, you will access Upper Burro Creek Canyon, which heads north. Follow the wilderness area's namesake drainage for a short way using an old vehicle way. When you reach the end of this road, you can continue following the canyon bottom for several miles. Occasional boulder chokes and deep pools may slow your progress, but the scenery and riparian plant growth make the effort worthwhile.

Access to the upper end of the Burro Creek Canyon is possible from the mining town of Bagdad. At Bagdad, you will need to stop at the entry gate for the Cypress-Bagdad Copper Mine to receive permission and directions for crossing the mine site. Beyond the mine, drop into the Boulder Creek drainage before climbing Bozworth Mesa to the north. After crossing the mesa, the road then drops steeply into Upper Burro Creek Canyon. With the creek forming the eastern boundary of the wilderness, you can park your vehicle at a cow camp on public land. A 4WD vehicle is needed for this drive. It should not be attempted during or after a rainstorm.

Dividing the wilderness area into two separate units is an old, unnamed road that heads north to eventually cross the Salt Creek drainage. This road may be reached by following the above-mentioned approach drive from the Nothing Store to where the natural-gas pipeline road turns right. Continue straight at this point and drive past a

Ocotillo growing above Upper Burro Creek

water tank to the Burro Creek crossing just beyond. If the creek is not too high, you can cross the creek, then continue north along a rough 4WD road for several miles before reaching Goodwin Mesa. Once on the mesa, you can hike a number of cross-country hiking routes east across the generally level mesa and explore the rim area of Burro Creek to the east.

Access to the western unit of the Upper Burro Creek Wilderness is possible by driving a road that turns east from US Highway 93 about 7.5 miles south of Wikieup, near mile 132. After following this good gravel road for nearly 8 miles east from the

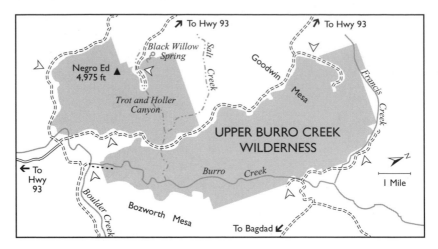

highway, turn left to follow the signs for Sycamore Camp. Continue north for nearly 5 miles to where a 4WD route turns right and drops into Cornwall Canyon. This road forms the wilderness area's southwestern boundary. By continuing another 3.4 miles on Sycamore Camp Road, you will reach a jeep road that takes off to the right. After driving 4.5 miles, turn right to access Black Willow Spring, which is located along the northwestern boundary of the wilderness. From this area, it is possible to explore portions of the western unit of the wilderness, including the above-mentioned butte, Negro Ed.

Hiking in this wilderness should be attempted only by experienced hikers. Water is available in Burro Creek, but it should be treated before drinking. Watch for snakes in the warmer months and for flash floods after heavy rains.

78 Rawhide Mountains Wilderness

Location: 80 miles NW of Wickenburg
Size: 38,470 acres
Status: Wilderness area (1990)
Terrain: Desert mountains and river canyon
Elevation: 800 feet to 3,927 feet
Management: BLM (Havasu Field Office)
Topographic maps: Artillery Peak, Rawhide Wash, Alamo Dam, Reid Valley

Two very different worlds are found in Rawhide Mountains Wilderness. As with other nearby wilderness areas, it features an extensive collection of desert foothills and mountains. Unlike most other wildernesses in the western half of the state, though, the Rawhide Mountains also offers the lush splendor of a riparian bottom land. This is thanks to an 8-mile stretch of the Bill Williams River, which flows west from Alamo Dam. Along this corridor, you will find not only a scenic 600-foot-deep canyon but also an interesting array of flora and fauna.

Seasons

Because summers are hot in this area, the best time to visit Rawhide Mountains Wilderness is between October and April. Winter nights may see temperatures dip below freezing, while March ushers in an impressive wildflower season, especially after wet winters. Depending on discharge from the Alamo Dam, stream flow can range from 25 cubic feet per second to 7,000 cubic feet per second.

Plants and Wildlife

Growing in the desert foothills and mountainous areas of the wilderness are scattered saguaro cactus, cholla, creosote bush, and paloverde, among other plants. Along the river bottom, the scene is strikingly different, as a number of cottonwood trees grow here, along with mesquite, willow, and tamarisk. In addition to the expected deer, desert bighorn sheep, coyotes, mountain lions, and desert tortoises that inhabit the desert areas of the wilderness, riparian areas also support populations of beavers, egrets, herons, and ducks. In addition to wintering along the river, a pair of bald eagles also nests in the gorge.

Geology

Divided by the Bill Williams River, Rawhide Mountains Wilderness encompasses portions of two different mountain ranges. Stretching north from the river are the Rawhide Mountains, a low but often rugged range. And rising south of the river is the eastern end of the Buckskin Mountains, which run west all the way to the Colorado River. Both ranges have metamorphic cores, exhibited in the white-and-dark-striped rock found within the Bill Williams River Gorge.

ACTIVITIES
Hiking

The Bill Williams River corridor is relatively accessible from Alamo Lake State Park, 80 miles northwest of Wickenburg. Upon reaching the state park, drive to the Bill Williams Overlook, which is located near the dam in the western end of the park. Park here and walk 1.5 miles down a service road to the river, just downstream from the dam. Completed in 1968, the Alamo Dam was built for flood control. Downstream from the dam, the wilderness begins just beyond a river gauging station. Within the next 0.25 mile, a deep pool walled in by vertical canyon walls forces hikers to swim (you will need an inner tube or raft to float your gear) during most levels of water flow. Beyond the pool, hikers will have to wade across the river on several occasions, but the rewards are certainly worth the effort. The scenery here is rarely matched in other parts of Arizona. The gorge may be closed in the spring to avoid disturbing a nesting pair of bald eagles. Check at the state park for details. From this end of the Bill

The Bill Williams River flows through the Rawhide Mountains Wilderness.

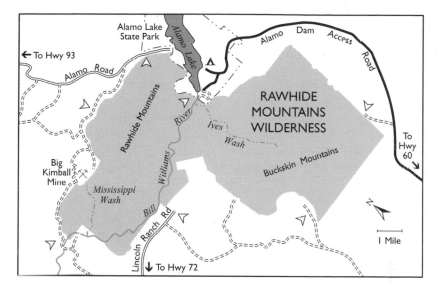

Williams River, you may also want to explore Ives Wash, a narrow side canyon that branches off to the south. Extending for more than 3 miles, this impressive drainage is passable to all who don't mind an occasional scramble.

The lower portion of the Bill Williams River is accessible by driving the high-clearance, 2WD Lincoln Ranch Road, which branches off Swansea Road to the south-west. Swansea Road begins on Arizona Highway 72, southeast of Parker. To reach the river at this access point, follow a 4WD route that turns north from Lincoln Ranch Road, about a mile west of the ranch. Here again, a pleasant riparian environment adds to the pleasures of hiking along the river. While this corridor can be followed for several miles in either direction, one possible destination is Mississippi Wash, which turns north from the river about 3 miles downstream. Some private land is encountered near the mouth of Mississippi Wash, but it can be skirted by walking on the north side of the fence that marks the boundary. Paralleling the westernmost boundary of the wilderness is an old road (it is now impassable to vehicles) that heads north for a few miles from the Bill Williams River to the abandoned Big Kimball Mine. With the aid of a topographic map, you can then find your way into the head of Mississippi Wash, thereby completing a loop hike of several miles.

From the river corridor, the wilderness extends southeast for 8 miles or so, across the eastern end of the Buckskin Mountains. Bounded by a power transmission line along its eastern border, this portion of the wilderness may be reached by driving different 4WD routes that branch off Alamo Dam Access Road—the paved road that leads to Alamo Lake State Park. Although no trails exist in this portion of the wilderness, it is possible to follow some of the washes or ridgelines that dissect the area. Check the topographic maps to find the best access routes.

Spanning a portion of the Rawhide Mountains, the northern half of the wilderness may be reached by driving Alamo Road, which is accessed from Wickieup along US Highway 93 via Chicken Springs Road. Some 4WD roads form much of the wilderness boundary here, and one abandoned jeep route enters the wilderness for about a mile. In addition, it is possible to hike along some of the drainages that head south from Alamo Road into the northeastern corner of the wilderness. The graveled Alamo Road is open to most vehicles.

Use extreme caution when hiking cross-country in the wilderness, or in any other backcountry area. Watch for rattlesnakes in the warmer months of the year, especially among the rocky canyon walls along the Bill Williams River. Although water is usually found in the Bill Williams River, it should be treated before drinking.

79 Swansea Wilderness

Location: 25 miles E of Parker
Size: 16,400 acres
Status: Wilderness area (1990)
Terrain: Desert mountains and river canyons
Elevation: 700 feet to 1,890 feet
Management: BLM (Havasu Field Office)
Topographic maps: Centennial Wash, Swansea, Planet

Like the Rawhide Mountains Wilderness a few miles upstream, Swansea Wilderness encompasses a stretch of the perennial Bill Williams River. While this section of the waterway is not encased in a spectacular canyon like the one found upstream, it does feature rocky bluffs, low cliffs, and verdant riparian growth. South of the river, Swansea Wilderness takes in a portion of the Buckskin Mountains, while to the north it includes part of Black Mesa—a scenic volcanic escarpment.

Seasons
The best times to visit this wilderness are between the months of October and April. Summers are very hot, although the Bill Williams River might offer temporary relief from the heat. Winters occasionally bring subfreezing temperatures at night. March is a good time to enjoy the many wildflowers of this desert area.

Plants and Wildlife
Riparian vegetation along the Bill Williams River includes occasional cottonwood, tamarisk, and willow. Bird life is plentiful, and the tracks of various species of wildlife are also evident along the muddy shores of the river. Among the desert hills and mountains, expect to find saguaro cactus, cholla, barrel cactus, creosote bush, and paloverde. Wildlife in the arid reaches of the wilderness includes mule deer, desert bighorn sheep, coyotes, mountain lions, Gila monsters, and desert tortoises.

Geology

Swansea Wilderness encompasses a section of the Buckskin Mountains, a metamorphic core range that runs southwest–northeast. By contrast, most other ranges in western Arizona trend northwest–southeast. The difference resulted in part because they were uplifted at different times. North of the Bill Williams River, the wilderness takes in a portion of scenic Black Mesa. Volcanic dikes, plugs, and dark basalt rock are found in this portion of the wilderness.

History

Just south of the wilderness are the remains of the old mining town of Swansea (named after a Welsh mining town in Britain). Beginning in 1908, copper and other minerals were mined in the area. The smelter was closed in 1912, and the ore was subsequently shipped all the way to Swansea, Wales, by way of the Colorado River and the Gulf of California. The mine closed in 1949, and today crumbling adobe walls, old foundations, and fenced-off vertical shafts are all that remain.

ACTIVITIES
Hiking

Access to the southern portion of Swansea Wilderness is possible along Swansea Road. From Parker, drive south on Arizona Highways 95 and 72 to Bouse. Turn left on the 2WD Swansea Road, continue 12 miles to an intersection, where Swansea Road bears left. Keep following Swansea Road, and in 5.6 miles, this route will reach a second intersection, where Swansea Road turns right. Beyond this point, the road becomes rougher and may require a high-clearance vehicle. In 2.8 miles, a secondary road branches left to access the southern tip of the wilderness. Although no trails exist in

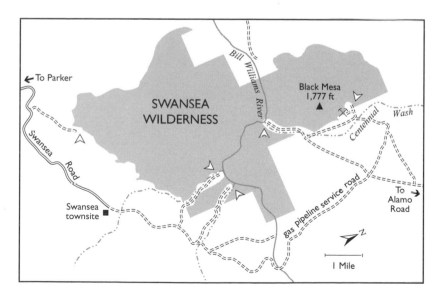

this area, it is possible to find several cross-country routes. A little more than 7 miles from the last intersection, Swansea Road reaches the ghost town of Swansea, beyond which the road becomes a 4WD route. It continues northeast for 3.5 miles, before dropping into an unnamed wash. Once in the wash, you can drive downstream along the normally dry drainage bottom to reach the Bill Williams River in 2.2 miles. This corridor has been cherry-stemmed from the wilderness. Once at the Bill Williams River, you may then hike the river bottom upstream or down for as far as you like. Plan on wading the river on several occasions, and watch for wildlife, including a variety of wading birds.

Access to Black Mesa and the northern third of the wilderness is possible, thanks to some 4WD routes that turn off from Alamo Road near Fools Peak. It is also possible to drive the above-mentioned route through Swansea to where the road crosses the Bill Williams River. This crossing may be impossible during high water levels. When the river is down, however, you can continue north from the crossing (the road is fairly good here as it follows a natural-gas pipeline) for about 3.5 or 4 miles to a left-hand turn. Dropping into Centennial Wash, this 4WD route eventually reaches the Bill Williams River, as it is cherry-stemmed out of the wilderness for its last mile or so. While the top of Black Mesa is well guarded by the precipitous escarpments along its east face, it may nevertheless be accessed by hiking in from an old mining area located adjacent to the northeastern boundary of the wilderness. To reach this access point, follow the natural-gas pipeline road about 5 miles north from the Bill Williams River crossing and turn left. The mines are less than 2 miles to the southwest.

Hiking cross-country in this wilderness can be hazardous and should be attempted only by experienced hikers. Water collected in the Bill Williams River should be treated before drinking. Watch for rattlesnakes when hiking during the warmer months. Be aware of the possibility of flash floods along wash bottoms after heavy downpours.

80 Aubrey Peak Wilderness

Location: 72 miles S of Kingman
Size: 15,400 acres
Status: Wilderness area (1990)
Terrain: Desert mountains and washes
Elevation: 1,600 feet to 2,953 feet
Management: BLM (Kingman Field Office)
Topographic maps: McCracken Peak, Centennial Peak

Isolated from major highways, Aubrey Peak Wilderness is a good destination for outdoor enthusiasts in search of solitude. The wilderness is dominated by the rugged Aubrey Peak and, while there are no established trails within its boundaries, the area's terrain is mostly open and ideal for hiking.

Seasons

Summers are quite hot in these low elevations and should be avoided. Late autumn is nice, as is much of the spring season. Winter months can see pleasant afternoon temperatures and cool nights. Watch for colorful wildflower displays in March, especially after wet winters.

Plants and Wildlife

Aubrey Peak Wilderness includes an interesting mix of plants characteristic of both the Sonoran and Mojave Deserts. Saguaro cactus, cholla, barrel cactus, ocotillo, paloverde, and creosote bush are some of the species that you can expect to find here. In addition, however, scattered Joshua trees offer visitors a nice surprise. Mule deer, javelinas, coyotes, mountain lions, kit foxes, and jackrabbits reside within this wilderness, as do desert tortoises, Gila monsters, and desert bighorn sheep. The Aubrey Peak area, in fact, has been identified as an important bighorn sheep lambing area.

Geology

Aubrey Peak Wilderness exhibits a complex mixture of volcanic structures, similar to those found in other Basin and Range mountains. Included here are most types of volcanic rock found throughout western Arizona: colorful tuff, dark basalt, volcanic plugs, and more. Erosion has had a field day within the wilderness, sculpting numerous precipitous cliffs, natural arches, spires, caves, and water-catching potholes. *Bajadas*

Joshua trees and saguaro cacti grow side by side in the Aubrey Peak Wilderness.

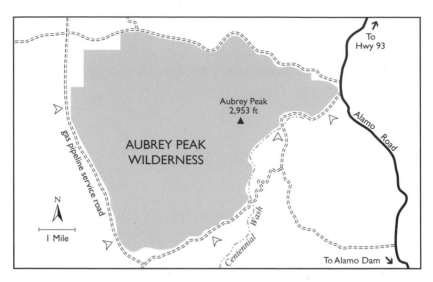

(alluvial fans) slope east, south, and north from the higher mesas and peaks—a distinctive feature in these deserts.

ACTIVITIES
Hiking

The best place to begin exploring Aubrey Peak Wilderness is along the southern boundary, where a road follows a powerline along Centennial Wash. To reach this portion of the wilderness from US Highway 93, turn west on Signal Road (it turns off the highway 66 miles northwest of Wickenburg) and drive 17.8 miles to Alamo Road. Turn left and drive 4.4 miles to where a powerline crosses the road. Turn right and follow this road for a short distance to reach the wilderness boundary. While Signal and Alamo Roads are gravel and passable to most vehicles, the last portion of the drive may require a 4WD vehicle. Eventually, this road begins following Centennial Wash, and about 3 miles in it passes through a narrow section between some rock bluffs. From this point, it is possible to hike northwest along ridgelines to the top of Aubrey Peak. Although the summit is less than a mile from the road, the going can be slow due to rocky terrain. It is also possible to hike across the gentler *bajadas* that extend east from Aubrey Peak. Beyond the above-mentioned access point, the road through Centennial Wash continues along the southern boundary of the wilderness for another 4 miles, before reaching the southwestern corner of the wilderness. From various points along this road, it is possible to hike into the gentler terrain that characterizes this portion of the wilderness. Bordered by a natural gas line and accompanying service road, the west side of the wilderness is also accessible.

Don't plan on finding water in Aubrey Peak Wilderness. Pack in at least a gallon per person per day. Watch for rattlesnakes during the warmer times of the year. Use extreme caution when hiking cross-country, as the hazards are many.

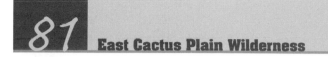

81 East Cactus Plain Wilderness

Location: 18 miles E of Parker
Size: 14,630 acres
Status: Wilderness area (1990)
Terrain: Desert sand dunes
Elevation: 1,250 feet to 1,654 feet
Management: BLM (Havasu Field Office)
Topographic map: Powerline Hill

Characterized by extensive sand dunes that are partially stabilized by established plant communities, the East Cactus Plain has long been of interest to botanists, as this dune system is unique in Arizona. Because the topography varies little, this wilderness may not be for everyone. Nevertheless, the intricate beauty of the desert flora found here is alluring. Cut off from East Cactus Plain Wilderness by the Central Arizona Project canal is the much larger (59,100 acres) Cactus Plain Wilderness Study Area. Bypassed for inclusion in the 1990 Arizona Wilderness Act, the area is similar to East Cactus Plain Wilderness and, therefore, warrants mention below.

A short-horned lizard

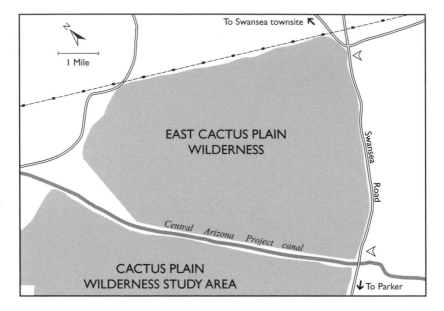

Seasons

Summers are typically too hot for hiking in this wilderness. The best times to visit are between the months of October and April.

Plants and Wildlife

The surprisingly dense vegetation that grows across the Cactus Plain has been recognized for its uniqueness by the Arizona Natural Heritage Program. Dominant species include big galleta grass, two types of paloverde, ironwood, creosote bush, ocotillo, two varieties of cholla, and saguaro cactus. In addition to populations of mule deer, coyotes, jackrabbits, and various rodents, East Cactus Plain Wilderness is also home to the Mojave fringe-toed lizard and the flat-tailed horned lizard—both of which are listed as special-status species.

Geology

Spread across nearly level lands, the low dunes of East Cactus Plain Wilderness have been stabilized by plant cover. Such expansive stabilized dunes are unique to the Sonoran Desert, and possibly to the Desert Southwest.

ACTIVITIES
Hiking

Bounded by a power transmission line to the northeast, a road to the southeast, and the Central Arizona Project canal to the southwest, East Cactus Plain Wilderness is easily accessible from many places. Because the terrain varies very little throughout, however, hikers need not be choosy in selecting a starting point. One good place to begin is at the wilderness's southern tip. To reach this point, drive 12 miles south from Parker on Arizona Highway 95 to Arizona Highway 72. Turn left and continue 15 miles to Bouse. Turn left here on the 2WD Swansea Road. Continue about 6 miles to where the route crosses the Central Arizona Project canal. Just beyond is a parking area and wilderness sign on the left. From this point, the walking is easy among the dunes but, because there are no outstanding landmarks, bring a compass. East of this parking area, the wilderness bounds Swansea Road for the next 6 miles, to where a transmission line crosses overhead. The wilderness boundary is also accessed by a road at the northern tip of the area.

Access to the southern portion of Cactus Plain Wilderness Study Area (WSA) is available along the first 6 miles of Swansea Road and along Arizona Highway 72. Because the topography is similar to that of East Cactus Plain Wilderness, the hiking strategy is the same: pick a convenient access point, then set off cross-country among the dunes, with compass in hand. In the northernmost portion of Cactus Plain WSA, several washes dissect the terrain, making for some suitable hiking routes. This area is accessed along the paved Shea Road, which heads east from Parker.

Use caution when hiking cross-country in East Cactus Plain Wilderness. No water is found within the area, so pack in all that you will need. Watch for rattlesnakes when hiking here in warmer seasons. Be sure not to trample cryptogamic soil in this, or any other, wilderness.

82 Gibraltar Mountain Wilderness

Location: 10 miles E of Parker
Size: 18,790 acres
Status: Wilderness area (1990)
Terrain: Desert mountains and plains
Elevation: 600 feet to 1,888 feet
Management: BLM (Havasu Field Office)
Topographic maps: Cross Roads, Black Peak, Osborne Well, Bobs Well

Dominated by its namesake summit in the south and Giers Mountain in the north, Gibraltar Mountain Wilderness encompasses the western end of the Buckskin Mountains. While these higher summits are rocky and rugged, the lower elevations are more open and easy to walk. Thanks to a paved road that skirts the area's southern boundary, the wilderness is easy to reach.

Seasons
Summers are too hot for hiking here, whereas late fall, winter, and early spring are ideal.

Plants and Wildlife

Vegetation is sparse within this wilderness. While you may find a few saguaro cactus growing here and there, cholla, beavertail cactus, and creosote bush are more common. Barrel cactus occasionally haunt the rocky ridges of the area, and paloverde is common in the washes. Among the species of wildlife that inhabit Gibraltar Mountain Wilderness are mule deer, desert bighorn sheep, coyotes, mountain lions, and a variety of birds of prey. The lower foothills of the wilderness also contain desert tortoises.

Geology

While the core of the Buckskin Mountains consists mostly of metamorphic rock, the western section of the range (specifically in the Gibraltar Mountain area) features plenty of volcanic material, including dark basalt rock and tuff beds. Mineral resources in the area have produced sizable amounts of gold, silver, and copper.

ACTIVITIES
Hiking

No maintained trails are found within Gibraltar Mountain Wilderness, but plenty of washes and open terrain offer ideal hiking possibilities throughout. A good place to begin is along the southern end of the wilderness. Drive south from Parker on Arizona Highway 95, less than 2 miles to the paved Shea Road, which turns left. Continue 10 miles to an unmarked dirt road (high-clearance, 2WD) to the north. Follow it for less than a mile to the wilderness boundary, which is marked by a BLM wilderness sign. From this point, you may follow the drainage north for a way into a nice little canyon.

A 4WD road that turns from Shea Road about 7 miles east of Arizona Highway 95 accesses some inactive mines in the vicinity of Gibraltar Mountain. Less than 4

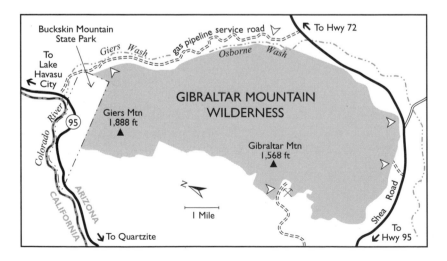

miles long, this secondary road provides the best access to the wilderness's namesake, as well as an entry point for an extensive canyon system in the central portion of the wilderness.

Accessing the eastern portion of the wilderness is easy because Shea Road parallels the wilderness boundary for a few miles as it bends north. Where Shea Road turns northeast, away from the wilderness, a 4WD road then continues up Osborne Wash, which roughly defines the wilderness boundary. Because the terrain in this area is comparatively open, the hiking is quite easy. Several smaller washes also fan out toward the west and northwest from the larger Osborne Wash.

A high-clearance road that services a transmission line runs along the northeastern boundary of the wilderness from Buckskin Mountain State Park. This route follows Giers Wash for a few miles before crossing into the head of Osborne Wash. The terrain in this area is more rugged, but there are some routes through it. This road is closed from January through June because of the desert bighorn sheep lambing season.

Hiking cross-country in this wilderness area can be hazardous, especially for novice hikers. Water is not available. Watch for poisonous snakes when hiking in the warmer months.

83 Havasu Wilderness

Location: 10 miles N of Lake Havasu City
Size: 17,801 acres
Status: Wilderness area (1990)
Terrain: Deserts and desert mountains
Elevation: 400 feet to 2,084 feet
Management: USFWS (Havasu NWR)
Topographic maps: Topock, Castle Rock

Although best known for its wetlands along the lower Colorado River, the Havasu National Wildlife Refuge also includes some 17,000 acres of desert wilderness—14,606 acres in Arizona and 3,165 acres in California. Spread along the eastern shore of the Colorado River, Arizona's share of the wilderness is highlighted by the Needles a cluster of dark volcanic spires that are plainly visible from nearby Interstate 40.

Seasons

Due to its low elevation, Havasu Wilderness is hot for much of the year. Summers may see temperatures above 110 degrees. Late spring and early fall are also hot. Winters are mostly pleasant, but late fall and early spring are probably the best times of the year for a visit. March often brings colorful displays of blooming desert annuals, with cactus blooms following shortly after.

Cholla cactus in the Havasu National Wildlife Refuge

Plants and Wildlife

While Havasu National Wildlife Refuge was established to protect wetlands along the Colorado River for migratory birds, it preserves an interesting swath of desert land as well. Although the vegetation is characteristically sparse, you will find paloverde, cholla, creosote bush, barrel cactus, and ocotillo growing here. Wildlife includes coyotes, bobcats, foxes, desert bighorn sheep, jackrabbits, and a variety of rodents. The refuge is home to a number of migratory bird species in the winter months, as well as peregrine falcons, bald eagles, and other raptors.

Geology

Spanning much of the Havasu Wilderness are the Mohave Mountains. Although rugged throughout, the Mohaves are highlighted by the dramatic spires of the Needles. These sharply rising pinnacles resulted from magma cooled within conduits of volcanoes that have since eroded and been transported away by wind and water. This volcanic activity is thought to date back to the Tertiary period. The Colorado River, which borders the wilderness to the west, has carved out a scenic canyon system known as Topock Gorge.

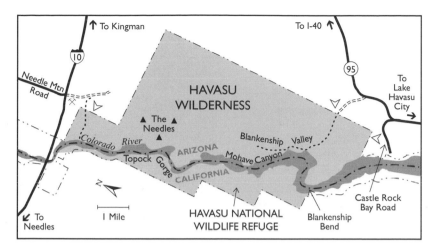

ACTIVITIES
Hiking
Although not maintained as hiking trails, a few old roads now closed to vehicles enter Havasu Wilderness, and the terrain is open and quite hikeable throughout. To enter the wilderness from the north, exit Interstate 40 at Needle Mountain Road, which is a few miles east of the Colorado River. Drive south through a gravel pit area and follow this high-clearance, 2WD road as it drops into a wash about 1.5 miles from the interstate. Follow the wash upstream for another 0.7 mile, to where it narrows and the road climbs out of the drainage. From this point it is possible to hike cross-country to the southwest toward the Needles. It is about 0.5 mile to the wilderness boundary and another mile to reach the heart of the Needles. Additionally, an old road leaves the above-mentioned wash to head west toward a gauging station located along the river, about 2 miles to the west. This route is closed to vehicles beyond the wilderness boundary.

Access to the southern end of the wilderness is possible from points along Castle Rock Bay Road, which turns off Arizona Highway 95 a few miles north of Lake Havasu City. Two possible destinations in this portion of the wilderness include Blankenship Valley and Mohave Canyon. A former vehicle way accesses Blankenship Valley, and the vegetation is sparse, making for easy cross-country travel throughout. The BLM road leading to this access point is closed from January 1 to June 30, however.

Water is not available within this wilderness, so bring plenty with you. Wear a hat and apply sunscreen to exposed skin. Watch for rattlesnakes in the warmer months.

River Running
Although the Colorado River has been excluded from this wilderness, canoeists can enjoy a day-long float down the river through Topock Gorge. The river has been stilled by nearby Lake Havasu, making this a flatwater journey. Since camping is prohibited along this stretch of the river, the entire 16 miles of the trip must be completed in a

day. Landmarks along the way include the Needles, the Devils Elbow, and Blankenship Bend. Due to very heavy motorboat traffic all along this route, it is best to avoid canoeing here during the weekends, especially Memorial Day, July 4th, and Labor Day weekends.

84 Warm Springs Wilderness

Location: 18 miles SW of Kingman
Size: 112,400 acres
Status: Wilderness area (1990)
Terrain: Desert plains and mountains
Elevation: 950 feet to 4,277 feet
Management: BLM (Kingman Field Office)
Topographic maps: Warm Springs, Warm Springs SW, Warm Springs SE, Mount Nutt, Boundary Cone, Kingman SW, Yucca NW, Yucca

Encompassing more than 100,000 acres, Warm Springs Wilderness is a vast parcel of desert that is mostly open for backcountry explorations. Dominating the northern and east-central portions of the wilderness is the 10-mile-long Black Mesa, which rises 1,000 feet above the desert floor. Surrounded by mountains in the south-central portion of the wilderness is a scenic inner basin that features the wilderness area's namesake. Rugged mountains typify the northwestern corner of the wilderness, and gently sloping *bajadas* (alluvial fans) stretch across the southern and easternmost portions of the area. Complex canyon systems that dissect Black Mesa and the mountainous areas add to the hiking possibilities within Warm Springs Wilderness.

Seasons
Because summers bring hot temperatures—100 degrees and higher—to this wilderness, autumn, winter, and spring are the best seasons for a visit to the area. Winter may see cool nights, but daytime temperatures are mostly pleasant. Following wet winters, early spring can produce a plethora of wildflowers in the wilderness.

Plants and Wildlife
Across the lowest elevations in the southern portion of Warm Springs Wilderness are found communities of mesquite, paloverde, catclaw, ocotillo, and a variety of cactus. At somewhat higher elevations, blackbrush grows in great abundance. Yucca is common throughout, and grasslands are found across the top of Black Mesa. This wilderness is home to a large herd of desert bighorn sheep and to a handful of feral burros. Coyotes, mule deer, and rabbits are common. Several species of raptors have been spotted in the area. Additionally, it is thought that Gila monsters and desert tortoises also live within the wilderness.

Rattlesnakes would rather avoid conflict when possible.

Geology

Mostly volcanic in nature, the geology of Warm Springs Wilderness has produced some spectacular scenery. Dominating much of the wilderness, the extensive Black Mesa resulted from a lava flow that occurred in relatively recent geologic times—approximately 2 million years ago. It is topped with dark basalt rock, hence its name. The mountainous reaches of the wilderness include the southern end of the Black Mountains, which feature colorful exposures of rhyolite, tuff, and other volcanic rock.

ACTIVITIES
Hiking

You can access Warm Springs Wilderness in several ways. Along the northern boundary, one interesting hike begins at Cool Spring, which is located at the end of a rugged, mile-long 4WD road. From the spring, the route follows an unnamed canyon for 2 miles into the northernmost portion of the wilderness. This canyon is ringed by several colorful cliffs and mountain summits. An old vehicle way actually continues along the entire route, but it may be faint in spots. To reach this hike, drive about 14.5 miles west on Oatman Road (the old Route 66) from Interstate 40. Oatman Road begins 4.5 miles south of Kingman at exit 44. The approach drive to Cool Spring crosses private land, so treat it accordingly.

Also accessed by Oatman Road is a cherry-stemmed 4WD road that continues nearly 5 miles into the eastern corner of the wilderness. Because it traverses the nearly level *bajadas* east of Black Mesa, this road accesses a variety of easy cross-country hikes, and it will also get you close to Black Mesa. For the best route up, check the topographic map first. The road eventually ends near Alkali Spring, which is situated a short way up a nice little canyon. This and other canyon systems may be accessed from

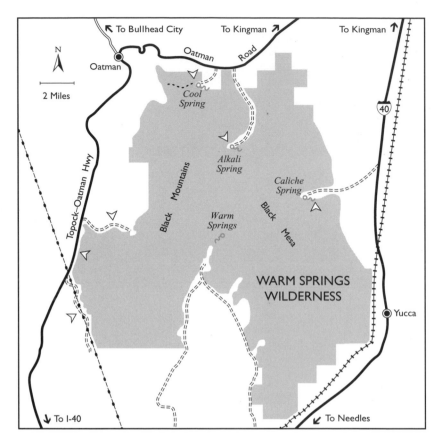

this approach. This road turns off Oatman Road, 13.5 miles west of Interstate 40.

Unfortunately the most direct access to the Warm Springs area is no longer possible because of a locked gate at the Franconia exit along Interstate 40. However, other access points are found along the Topock–Oatman Highway, a paved route that runs west of the wilderness boundary for 2 miles, beginning about 9.5 miles north of the Topock exit on Interstate 40. Some short but rugged canyons head east into the wilderness from this portion of blacktop.

Heading southeast from the Topock–Oatman Highway is a transmission line and accompanying service road. It forms more than 4 miles of the wilderness boundary, providing access to the mostly gentle *bajadas* that typify the southwestern corner of the wilderness. At one point, this difficult 4WD route also crosses Fivemile Wash, which also offers a convenient hiking route.

About 12.5 miles north of Interstate 40, the wilderness boundary turns east from the Topock–Oatman Highway to follow a 4WD road that is still open to vehicles. Although rough in places, this route provides access to a handful of canyons that head east into the northwestern corner of the wilderness.

Because there are no maintained trails within this wilderness, visitors should be skilled in cross-country orientation and travel. Water is scarce in the area, and it is essential that you pack in all you will need. Watch for snakes during the warmer months, and be wary of lightning in the higher, exposed reaches of the wilderness.

85 Wabayuma Peak Wilderness

Location: 17 miles S of Kingman
Size: 40,000 acres
Status: Wilderness area (1990)
Terrain: Desert plains and mountains
Elevation: 2,480 feet to 7,601 feet
Management: BLM (Kingman Field Office)
Topographic maps: Wabayuma Peak, Kingman SE, Hualapai Peak, Yucca NE

Encompassing a rugged stretch of the Hualapai Mountains, the Wabayuma Peak Wilderness offers hikers an inviting collection of desert foothills and midelevation peaks. Although not the highest peak in the Hualapai Range, the wilderness area's namesake tops the 7,500-foot mark. Here, you will find cool forests of ponderosa pine and Gambel

Looking south from a ridge in the Wabayuma Peak Wilderness

oak. In the wilderness area's lower elevations—below 3,000 feet—grow some of the northernmost stands of saguaro cactus. This wilderness offers a great variety of terrain and ecosystems.

Seasons

Because of the considerable elevation change found in Wabayuma Peak Wilderness, visitors can enjoy year-round hiking opportunities here. During the summer months, the lower elevations can be very hot, while the higher terrain remains relatively cool. Winter occasionally brings cold temperatures and snow to the high country. The ideal times to visit all sections of the wilderness are late fall and spring.

Plants and Wildlife

Growing in the lowest elevations of the wilderness is an eclectic mixture of vegetation characteristic of two major desert ecosystems: the Mojave and Sonoran Deserts. These plants include creosote bush, paloverde, ocotillo, pricklypear cactus, cholla, Joshua trees, and saguaro cactus. Higher up in elevation, plant communities include shrub live oak, manzanita, juniper, pinyon pine, and agave. The highest reaches of the wilderness are home to small stands of ponderosa pine and Gambel oak. Finding suitable habitat in this wide range of ecosystems are many species of fauna. Javelinas and mule deer are common. The western end of the wilderness is home to a small population of endangered desert tortoises. Ranging across the higher elevations is a small herd of transplanted elk. A variety of birds of prey—including goshawks, golden eagles, and merlins—also frequent the wilderness.

Geology

Continuing for 50 miles along a northwest–southeast axis, the Hualapai Mountain Range is typical of many mountain ranges in the Basin and Range province. It consists mostly of Precambrian granite, gneiss, and schist and rises quite suddenly from the broad desert floor. As faulted blocks, ranges such as the Hualapai Mountains formed during a geologic period when the earth's crust became riddled with faults and large blocks of rock were tilted skyward.

ACTIVITIES
Hiking

Bordered by backroads along much of its boundary, Wabayuma Peak Wilderness is accessible from all directions. A 3-mile-long trail accesses the summit of Wabayuma Peak. To reach the trailhead for the Wabayuma Peak Trail, drive south from Kingman to the Pine Lake community, which is near Hualapai Mountain Park. Turn right onto the 4WD Hualapai Ridge Road. Continue 20 miles south on this road to the signed trailhead. A second approach to the trailhead begins at the Yucca exit off Interstate 40, south of Kingman. Follow Alamo Road 3.2 miles to where it turns south. Continue straight on Boriana Canyon Road and drive about 15 miles east and north. The last

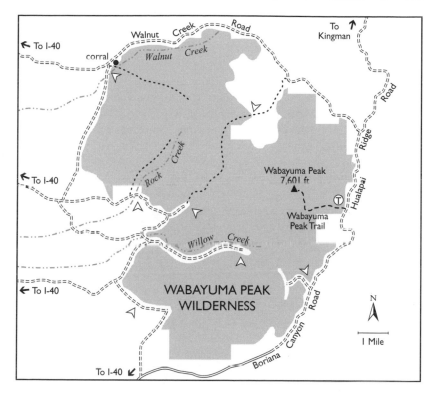

few miles of this approach may require a 4WD vehicle. Following an old vehicle track for the first 2 miles, the Wabayuma Peak Trail then branches off to the left, near where the road bends to the north. In this last mile, the trail completes about two-thirds of its 1,550-foot climb.

Before reaching the Wabayuma Peak Trail, Boriana Canyon Road accesses portions of the wilderness area's southern and southwestern borders. One possible hiking route in this section follows an old road that has been cherry-stemmed outside the wilderness. Although it is legally open to vehicles, this road becomes quite rough and impassable within a mile or so. It is best to park at an old corral that is located along Boriana Canyon Road, nearly 12 miles from where it turns off Alamo Road, then walk 2 miles to the top of a ridge west of Boriana Canyon.

Spreading out along the wilderness area's west side are low desert lands that lend themselves well to cross-country hiking. A good place to begin is along the wilderness area's northwestern corner. It may be reached by turning off Interstate 40 at the Griffith exit and driving approximately 5 miles east to an old corral. The wilderness boundary begins just beyond the corral and runs adjacent to the south side of a road, which follows Walnut Creek east toward its headwaters. Two very faint jeep tracks penetrate the wilderness—one from the corral area and the other about 2.5 miles beyond—to follow some interesting canyons for a couple of miles. Farther up, Walnut Creek Road is gated and closed to the public.

From the corral in the northwestern corner of the wilderness, another old vehicle way heads south to form the western boundary of the wilderness. While this road is legally open to vehicles, it is so overgrown that it is best to walk the route. About 4 miles south of the corral, the road reaches the Rock Creek drainage, which forms a sizable break along the mountain range's western facade. A closed-off road enters the wilderness and follows Rock Creek for a couple of miles. About 1.5 miles southeast of Rock Creek, another closed-off 4WD route enters the wilderness and heads northeast along ridges and drainages before reaching the upper end of Walnut Creek. Private lands in these areas may prevent access in some cases.

From Boriana Canyon Road, it is also possible to access the Willow Creek drainage, which includes about 3 miles of cherry-stemmed road. Although rough, this route provides access to the upper reaches of the Willow Creek drainage at the heart of the wilderness. Beyond road's end, hikers must travel cross-country over occasionally rough terrain.

Cross-country hiking within the wilderness can be risky for inexperienced hikers. Although water is available at some springs, it must be treated before drinking. It's best to pack in all that you will need. Watch for rattlesnakes during the warmer seasons and lightning in the higher areas, especially during summer thunderstorms.

86   Mount Nutt Wilderness

Location: 15 miles W of Kingman
Size: 27,660 acres
Status: Wilderness area (1990)
Terrain: Desert mountains
Elevation: 2,300 feet to 5,216 feet
Management: BLM (Kingman Field Office)
Topographic maps: Mount Nutt, Oatman, Union Pass, Secret Pass

Characteristically rugged, the Mount Nutt Wilderness offers an inviting array of canyons, wash bottoms, sheer mountain faces, isolated mesas, buttes, spires, and imposing volcanic plugs to explore. Although no established trails are found within the area, there are lots of cross-country hiking possibilities. Mount Nutt Wilderness is one of three wilderness areas that encompass a portion of the Black Mountain chain.

Seasons

As Mount Nutt Wilderness is very hot in summer, the best time to visit is between late autumn and spring. Winter may bring occasional freezing nighttime temperatures but the days are mostly pleasant.

Cacti growing in Gutt Canyon in the Mount Nutt Wilderness

Plants and Wildlife

At the lower elevations, creosote bush and blackbrush predominate. Mojave yucca, ocotillo, and cholla are common in many places. In the higher reaches are found desert grasslands, along with California juniper and shrub live oak. Springs in the area, and a few streambeds, support riparian growth, such as cottonwood and willow. Among the wildlife that inhabit the wilderness is a sizable herd of desert bighorn sheep. Mule deer are common, as are coyotes and a host of other desert species. Feral burros are found throughout the wilderness. Birds of prey include golden eagles and peregrine falcons.

Geology

Although a few outcrops of granite and gneiss are found within this stretch of the Black Mountains, much of Mount Nutt Wilderness features such volcanic rocks as rhyolites, andesite, tuffs, and agglomerates. The result is a colorful mix of cliff faces, spires, slot canyons, and other rock formations.

ACTIVITIES
Hiking

Although it lacks established trails, Mount Nutt Wilderness does feature some interesting natural hiking corridors along wash bottoms. One of the easiest to reach of these routes is located in the southeastern corner of the wilderness. From Kingman, drive about 4 miles west on Interstate 40 to exit 44 and Oatman Road. Follow Oatman Road west for 9 miles to Navajo Road. Continuing for 3.3 miles before reaching its end at the wilderness boundary, Navajo Road eventually deteriorates into a high-clearance, 2WD route. From road's end, you can then drop into scenic Gutt Canyon (locals call it the Devil's Garden), just to the north. The going can be rocky and rough along the drainage bottom.

Also in the southeastern corner of the wilderness is Thimble Mountain, a striking volcanic plug that rises above the surrounding desert terrain. It is possible to approach the base of Thimble Mountain by hiking cross-country from the Gold Trail Mine area, which lies a couple of miles north of Oatman Road. The turnoff for the Gold Trail Mine is approximately 3 miles west of the turnoff for Navajo Road.

North of Navajo Road, a number of dirt roads access the eastern boundary of Mount Nutt Wilderness. Although some of these roads cross private land, others are open to the public. These routes, in turn, access some interesting, unnamed canyons that cut into the eastern face of the Black Mountains. One of these is Guthrie Road, which leads to Cave Spring. From the spring, it is possible to hike upcanyon for a few miles.

Another interesting hiking route on the eastern side of the wilderness is Secret Pass Wash, which cuts across the northeastern corner of the wilderness. Flowing east from the wilderness, Secret Pass Wash is mostly open. However, as it continues upstream toward Secret Pass, it becomes more interesting. Rather than following the above-mentioned approach from Oatman Road, it is best to drive north of Kingman on US Highway 93 to the turnoff for Arizona Highway 68. Continue west for a little more than 9 miles to the paved Estrella Road. Turn south and drive 4.7 miles to the unpaved Shinarump Road. Turn right and drive a short distance to Kaibab Road. Turn left and drive 2 miles south to a jeep road. Turn right here and drive another mile to the wilderness boundary.

Secret Pass Wash is also accessible from the north, where a cherry-stemmed road follows the wash downstream for nearly a mile. This 4WD road is accessed from the above-mentioned Estrella Road, which turns off Arizona Highway 68. You will then

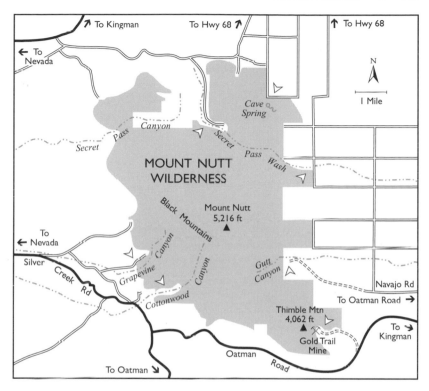

have to turn on Bulsa Drive, Gisela Road, Chukar Drive, and Ganado Road, respectively. Exact directions can be obtained from the BLM in Kingman. From Secret Pass, Secret Pass Canyon drops west, where it briefly crosses the northwestern corner of the wilderness. In its upper reaches Secret Pass Canyon is especially scenic, with narrow canyon passages and rugged spires of volcanic rock. A 4WD vehicle is needed to reach this access point.

Several 4WD roads access the west side of the wilderness, which, like the east side, features numerous canyons and washes. Two of these drainages are Grapevine and Cottonwood Canyons, which can be reached from Silver Creek Road. Silver Creek Road links Oatman to Bullhead City. Both of these canyons run for 3 miles or more before reaching the headwaters of their respective creeks at the higher reaches of the range.

Although running close to Oatman Road, the southern boundary of the wilderness is not readily accessible, due to thick desert brush, rough terrain, and parcels of private land.

As with all cross-country travel, a topographic map is a must, and extreme caution must be used. Although springs are located in Mount Nutt Wilderness, water must be treated before drinking. You should pack in all the water you will need. Watch for rattlesnakes and a variety of other poisonous creatures during the warmer months.

87 Mount Tipton Wilderness

Location: 24 miles N of Kingman
Size: 30,760 acres
Status: Wilderness area (1990)
Terrain: Desert and mountains
Elevation: 3,440 feet to 7,148 feet
Management: BLM (Kingman Field Office)
Topographic maps: Chloride, Mount Tipton, Mount Tipton 3 SE, Grasshopper Junction

Mount Tipton Wilderness includes the northern half of the Cerbat Mountain Range, which reaches its high point at 7,148-foot Mount Tipton. Typically rugged, the Cerbat Mountains are laced by several deep canyons and feature the Cerbat Pinnacles—a rugged collection of rock spires. Adding to the variety of wilderness experiences found here is a wide range of vegetation types—from Joshua trees in the foothills to ponderosa pines in the highest reaches of the range.

Seasons

Summers are typically too hot for hiking in this wilderness, although the highest elevations are somewhat cool. Winters occasionally bring wisps of snow to the upper reaches, but it rarely if ever precludes access to the wilderness.

Plants and Wildlife

Draped across much of the lower and midelevations of Mount Tipton Wilderness is a chaparral mixture of shrub live oak, manzanita, and beargrass. Scattered pinyon pine and juniper are also common. This growth is often quite thick and thorny, making hiking impractical. At the lowest elevations, a sparser mixture of plants common to the Mojave Desert may be found. These include cholla, yucca, and Joshua trees. A few ponderosa pines grow in isolated stands. These are mostly found on the northeastern slope of Mount Tipton, where it is cooler and moister. Wildlife of the wilderness includes such common species as mule deer, coyotes, and jackrabbits. The Cerbat Mountains are also home to a herd of feral horses, and peregrine falcons are known to nest among the Cerbat Pinnacles.

Geology

In keeping with many mountains within Arizona's Basin and Range province, the Cerbats trend northwest–southeast and include many outcrops of granite, gneiss, and schist. In contrast to these exposures of Precambrian rock, the Cerbat Pinnacles were formed by volcanic eruptions that occurred during the Tertiary period. Composed of

Free-roaming horses in the Mount Tipton Wilderness

material eroded from the mountain range over many years are pronounced *bajadas,* which slope gently away from the foothills surrounding the range.

ACTIVITIES
Hiking

There are no established trails in Mount Tipton Wilderness, but some washes and canyon bottoms offer possible cross-country routes. Furthermore, there are a number of different access points scattered along the wilderness boundary.

From the area of Dolan Springs, it is possible to enter the northern tip of the wilderness by way of Antelope Canyon. This can be reached by driving 29 miles north of Kingman on US Highway 93 to Pearce Ferry Road. Turn right and drive through the small community of Dolan Springs to 19th Street. Follow this road for 0.6 mile, then turn right onto Ocotillo Street. Drive a short distance, then turn right again on North Olive Street. Drive 0.5 mile to 16th Street, turn left, and drive one block to an unnamed road that turns right. The wilderness boundary is reached in 0.5 mile, but the road continues for another 1.3 miles to a water tank. The last mile is rough and requires

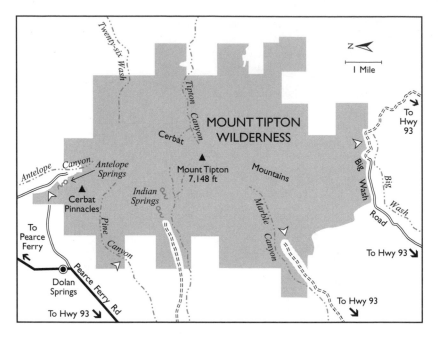

a high-clearance vehicle. The terrain here is open enough to allow for exploration. Antelope Springs lies a short distance south, with the canyon itself offering the best views of the Cerbat Pinnacles to the south.

Views of the Cerbat Pinnacles can also be enjoyed from the confines of Pine Canyon. This major drainage along the range's west side is reached by driving south from Dolan Springs for about a mile. There is a 40-acre parcel of private land within the canyon.

Marble Canyon, which is located in the southwestern corner of the wilderness, is also accessible by a cherry-stemmed road. The turnoff for this route is located about 23 miles north of Kingman along US Highway 93. The wilderness boundary is reached about 3.5 miles from the highway. A 4WD vehicle is required for this approach. Marble Canyon can be hiked via wash bottoms.

Running along 4.5 miles of the southern boundary of the wilderness is Big Wash Road. It turns east from US Highway 93 about 20 miles north of Kingman. Although the mountain slopes in this southern section of the wilderness are covered with especially thick chaparral, a few drainage bottoms provide access to some areas. The southern end of the wilderness is also home to most of the area's feral horses.

Because cross-country hiking in this and other wilderness areas can be hazardous, caution should be taken. No permanent streams are found within Mount Tipton Wilderness, but some springs are located within its boundaries. To find out about their condition, check with the BLM in Kingman before setting out (but always treat water before drinking). Your safest option is to pack all the water you will need.

Mount Wilson Wilderness

Location: 60 miles N of Kingman
Size: 23,900 acres
Status: Wilderness area (1990)
Terrain: Desert *bajadas* and mountains
Elevation: 2,000 feet to 5,445 feet
Management: BLM (Kingman Field Office)
Topographic maps: Mount Wilson, Petroglyph Wash

Nestled alongside the Lake Mead National Recreation Area, Mount Wilson Wilderness encompasses nearly all of the Wilson Ridge, at the northern end of the Black Mountains. The wilderness area's overall low elevation gives it a stark, open, yet visually interesting look that beckons cross-country hikers.

Seasons

Summers are usually too hot for hiking in Mount Wilson Wilderness. Winters are not overly cold, and snow is a rare phenomenon here. Late autumn is pleasant, as is spring. Springtime may be the best time of year for a visit because of the promise of desert flowers.

Plants and Wildlife

Although somewhat barren of vegetation, Mount Wilson Wilderness is home to some interesting desert flora and fauna. Plant species within the area include creosote bush, yucca, cholla, barrel cactus, and catclaw. Within this arid environment are found a large herd of desert bighorn sheep, along with mule deer, coyotes, and jackrabbits. Feral burros also reside here.

Geology

Encompassing the northern portion of the complex Black Mountains, Mount Wilson Wilderness is characterized by light-colored exposures of Precambrian gneiss and granite. Volcanic activity is also evident in Mount Wilson Wilderness in the form of landmarks such as Black Butte, a perfectly shaped butte of dark basalt. Sloping gently away from the rugged core of Wilson Ridge, which runs north–south through the wilderness, are alluvial deposits of sand and gravel, known in the Southwest as *bajadas*.

ACTIVITIES
Hiking

No designated trails enter Mount Wilson Wilderness, but two former vehicle ways do offer access to the southern and eastern portions of the wilderness. One of these access routes is reached by driving 52 miles north from Kingman on US Highway 93 to

Temple Bar Road. Turn right and drive 10.7 miles to a faint roadway, which heads off to the northwest. Crossing about 2 miles of Lake Mead National Recreation Area land administered by the NPS before reaching BLM lands, this faint, high-clearance route is closed at the wilderness boundary 3 miles from Temple Bar Road. Beyond this simple blockade of stones, it is possible to walk along the old road for another 2 miles to

Yucca in the Mount Wilson Wilderness

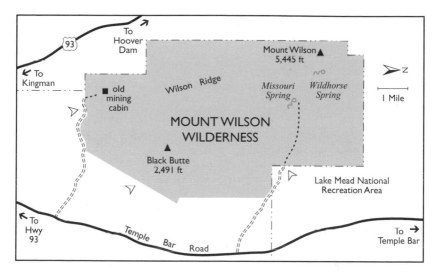

Missouri Spring and an old mine just east of the Mount Wilson summit (5,445 feet). Access to the summit of Mount Wilson is possible by continuing up the drainage beyond the springs.

Because vegetation across the *bajada* areas of Mount Wilson Wilderness is mostly open, it offers few obstacles to cross-country hiking. From the road mentioned above, it is possible to explore much of the eastern foothills. It is also possible to hike into the Black Butte area from Temple Bar Road. It is about 1.5 miles from the road to the wilderness boundary.

A second old vehicle way turns north from Temple Bar Road, a short distance north of mile 5. Continuing for 4 miles, this high-clearance route forms the southern boundary of the wilderness for about 1.5 miles. At road's end, which is less than 0.25 mile inside the wilderness boundary, are the remains of an old cabin. Intrepid hikers could climb up Wilson Ridge, which can then be followed north for several miles. From this high route, the views take in nearby Lake Mead, California, to the west, and the Grand Canyon to the east.

Cross-country hiking in this and other wilderness areas requires that you be extremely careful. The only surface water found within Mount Wilson Wilderness comes in the way of a few small springs that may be hard to find. All water should be treated before drinking. It is best to pack in all the water you will need for your hike. Watch for rattlesnakes during the warmer months.

APPENDIX: RECOMMENDED RESOURCES

NATIONAL FORESTS

Apache–Sitgreaves National Forest
www.fs.fed.us/r3/asnf

> Alpine Ranger District
> P.O. Box 469
> Alpine, AZ 85920
> 520-339-4384

> Springerville Ranger District
> P.O. Box 760
> Springerville, AZ 85938
> 520-333-4372

Coconino National Forest
www.fs.fed.us/r3/coconino

> Beaver Ranger District
> HC 64, Box 240
> Rimrock, AZ 86335
> 520-567-4501

> Peaks Ranger District
> 5075 North Highway 89
> Flagstaff, AZ 86004
> 520-527-3630

> Sedona Ranger District
> P.O. Box 300
> Sedona, AZ 86339
> 520-282-4119

Coronado National Forest
www.fs.fed.us/r3/coronado

> Douglas Ranger District
> 3081 N. Leslie Canyon Road
> Douglas, AZ 85607
> 520-364-3468

> Nogales Ranger District
> 303 Old Tucson Road
> Nogales, AZ 85621
> 520-281-2296

> Safford Ranger District
> P.O. Box 709
> Safford, AZ 85548-0709
> 520-428-4150

> Sierra Vista Ranger District
> 5990 South Highway 92
> Hereford, AZ 85615
> 520-378-0311

> Tucson Ranger District
> 5700 North Sabino Canyon Road
> Tucson, AZ 86750
> 520-749-8700

Kaibab National Forest
www.fs.fed.us/r3/kai

> North Kaibab Ranger District
> 430 South Main
> Fredonia, AZ 86022
> 520-643-7395

Williams Ranger District
742 South Clover Road
Williams, AZ 86046
520-635-2676

Prescott National Forest
www.fs.fed.us/r3/prescott

Prescott Ranger District
2230 East Highway 69
Prescott, AZ 86301
520-771-4700

Verde Ranger District
P.O. Box 670
Camp Verde, AZ 86322
520-567-4121

Tonto National Forest
www.fs.fed.us/r3/tonto

Globe Ranger District
7680 South Six Shooter Canyon
Road
Globe, AZ 85501
520-402-6200

Mesa Ranger District
P.O. Box 5800
Mesa, AZ 85211-5800
602-610-3300

Payson Ranger District
1009 East Highway 260
Payson, AZ 85541
520-474-7900

Pleasant Valley Ranger District
P.O. Box 450
Young, AZ 85554
520-462-4300

Tonto Basin Ranger District
HC 02 Box 4800
Roosevelt, AZ 85545
520-467-3200

BUREAU OF LAND MANAGEMENT
www.az.blm.gov

Arizona Strip Field Office
345 East Riverside Drive
St. George, UT 84790
435-688-3200

Havasu Field Office
2610 Sweetwater Avenue
Lake Havasu City, AZ 86406-9071
520-505-1200

Kingman Field Office
2475 Beverly Avenue
Kingman, AZ 86401-3629
520-692-4400

Phoenix Field Office
2015 West Deer Valley Road
Phoenix, AZ 85027-2099
623-580-5500

Safford Field Office
711 14th Avenue
Safford, AZ 85546
520-348-4400

Tucson Field Office
12661 East Broadway
Tucson, AZ 85748-7208
520-722-4289

Yuma Field Office
2555 East Gila Ridge Road
Yuma, AZ 85365-2240
520-317-3200

NATIONAL PARKS AND MONUMENTS

Chiricahua National Monument
HCR 2, Box 6500
Willcox, AZ 85643
520-824-3560
www.nps.gov/chir

Grand Canyon National Park
P.O. Box 129
Grand Canyon, AZ 86023
*www.nps.gov/grca/grandcanyon
trip_planner*

Organ Pipe Cactus National
Monument
Route 1, Box 100
Ajo, AZ 85321-9626
520-387-7662
www.nps.gov/orpi

Petrified Forest National Park
Box 2217
Petrified Forest National Park,
AZ 86028
520-524-6228
www nps gov/pefo

Saguaro National Park East
3693 South Old Spanish Trail
Tucson, AZ 85730
520-733-5153
www.nps.gov/sagu

Saguaro National Park West
2700 North Kinney Road
Tucson, AZ 85743
520-733-5158
www.nps.gov/sagu

NATIONAL WILDERNESS PRESERVATION SYSTEM
www.wilderness.net/nwps/

NATIONAL WILDLIFE REFUGES

Cabeza Prieta National Wildlife Refuge
1611 North Second Avenue
Ajo, AZ 85321
520-387-6483
*http://southwest.fws.gov/refuges/
arizona/cabeza.html*

Havasu National Wildlife Refuge
P.O. Box 3009
Needles, CA 92363
760-326-3853
*http://southwest.fws.gov/refuges/
arizona/havasu.html*

Imperial National Wildlife Refuge
P.O. Box 72217
Yuma, AZ 85365
520-783-3371
*http://southwest.fws.gov/refuges/
arizona/imperial.html*

Kofa National Wildlife Refuge
356 West First Street
Yuma, AZ 85364
520-783-7861
*http://southwest.fws.gov/refuges/
arizona/kofa.html*

INDEX

ABOUT THE AUTHOR

Scott S. Warren has lived in the Southwest for the last thirty years. He has spent much of that time in Arizona, exploring its many different natural areas. "What I really love about hiking in Arizona is the incredible variety of terrain and plant life," Warren says. "From cactus forests and canyon bottoms to lush forests and high alpine summits, Arizona has it all." In addition to writing about the outdoors, Warren is also a photographer. He holds a bachelor of fine arts degree in photography from Utah State University, and his images have appeared in *Audubon, Outside, Sierra, Smithsonian, Travel & Leisure,* and various National Geographic publications. Warren is also a 1999 Alicia Patterson Fellow.

THE MOUNTAINEERS, founded in 1906, is a nonprofit outdoor activity and conservation club, whose mission is "to explore, study, preserve, and enjoy the natural beauty of the outdoors . . . " Based in Seattle, Washington, the club is now the third-largest such organization in the United States, with 15,000 members and five branches throughout Washington State.

The Mountaineers sponsors both classes and year-round outdoor activities in the Pacific Northwest, which include hiking, mountain climbing, ski-touring, snowshoeing, bicycling, camping, kayaking and canoeing, nature study, sailing, and adventure travel. The club's conservation division supports environmental causes through educational activities, sponsoring legislation, and presenting informational programs. All club activities are led by skilled, experienced volunteers, who are dedicated to promoting safe and responsible enjoyment and preservation of the outdoors.

If you would like to participate in these organized outdoor activities or the club's programs, consider a membership in The Mountaineers. For information and an application, write or call The Mountaineers, Club Headquarters, 300 Third Avenue West, Seattle, Washington 98119; 206-284-6310.

The Mountaineers Books, an active, nonprofit publishing program of the club, produces guidebooks, instructional texts, historical works, natural history guides, and works on environmental conservation. All books produced by The Mountaineers fulfill the club's mission

Send or call for our catalog of more than 450 outdoor titles:

The Mountaineers Books
1001 SW Klickitat Way, Suite 201
Seattle, WA 98134
800-553-4453
mbooks@mountaineers.org
www.mountaineersbooks.org